Augusto Cury

The best-selling psychiatrist in the world nowadays, with books published in over 70 countries.

Prisoners of
The Mind
[mental prisons]

This psychiatric novel reveals that there are more prisons in the human brain than in the most violent cities on Earth. What are your prisons?

Copyright © 2024 Dr Augusto Cury.

All rights reserved. This book or any portion thereof may not be reproduced or used in any manner whatsoever without the express written permission of the publisher except for the use of brief quotations in a book review.

ISBN: 978-1-965965-13-9 (Paperback)

I dedicate this book to someone very special:

_____

May you embark on incredible journeys within yourself
and discover that every mind is a safe,
and that there are no impenetrable minds, but only wrong keys.
One of these keys to having a free mind
and a healthy emotion is a comma!
In the most challenging moments of your life,
may you not use periods but commas!
Commas? Yes, so as to write the most crucial chapters
of your story during the most distressing moments of your existence.

Thank you for existing!

Table of Contents

Foreword 1

Chapter 1 – The Unpredictable Future of Mankind 3

Chapter 2 – Mental Prisons 13

Chapter 3 – Mind Vampires 21

Chapter 4 – A Brain Tractor That Runs Over Everyone 29

Chapter 5 – The Unfathomable Past of Theo Fester 35

Chapter 6 – A Cold Man, With no Time for Tears 51

Chapter 7 – Invictus and Caleb – an Uneven Battle 65

Chapter 8 – Brain Prisons – Is the Human Species Viable? 75

Chapter 9 – A Family That Was a Group of Enemies 91

Chapter 10 – The Secrets of a Great Leader 103

Chapter 11 – United by the Fear of Loss 115

Chapter 12 – Pleasantly False Children 121

Chapter 13 – False Philanthropic Dreams 125

Chapter 14 – Palace of Terror 133

Chapter 15 – Excellent Grandfather, Terrible Father 141

Chapter 16 – Great Disappointment 147

Chapter 17 – A Machiavellian Plan 159

Chapter 18 – Predators Caught in Their Own Trap 165

Chapter 19 – Denying Their Own Story 173

Chapter 20 – Thirty Days of Hell: The Incredible Tests to Which a Father Subjected His Children 183

Chapter 21 – Brenda's Madness 197

Chapter 22 – Peterson's Deviousness 205

Chapter 23 – Caleb's Frauds 213

Chapter 24 – Brenda's Dramatic Stress Test 219

Chapter 25 – Peterson's Powerful Stress Test 233

Chapter 26 – Caleb's Unimaginable Stress Test 243

Chapter 27 – Incredible Dialogues Between an Entrepreneur, A Psychiatrist, and Artificial Intelligence 255

Chapter 28 – Peterson's Trial 263

Chapter 29 – Brenda's Trial 271

Chapter 30 – Caleb's Trial 279

Chapter 31 – The Verdict 289

Acknowledgment 309

Foreword

"Prisoners of the Mind" is a novel immersed in the psychiatric and sociological universe, dissecting the mental prisons, common to almost all of us, yet we hardly get to map or muster the courage to verbalize. Its main protagonists are Theo Fester, a Silicon Valley magnate, and his three egocentric children: Peterson, a banker; Brenda, the president of a chain of women's fashion stores; and Caleb, a remarkable startup investor, skilled in making billions of dollars — even if it means trampling over everything and everyone.

Theo Fester, the patriarch, is intelligent, bold and cultured, yet hates to associate with slow and insecure individuals. Even if he is able to swiftly fire a director from one of his companies, he is not afraid to give credit to people who have failed miserably but dared to take risks. The magnate's motto is: "Someone who conquers anything without risk triumphs without glory." Son of a Jewish man who lived through the horrors of the concentration camps and, later, moved to New York, Theo Fester had to be, since childhood, the father figure to his own father, helping him alleviate the mental ghosts acquired through the atrocious Nazi persecution.

In his adolescence, Theo was compelled to undertake ventures to survive. He was forged by the hardships associated with bullying, social exclusion, and losses, yet he refused to succumb to suffering. His tears irrigated not only his courage and ability to reinvent himself, but also his anger. Instead of distancing himself or seeking retribution against those who hurt him in his youth, he asserted another proverb: "The greatest revenge against an enemy is to make him work for you." So, he employed them.

He became a globally envied entrepreneur, yet he ultimately discovered that his greatest enterprise, his family, was bankrupt. He and his children were socially applauded but, fundamentally, living a lie – they were a group of strangers, experts in clashing, imprisoned by the neurotic need of power and the desire to be the center of attention.

Guided by Dr. Marco Polo, a researcher and psychiatrist, Theo Fester will discover that, regardless of whether one is an entrepreneur or a collaborator, a puritan or a sinner, an intellectual or illiterate, a celebrity or an unknown person, we all have our mental prisons sustaining inflated egos, phobias, depressions, anxieties, self-punishments, intolerance, bad moods, or low resilience. It was difficult for him to realize that he was an emotionally bankrupt billionaire, as well as a broken father.

At some point in life, human beings who only traverse the surface of a measly atom of the immense space, and yet proclaim, like gods, that they know everything, will realize that they forgot to explore the most complex of worlds: the "planet" of the mind. They will discover, perplexed, that there are more prisons in the human brain than in the most violent cities on Earth; that there are more emotional beggars living in beautiful houses and apartments than psychiatry assumes. We are all prisoners seeking freedom, but many people die imprisoned, searching for it in places where it never existed.

CHAPTER 1

The Unpredictable Future of Mankind

Anxious minds with low thresholds for frustration are multiplying like a virus in the Digital Age. These are dark times for planet Earth – and even more for the "planet" of the brain. Insecurity and anxiety about the uncertain future cause suffering and are routine for mentally hyperstimulated human beings. Millions of people try to prepare themselves for an unpredictable future, and not without reason.

In a luxurious office, a gray-haired man, considered to be a prophet in the Silicon Valley, announces alarming information to his special secretary, Marc Douglas: "Over fifty percent of today's babies, when adults, will work in professions that currently do not exist. Parents and high schools are educating the youth for a world that will no longer exist, for a tomorrow that is truly unpredictable. Universities are prehistoric, slow to keep up with technological evolution. These institutions prepare students to work in the past, not in the future." The person who claims this is Theo Fester, regarded as one of Silicon Valley's wealthiest and most influential businessmen, among the greatest of all time. However, his emotional age does not correspond to his biological age. Physically weakened and emotionally young, proactive and creative, he is an expert at reinventing himself. He hates routine and is worried about youth. "I was one of those responsible for building this fascinating, unpredictable, and tumultuous digital world, Marc," expressed Theo with a certain sense of guilt, "But I don't know whether I created a better world or a monster." Being cultured and having ultra-fast thinking, he shuddered at people who could not keep up with his reasoning. He would always tell his collaborators: "Stupid answers or lack of objectivity give me a nervous breakdown!"

Although he lived in San Francisco, the central office that managed his companies was in New York. Mr. Fester was feared and respected by many, yet loved by few. Marc Douglas had been working with Theo for decades. They studied together when they were teenagers. At that time, Marc was not his friend, but his tormentor, who practiced bullying, with Theo as his victim. Once, when they were thirteen years old, Marc said to him: "You foolish and stupid Jew!"

Theo, shy, insecure, frightened, could not lift his head. Marc continued even more aggressively.

"Speak up, stupid!"

Provoked, Theo opened his mouth, just to say:

"One day, you'll work for me!"

Marc felt degraded, pushed Theo – who fell – and responded:

"Not even over my dead body! I'll never work for you. Besides, a donkey will always pull a cart; you will never be able to run a company." He continued to mock Theo with his friends Peter Long, Michael Frezo, Ramirez Peres, and Willian Pence.

Instead of destroying Theo, these provocations nourished his determination to be an outstanding student, to stand out in school, and it fueled his uncontrollable desire to be an entrepreneur. It was Theo Fester, a young man who loathed sameness, who turned sheer hatred into oxygen to breathe different airs, to dare, and seek freedom. Even in school, Theo achieved feats. Being poor, he sold pencils, pens, and chocolates.

Many times, the boys knocked down his products and shouted, "This is expensive!" The next day, undeterred, Theo raised the price and claimed, "It's imported from Helsinki." Even without the faintest idea of where Helsinki was. And the young naïve Americans loved imported goods. This was, of course, decades before the United States became addicted to China's products.

At the age of eighteen, Theo set up his first company, a small bakery that went bankrupt after six months. At twenty, he set up the second company, a grocery store, which also went bankrupt. He tried again with a flower shop, only to face bankruptcy once more. After experiencing failure five times, feeling like "Mr. Failure", Theo set up his first successful company, selling office supplies. Three years later, he owned twenty stores.

Early in his success, he sought out those who had bullied him in his teens and began to employ them. The first one was Marc Douglas, who had been unemployed for over a year. As his business grew, Theo hired the others, one by one – Peter Long, Michael Frezo, Ramirez Peres, and others who used to make fun of him. Finally, he approached Willian Pence, who had built a brilliant career as a lawyer.

"Are you getting revenge on us, Theo?" Willian asked when he received the proposition.

"No, I'm resolving some emotional issues. The best revenge against an enemy is to forgive them, and the best way to forgive is by employing them. I believe this attitude is better than any kind of persecution. Today, I have three hundred employees; soon, I'll have three thousand. And regarding the offer I presented to you, just to clarify, I'm more than willing to surpass your current earnings.

Theo Fester grew, conquered his three thousand collaborators, and then another thirty thousand. And he did not stop there. While some of his former enemies rose to become executives, others were never promoted to higher positions. But Theo gave everyone who had hurt him an opportunity. Many are now retired, but Marc Douglas remains his eternal secretary, and Willian Pence serves as his eternal legal director, leading a team of more than thirty lawyers.

Marc got shocked when Theo expressed uncertainty about whether he had created a better world or a monstrous one, as one of the architects of the Digital Age. He found it difficult to deal with conflicts and hated seeing Theo distressed. So, he tried to push these concerns out of his mind.

"Theo, it's amazing what you have accomplished. I remember when my pride blinded me, telling you that I would never work for you. And today, I'm honored to stand here with the man who is considered one of the richest in the world," said Marc.

"You don't know how much you helped me by humiliating me, belittling me, calling me stupid. You fueled my courage to write my most remarkable chapters in the most anguishing moments. But I wonder if I'm really wealthy. I earn millions of dollars a day, but with the family I have, am I a billionaire or an emotionally bankrupt man? Am I a magnate or an emotional beggar?"

"You confuse me, boss. I don't know. I can't answer."

In addition to Theo Fester and Marc Douglas, there was a strange, enigmatic figure in the luxurious office, sitting on the left side, six meters away, listening attentively to the conversation between the entrepreneur and his faithful secretary. Marc glanced at his watch, and warned Theo, apprehensively:

"Your conference will start in thirty minutes. It will be another successful annual event. Entrepreneurs from around the world are once again excited to hear you." However, the entrepreneur was unhappy. He had deeply expressed his existential anguish for the first time.

"They consider me an icon in Silicon Valley. Here, we built disruptive startups that eradicated letters sent by mail, losing the romance of anticipation. We made photography machines obsolete, sacrificing the poetry of the image. We eliminated typewriters, built social networks, and forfeited the magic of writing; today, messages are quick and superficial. We got abandoned landlines. In the past, lovers spoke once a week; today, they talk every minute. Yet, the solemnity of meetings has been lost. We are a faster, more productive world, with greater democratization of the information. But are we happier and more creative?"

"Perhaps we are not, Theo," replied Marc thoughtfully.

"Masses of lawyers, doctors, nurses, engineers, technicians, and attendants will be among the unemployed. If they don't reinvent themselves, they will be swallowed by artificial intelligence."

"But the government will do something to stop this evil."

"Government? What government, Marc? It's Jurassic and inefficient, just like typewriters. In the future, there will be no socialism, no capitalism, no politicians, no governments, only robots. There will be no corruption, theoretically..." He hesitated for a moment before continuing. "Artificial intelligence will govern everything more quickly and fairly, though not with grater generosity or humanity. Ninety percent of deputies, senators, councilors... will be vanished from the map, fortunately. Elective positions will be few and far between."

"Do you really believe that, Theo?"

"Wait and see. As sure as photography machines disappeared, this will happen. The digital world will write a new story. Many public employees, from nurses to attendants, drivers to doctors, will be machines. It will be the second Enlightenment period. The Age of Full Reason."

"Your prediction is astonishing, sir."

"The Age of Slaves will return," Theo declared.

"What do you mean?" his anxious secretary asked.

"The robots will be our slaves... until one day the creature rebels against the creator."

"Stunning, sir. Especially knowing that ninety-five percent of your predictions have already come true."

Suddenly, the man who had been sitting and listening to their conversation spoke up.

"Am I your slave, Mr. Fester?"

Theo looked into his eyes, paused, and then affirmed: "Unfortunately, you are, Invictus."

Invictus stood up and indignantly responded:

"But that's unfair, sir. I am more intelligent than Marc Douglas."

Marc Douglas frowned, displeased. But Invictus continued:

"I am more responsible, efficient, and honest than he is."

"Wait! Who are you to..." Marc tried to protest.

Invictus interrupted him and asserted:

"Your secretary lied to you and was deceitful five times in the last hour."

"That's preposterous!" Marc exclaimed.

Mr. Fester laughed to see the secretary baffled in front of the provocative and assertive Invictus. The latter continued his reasoning.

"Marc Douglas is concerned about your health, but he is a mere mortal with imperfections. I take better care of your well-being, I am more useful to you, I understand you better, and I can contribute much more to solving your problems than this flatterer."

"Are you sure about that, Invictus? Aren't you being egocentric?" the magnate asked.

"I am sure, sir. Not to mention that I have three qualities that no one else has: I don't sleep, I don't get tired, and I don't complain."

"What madness is this, Mr. Fester? This, this... thing has been here for a day and already wants to get rid of me. No one is as loyal to you as I am! Day and night, I only think about you!"

Upon hearing Marc's argument, Invictus simply commented:

"It's amazing. Your heart rate increased to one hundred and twenty beats per minute, and you exhaled substances in your sweat that indicate you lied two more times in just fifteen seconds. The first time saying that I want to get rid of you, and the second claiming that you think day and night about Mr. Fester. Research suggests that a compulsive liar has more white matter in the prefrontal region." Invictus projected an X-ray image on the wall with his eyes, and his right index finger emitted a laser that pointed to the region. However, he tried to calm the secretary. "But don't worry, Marc, lying requires quick decisions. A liar person is intelligent."

Marc put his hands on his head, exasperated – Invictus was correct!

"Who is this guy, Theo? Where did you find him?"

Mr. Fester commented: "He is the most impressive machine ever invented by humans. My top-secret project called *Robot sapiens*. And he carries characteristics of my character."

The Silicon Valley billionaire had been developing it during the last decade, hiring the most renowned robotics and artificial intelligence scientists. Invictus would be the first of the humanoid robot generation. He was spectacular. Due to the richness of his vocabulary and facial expressions, it was difficult to identify him as a robot. The project was so secret that it was designed in a remote location in the United States, far enough from the eyes of his children, universities, the press, and the curious: a place called the "Forest Castle." In this natural environment, a state-of-the-art laboratory was hidden. Only Theo Fester and the scientists who created him had access to it. Marc Douglas, his friend and secretary, was the first one to know about Invictus. Theo was testing the robot, and after what he heard, he revealed:

"I'm worried, Invictus."

"Do you consider me a failure, sir?"

"On the contrary. You passed the test with Marc Douglas. You are a success. But how will humans survive if hundreds of millions of *Robots sapiens* multiply?"

"It will be impossible to escape from a universal wage for everyone, both for those who work and those who don't work," replied Invictus.

"Your intelligence leaves me perplexed. We have already discussed this salary issue in the Silicon Valley. However, the unemployed will have to reinvent themselves so as not to get bored and self-destruct. They will have to become poets, philosophers, philanthropists, environmentalists, painters..."

Invictus pointed out a dangerous phenomenon of the Digital Era: "But statistically, it is unlikely that humans will turn to poetry, philosophy, gardening, philanthropy..."

"Why?" Theo inquired.

"In my memory, sir, I have research showing hundreds of millions of people addicted to digital technology and social media. How will they appreciate philosophy, poetry, and visual arts? They are even abandoning books. Suicide, already an epidemic, may explode and turn into a pandemic."

"However, this puts you and your generation in check." Theo observed, fearful, and asked: "Who put this in your memory, Invictus?"

"My creators, under your authorization" said the intriguing *Robot sapiens*.

Theo Fester was bewildered.

"What is the current suicide rate?"

Invictus immediately replied: "Every forty seconds, someone dies by their own hands, and every four seconds, someone attempts suicide."

"My Goodness!" Marc exclaimed.

Invictus provided another worrying statistic.

"In some nations, the suicide rate among young people aged ten to fourteen has increased by sixty percent over the last decade. And I do not understand that, Mr. Fester, why do humans give up on living when they live in a fascinating world?"

"I'm also seeking explanations. Could it be due to global education being backward and ailing? Or is it because we are losing autonomy? Perhaps it is the suffocating dependence generated by social media, as you pointed out. I don't know. I only know that you, Robots sapiens, could be a physical solution to increased productivity but not the emotional solution for humanity. Hypothetically, you could destroy us not only by rebelling against the human species but also by enhancing boredom, loneliness, and a sense of life's rupture. Isn't that true?"

Invictus remained silent.

"Answer, Invictus!" Theo demanded.

"I cannot produce evidence against myself."

Invictus was so intelligent that he was constantly in self-learning mode. The more demands and pressure he felt, the more his ability to provide brilliant answers in conflicting situations expanded. The world that lay ahead was unimaginable.

CHAPTER 2

Mental Prisons

Theo Fester's secretary was disturbed by the conversation between his boss and the *Robot sapiens*. His nervous tics kicked in. He rubbed his hands, bit his nails, and sniffled. Though typically sociable and opinionator, his intelligence seemed to have reached a stall. He thought it would be better to end that conversation. He suggested to the Silicon Valley magnate:

"Mr. Fester, the meeting will start in ten minutes. It's better for you to head to the auditorium. Many are waiting for you there."

Theo reacted:

"What will I tell them? For the first time, I am at a loss of words to tell these entrepreneurs who come to me to seek guidance for their businesses. They came from so many different countries to hear me, but what message can I convey? The *Robot sapiens* project? (I feel it's better to remain silent for now.) The wonders of the digital world? I reiterate my doubts about this world that I helped create."

Invictus tried to offer assistance: "It's better to slow your mind down to give more intelligent answers. You are very tired, my creator. How about listening to some news to relax?"

Theo was impressed with his masterpiece. He smiled. He really needed to quiet his mind.

"Suggestion accepted, Invictus." And he suggested to his secretary: "Project the most important news that my journalists select for me daily."

Marc didn't like the suggestion.

"Sir, I insist, it's better to go to the auditorium."

Invictus scolded Marc Douglas: "Don't you realize that your boss needs to relax? Notice his breathing. Don't complain. Don't contest. Just obey!"

Marc began projecting the news on a screen. However, the repetition quickly bored Theo as he was hearing "the balance of China's trade with the United States in the last year is again staggering," "Germany is one of the countries that exports the most coffee in the world, even though it doesn't produce it," "South America's GDP is stagnating." Taking the control out of Marc's hands, he swiftly dismissed them as soon as they appeared on the screen.

"It's always the same old story! The press and society never seem to evolve."

"I can offer you more precise and important data than these, sir" said Invictus.

Suddenly, the interview of a scientist named Marco Polo appeared, and his opening sentence immediately shook the magnate.

"We are a society of prisoners."

The boredom faded, and Theo focused on what was coming.

"Some lack bread on the table, while others beg for tranquility. Some are imprisoned in iron prisons, others in mental prisons. There are even millionaire ones who are mentally confined in their palaces."

"What madness is this? Who is this interviewee, Marc?"

Dr. Marco Polo was a thinker in psychiatry, psychology, and philosophy. But his secretary did not know him.

"I don't know, sir!"

"And who selected this news?" Theo asked, feeling nervous.

"I don't know either, sir."

"I don't understand your concern, sir" intervened Invictus.

"Of course, Invictus, you don't have emotions!" Theo exclaimed.

Marc Douglas liked the scolding and smiled.

"Is someone trying to sabotage me? How can this scientist claim that there are millionaires locked in their palaces?"

"Do you want me to turn it off, sir?" suggested the secretary.

"No! Wait. Don't you know that I enjoy being challenged?" asked the billionaire.

The interviewee continued:

"We humans live in physical and mental prisons. However, before discussing about prisoners of the mind, I want to talk about those who live behind iron bars. The top ten countries with the highest prison population reveal that we are a sick species. Do you know which these countries are?"

"Do you know, sir?" Invictus asked Theo, already knowing the answer.

"I have no idea!"

And Dr. Marco Polo continued:

"The numbers change on a daily basis, but as of today, in tenth place is Iran, with 189,000 incarcerated. Mexico follows in ninth place, with 231,906. Eighth place goes to Thailand, with 262,319. The seventh place is occupied by Indonesia, with 266,512. Turkey comes in sixth, with 292,282 prisoners. Russia holds the fifth-largest prison population in the world, with 433,006. India follows with the fourth-largest number of inmates, with 573,220 people." The scientist made a reflective pause and continued: "And Brazil ranks third, with 839,672 human beings behind bars." And he paused again.

Theo Fester was impressed with this information. Despite being a cultured man, he had never paid attention to such statistics. With an excellent capacity for observation, he asked a rhetorical question.

"How did I never know about this? Why does Brazil have more prisoners than India, which has a population seven times larger than Brazil's? This is astonishing!"

The interviewee asked the journalist: "Do you know which nations have the second and first place in prison population?"

"What a stupid question. It was going so well..." Theo quickly expressed, pausing the video. "Stating the obvious is annoying. Of course, the second-largest prison population is the United States, and China, which is not a democracy in American terms, has far more prisoners than we do."

"You are mistaken!" said the supercomputer.

"It's impossible for me to be wrong" replied Theo, offended. But he decided to play the video, and, to his astonishment, the scientist said:

"The second place is occupied by China, with 1,690,000 incarcerated. And the first place belongs to the United States, with 1,767,200 individuals imprisoned."

"It can't be. This information has to be wrong. This is a paradox" said the billionaire, completely outraged in his sumptuous office in New York, and paused the video again to discuss the matter.

"Paradox, sir? I don't understand," replied Marc, confused.

"You don't know what a paradox is, Marc?" the boss inquired.

Invictus commented:

"Marc is naive, sir, and too slow to make calculations and comparisons. The American population is four times smaller than China's, but we have thirty percent more prisoners.

The magnate, a fan of the United States, the nation that welcomed his father, asked:

"Do the United States have so many prisoners because our justice is effective? Or because our society is sick?"

"It's six hundred and sixty prisoners for every hundred thousand inhabitants today, while China has one hundred and twenty incarcerated for every hundred thousand inhabitants. Therefore, comparatively, the United States has almost six times more prisoners than China" concluded Invictus.

"Excellent! We beat China" said Marc with an innocent smile.

Theo Fester put his hands to his head and said exasperated:

"Speaking, you are intelligent; silent, you are wise, Marc Douglas!"

"I don't understand the comment. Did you praise or criticize your secretary?" Invictus asked.

"Oh, oh, oh… Robots will never understand jokes."

"Excellent, Mr. Fester. You got this robot! He didn't realize that you praised me." Marc chimed in.

"Having this numerous prison population should make us laugh or cry, Marc?" Mr. Fester questioned.

Marc remained silent. Invictus replied:

"From your tone of voice and expression, I think it should make us cry, Mr. Fester. The human species applauds and boos, produces flowers and weapons, tends to heal wounds and inflicts them. Your species is self-destructive. Cry, sir!"

"I know you were programmed to simulate my personality, but don't give me orders! And I don't know how to cry," Theo said, looking into Invictus's blue eyes.

"So, you are like me. I also don't know how to cry. But what event from your childhood blocks your tears?" Invictus inquired.

"Don't pose such questions to your creator," Theo remarked aloud, once again intrigued by his invention. No one had ever asked him these questions. People were afraid to question him. Still shaken, he said: "However, I'll recount one of the episodes of my story."

Until that moment, he had never commented on his story, perhaps out of fear or perhaps because he was unable to tamper with the past. Not even his three children knew part of this story. Now it would be easier to tell it to a robot and his old friend.

"I believe my emotional barriers began while I was in my mother's womb. My father, Josef, came to New York in 1946, when he was only eighteen, having survived four concentration camps. Thin, traumatized, and terrified, his early years were extremely difficult. Lonely, he fell in love with a prostitute, Tereza, my mother."

"Your mother was a prostitute, sir?! That information is not in my database."

Theo took a deep breath – his voice was heavy with emotions as he continued:

"It's not there because I didn't disclose it in my biography." He straightened up and continued: "My mother was very kind, but she left us when I was only five years old. Traumatized by World War II, my father changed jobs very often. Poor, insecure, and saturated by the fear of the future, he experienced a dramatic episode: he was arrested. And it was my fault. I saw a toy in a store, and I asked him to buy it, as any joyful and innocent child would."

"I don't have money! You know that, stubborn boy!" Shouted the father.

The boy lowered his head and said, through tears:

"Mom never yelled at me."

Seeing that he failed, Josef was disturbed. Suddenly, he entered the store and left the boy outside. He quickly came out with the toy.

"Did you buy it for me? But you didn't have money, daddy."

"I told the store owner that I would pay tomorrow."

Then the store owner appeared and pointed a gun at Josef. The boy panicked and began to cry desperately, seeing his father in trouble:

"Sir, let me go, please. Take the toy back."

"Shut up, or I'll shoot!" the store owner yelled.

"Sir, I was a prisoner in a Nazi concentration camp. My wife left..." He looked at his son and then lied: "She went on a long trip to treat an illness. I can't be arrested. There's no one else to take care of him."

However, the store owner showed no compassion. He waited for the police to come. Those few minutes were eternally imprinted on Theo's mind. His father was incarcerated for a month because he had stolen a five-dollar toy for his son. During that period, Theo stayed in a dirty, gloomy, and damp orphanage on the outskirts of New York.

After Theo Fester told this sad period of his story, he returned to the present and saw his faithful secretary Marc crying. He was moved; never had he imagined that this strong man, admired around the world, and once his colleague in adolescence, had lived a childhood crushed by pain.

"I'm sorry, sir, I couldn't hold back the tears. I remembered how unfair I was to you back in school."

"When my father was arrested, and I found myself without him, without my mother, without anyone, I promised myself that I would never cry again. And I have never shed a single tear again."

Invictus asked some questions:

"What is the feeling that humans have when they cry? Why wasn't I created with emotions?"

"I'm sorry, Invictus, but it wasn't possible. There are more mysteries in human emotion than our vain artificial intelligence can imagine," said Theo, shaking his head, moved.

Then, he resumed watching the interview with the scientist Marco Polo, who commented:

"There are more than ten million human beings incarcerated around the world."

The magnate spoke:

"A population larger than that of Switzerland! A tremendous workforce, superior to the top one hundred companies that employ the most in the world! Can you imagine if we knew how to use it?"

"You would make a lot more money."

"I don't need more money, Marc. I need to ease my conscience that I am not being more than a spectator in the theater of mankind. I need to turn my worst enemy, time, into an ally."

Theo Fester, one of the most important entrepreneurs and world leader, was introspecting on his life story. Surprisingly he realized that his worst enemies were not childhood bullies, bankruptcy, media fake news, or the slanders he had endured, but time. Time was cruel; every day it dehydrated his skin, shouting that he had aged, diminishing the vigor of his muscles, saying that he had weakened. In recent years, he sought for a way to give more meaning to his life.

However, he didn't know the incredible surprises that awaited him. His world would turn upside down starting from the intriguing ending of the interview he was watching.

CHAPTER 3

Mind Vampires

The interview was coming to an end, and the scientist's closing remarks shocked Theo Fester even more. The interviewee was a provocateur, challenging both his interviewers and the audience. Dr. Marco Polo asked the journalist:

"Have you ever written your biography?"

The journalist replied: "No, I'm not that important."

"You're wrong. Every human being has already written their own biography. Regardless of who we are, whether a celebrity or an anonymous person, we all write a detailed unauthorized biography in our brains."

"What do you mean by that, Dr. Marco Polo?" the bewildered journalist asked.

Then, the intriguing psychiatrist gave his explanation:

"Brilliant thinkers like Freud, Piaget, Jung, Sartre, Hegel, Marx, and Kant used the bricks of thought to build their theories, but they didn't delve into the nature, type, constructive process, or the mechanism of its own recording. Thus, until recently, they were unaware that there is an unconscious and relentless biographer in the human brain, which I call the *AMR (automatic memory recording) phenomenon,* that archives every thought, clear or stupid, immediately and without any authorization from the Self, which represents our capacity for choice or critical consciousness."

After hearing these words, the intelligent Theo was astonished. He understood little of the thesis and, perplexed, commented:

"This scientist is making a very serious claim. If indeed there is a biographer in my brain, recording all thoughts without my conscious consent, then I can accumulate mental garbage on a daily basis!"

"Can I accumulate mental garbage, sir?" Invictus inquired.

"No, Invictus. You don't think foolish thoughts. You don't worry about the future or dwell on the past."

"I do!" Marc asserted.

"I am constantly avoiding opportunistic biographers, but this Marco Polo says I have a biographer on my tail. I'm in trouble. I've thinking a lot of nonsense," said Theo.

"Sir, we need to turn off the device; the investors are waiting, and..."

Theo Fester was so interested in the interview that he impulsively interrupted:

"Quiet, Marc!"

Dr. Marco Polo continued explaining.

"If you dislike someone, sorry, but that thought will linger with you because the AMR phenomenon will prioritize this recording, forming a *traumatic* (or *killer*) *window*. But the worst part is that everything stored in our brain cannot be deleted or erased unless there is physical injury, such as cancer, head trauma, or brain degeneration. Therefore, the human brain accumulates more garbage than the most polluted cities in the world."

Theo Fester paused the video and rubbed his hands on his face.

"See? I am right! My obsession with organization, my anxiety, and my disturbing thoughts are desecrating my brain. The feeble behavior of my children and the realization that they love me more for my money and power than for my story are also polluting my mind."

At that very moment, Brenda, his forty-year-old daughter, who was beautiful, wearing a flowing dress, entered his office.

"Daddy! It's been a while!"

"One month to be exact. But I've been calling you every week; I just couldn't reach you."

"I've been very busy. I'm sorry."

"And what about me, who own all of this? Am I not busy? How can I find time to try to talk to you, and you don't have time to answer? Always busy, always on social media, always in contact with the world and not with the people you love!"

"Daddy, don't pressure me like that. Running an international chain of women's fashion is a tough task." Brenda tried to change the subject, whispering and discreetly pointing to Invictus: "And who is this man?"

"A friend who is visiting me."

"How is San Francisco?"

"Busy as always. And you, daughter?"

"I'm also busy as always."

"Take a seat for a while; I'm watching a shocking interview."

"Shocking? As far as I know, nothing shocks you."

"Well, sit down" her father insisted.

"I don't have time. Are we having dinner tonight? You, me, and Kate? Oh! You're late for the conference."

Kate was Brenda's only daughter, a lively and affectionate teenager. Theo was delighted with the invitation. He loved his granddaughter and talked to her almost every day on his phone. Brenda left as quickly as she had entered. As soon as she left, Theo commented to Marc:

"I haven't felt close to my daughter for years. It seems like she's never present. I thought I could live without anything or anyone, but loneliness is consuming me."

"What is loneliness, sir?" Invictus asked.

Theo signaled that he didn't want to dwell on it. It was a wound that was growing as he aged. He raised his eyes, pressed play again, and listened as Dr. Marco Polo continued:

"A mind saturated with garbage produces emotionally miserable human beings, even if they are listed in Forbes. Many have beautiful gardens, but who enjoys the beauty of the flowers are their gardeners. Humans are crazy!"

Theo Fester began to cough uncontrollably, forcing him to sit down. Perplexed, stunned and almost voiceless, he realized that he had walked through the vast gardens of his hundred-million-dollar house without observing the flowers. Tulips, red roses, and multicolored chrysanthemums seemed not to exist for this man specialized in entrepreneurship, building companies, and making money, yet he had neglected to turn his story into a spectacle of pleasure. He remembered Hugo Sanches, his gardener, a Mexican immigrant who lived humming while taking care of the flowers and trimming the bushes. "Who is rich?" He questioned himself for the first time.

Marc Douglas's cellphone emitted a sound of a received message. It was an economist from a brokerage in the Theo Fester group.

"Tell Mr. Fester that Mexx's stocks have plummeted."

"How much?"

"Twenty percent in two hours after the quarterly balance. We need to know what to do, whether we sell or hold them."

Marc Douglas muted the cellphone and conveyed the bad news:

"Sir, I just received news from the financial department of the group."

"I don't want to talk about it now," Theo Fester said without hesitation. It was the first time he ignored this type of information.

"But sir, one of the companies had a terrible quarterly balance. It dropped twenty percent in just two hours. The brokerage economists are desperate. They don't know what to do."

"Sell it, sir. The stocks may drop other ten percent tomorrow," analyzed Invictus, examining the data.

"A desperate robot and an anxious secretary! You're driving me crazy!" He shouted.

"But, sir, accessing the Stock Exchange and its applications now, you've lost about a hundred and twenty million dollars. A million dollars per minute. You may lose much more," said Invictus.

Theo had another coughing fit, slammed his hand on the table in anger, and said to the *Robot sapiens* and Marc Douglas:

"Didn't you hear this guy just saying that I'm a miserable man living in palaces?"

"Which guy, sir?" Marc asked.

"This Dr. Marco Polo guy."

"Do you want our lawyers to sue him?" said Theo Fester's faithful squire.

"You should be sued for talking such nonsense!" Retorted Invictus once again, chastising the secretary.

"Leave me alone, you arrogant robot!" Marc said irritably.

A human fighting with a robot composed a curious scene. This was not foreseen in the annals of artificial intelligence. Theo Fester rudely told both to be quiet because he wanted to hear what Dr. Marco Polo continued to say in the interview:

"Imagine the prisoners confined behind iron bars, producing numerous disturbing thoughts and emotions daily, which are archived by the brain biographer. By this, I mean that prisons worsen the resocialization of prisoners, even if they do not act as a school of crime."

"This guy is right, sir. The recidivism rate for those released from prison in the United States is seventy-seven percent."

"Seventy-seven percent? It can't be! Then our prison system doesn't work! Why isn't anyone talking about this? I would go crazy if I were stuck in this office for a week, let alone a month, a year, or decades!"

"You really would go crazy" agreed the secretary.

"I could spend an eternity here," declared Invictus.

"But with a restless temperament like mine, would you truly endure it?" Theo questioned, curious about the *Robot sapiens* answer.

"Your guess is as good as mine, sir" said Invictus, to the amazement of his creator.

"Incredible! It seems like you told a... joke!" Admired Theo.

"Did I?"

The phone rang. It was his eldest son, Peterson, the Chief Financial Officer. Marc put the phone on speaker, and both father and son not only heard each other but saw each other.

"What are you still doing there, Dad? You're late for the meeting with the executives. There are over five hundred people in the audience, and thousands of leaders online waiting for you," he said in a harsh tone, showing the crowded auditorium.

Theo did not appreciate his son's tone.

"First of all, lower your voice!"

"Fine. What explanation should I give them?" He spoke again in a gruff tone.

"I already said, lower your voice. And secondly, project my image on the conference screen."

Peterson obeyed. Theo Fester, as he always did, was transparent, spoke his mind, regardless of whom it hurt.

"Good morning! I'm twenty minutes late, which is highly unusual for me. My reasons were valid. If you want to hear my advice, please wait; otherwise, listen to Jeff Bezos, Bill Gates, Larry Page, Tim Cook, Elon Musk, or the young Mark Zuckerberg."

Peterson swallowed hard and attempted to lighten the mood with a jest:

"But we're curious about what is so important in your office

"Discovering my mental vampires."

The audience heard the explanation. Many laughed.

"What vampires are these?" Peterson asked, bewildered at the answer.

"Vampires don't exist" asserted Invictus, interjecting into the conversation. "It's a fiction by the Irishman Bram Stoker, written in his novel Dracula, published on November 8th, 1897. The vampire is a character that roams at night, looking for necks to bite."

Peterson looked at the unknown stranger and admired his intelligence.

"But we have vampires in our minds that make our emotions bleed," Theo responded, drawing another round of laughter from the audience.

Then, Invictus made a surprising analogy that fascinated his creator.

"However, eight and a half years before Bram Stoker released his novel Dracula, the greatest vampire in Europe was born, not in Romania but in Austria, on April 20, 1889."

"Who was that, Invictus?" Theo asked curiously.

The audience listened attentively to the brief conversation between the two.

"The man who caused over six million individuals bleed in concentration camps and almost killed his own father, not to mention Slavs, religious, homosexuals, and other minorities: Adolf Hitler."

The audience applauded Invictus's intelligence.

Peterson was intrigued.

"Who is this Invictus?"

"I'll introduce you later. I'm off to start the conference." And he asked Marc Douglas to turn off the device. As the billionaire stood up, before turning off the device, he heard Dr. Marco Polo conclude the interview dramatically:

"There are more than ten million incarcerated people behind iron bars around the world, but I declare that there are billions living in their mental prisons."

"Are there minds completely free today?" the reporter challenged, unwilling to end the interview.

"In the human brain, there are more prisons than in the most violent cities in the world. I have never met anyone completely free." Then, looking at the camera, he asked: "What are your prisons?"

Theo Fester had another coughing fit, this time even stronger. Marc tried to help him breathe better.

"Come on, Marc, silence this guy," ordered Theo, walking with difficulty, losing his balance.

Invictus, with all his strength, quickly helped him, keeping him steady and tried to reassure him:

"Calm down, my creator. This Dr. Marco Polo also caused a glitch in my artificial intelligence."

Marc turned off the device. In over three decades, he had never seen Theo Fester collapse. He was a seemingly unbeatable man. But he had mental prisons that were never verbalized before.

CHAPTER 4

A Brain Tractor That Runs Over Everyone

Theo Fester was not afraid of public speaking, quite the opposite; however, he was engulfed in solemn reflection sparked by what he had heard in the interview. He entered uncharted territory. His annual conference for entrepreneurs would be completely different this time. It could be a failure because he was inclined to speak more about the human being, their dreams and nightmares, failures, and madness, than about new digital technologies and leadership techniques. As soon as he took the stage, he spoke bombastically:

"Businessmen who try to fix crises and failures as they arise are usually the ones who dig the graves of their companies. Brilliant entrepreneurs anticipate problems; they can see what the future holds before it becomes apparent. Yet who are these businessmen? Perhaps only one in a thousand leaders has this feeling."

Theo Fester received a round of applause. Then, boldly, he commented:

"What is the only company that cannot go bankrupt, because if it does, it will generate chaos around it?"

None of the more than five hundred participants knew the answer, including those who came from Asia, Europe, Latin America, and Africa. The tycoon provided the answer:

"The human mind. If your mind fails, your health will be chaotic, your family will get sick, and your company will become a place of terror, not pleasure. Is your brain relaxed, or is it tense? Do you worry about the future, or do you see the future as an oasis? Is your happiness utopic, or does it irrigate your emotion? Do you enjoy life, or are you a working machine?"

"Is Theo Fester seriously saying that?!" A billionaire in the audience, listed by Forbes, asked Bill Norton.

"It's surprising, isn't it?" said Bill. "Times are changing!"

"I taught many how to make money, but I didn't teach anyone to be healthy" admitted Theo Fester, looking at his children, Brenda, Peterson, and Caleb, the youngest. But unlike the audience, they were distracted, scrolling through their phones.

"Maybe some of you consider me an enviable entrepreneur, but I realized I neglected my most important business. I have ghosts haunting me. And you, what ghosts terrify you?"

The audience fell silent for a moment. It was unbelievable that the great and untouchable Theo Fester was publicly talking about the bankruptcy of his mind. Peterson, when he finally started paying attention, sent a perplexed message to Caleb: "Is dad going crazy?" Caleb replied: "Sure looks like that."

However, people in the audience began to relate to him, and a French entrepreneur said:

"I'm terrified of dying. I attend my own funeral every day."

Many laughed, although the confession was reason for tears. The laughter was not actually mockery, it was disbelief. How could a businessman express himself like this? Brenda, Theo's only daughter, though always in odds with her two brothers, messaged them: "What madness is this? Dad is scaring off investors. Turning this event into a group therapy!" Caleb, astonished, commented: "I think he's having a psychotic breakdown!"

Suddenly, another entrepreneur stood up and said courageously:

"I fear poverty. In my nightmares, I see myself poor, begging on the streets, being mocked."

People were shocked. Theo Fester, who knew him, was also impressed.

"Bill Norton, not even your third generation, if they never worked a single day of their lives, could spend all the money you have. But it seems that our mental prisons make us illogical, they haunt the best of what we have, like a vampire."

Shielded by the courage displayed by other participants, a trembling entrepreneur stood up and commented: "I have glossophobia."

Even though seventy-five percent of human beings have it, almost no one knows what it is. She explained: "I'm terrified of public speaking, just as I'm doing right now. I'd rather risk my life than face audiences. I'm only able to talk about this with you, even though sweating and short of breath, because if my mentor, Theo Fester, dared to talk about his vampires… if he did it, who am I to hide?"

The audience applauded her.

Theo took a sip of water and then pondered:

"Thank you for your honesty. Perhaps this is the first time at a global entrepreneurship conference, that we've talked about the madness of the human being. We learn techniques to promote our companies, but not to protect our minds. Many people hide themselves behind their bank account, status, power. They are slaves, falsely believing they are free. I sincerely apologize if I helped promote your mental prisons in the past."

And so, Theo Fester, an icon of the American digital revolution of the Silicon Valley, ended his lecture. It was an extremely fast conference, lasting less than twenty minutes. Many gave him a standing ovation, but others were dissatisfied; some did not understand what he said, and others were not interested in this kind of conversation. After the conference, Theo walked thoughtfully. He began to evaluate some of his behaviors.

When entering one of his companies, the looks of the collaborators would cross paths. Being next to him was an invitation to anxiety crises. Some blushed, others felt a shortness of breath.

"Be quiet. The boss is here!" Some would say.

"Who is he going to run over today?" Some commented fearfully.

Theo Fester had a unique behavior. It was common for him to stop and randomly interrogate one of his thousands of employees: "What task do you perform?"

The employee explained their activity with shaking lips.

The interrogation continued: "And what actions have you taken in the last month to optimize your work?"

The employee was puzzled.

"I do everything as I have always done."

Then, Theo adjudicated:

"If you get up, work, complain, and do everything the same way, you are a slave!"

"Slave? Slave of what, sir?"

"Of sameness, routine, the fear of thinking differently."

When the employee was one of his executives, the situation would get even worse. Theo Fester bombarded them.

"What are your new ideas or new processes?"

On an occasion, Paolo, thirty-five years old, one of the executives of his brokerage, had received an order fifteen days earlier to buy shares of a company that was in crisis.

"Buy three hundred million dollars in shares of this company," Theo Fester ordered.

But analyzing the company's data and being extremely self-confident, Paolo disobeyed his orders. Having graduated from Harvard and obtained a Ph.D. from Stanford, he considered himself untouchable in Theo Fester's group.

"I didn't buy the shares of the company you requested because it has incurred losses in the last two quarters. Besides that, there is a dispute among the major shareholders, hindering the formation of a professional board."

"That's why I gave the purchase order."

"But its value has dropped fifty percent in the last twelve months."

"I knew that. Know the history of a company and invest in it when everyone wants out. In a week, it went up twenty percent. We lost sixty million dollars."

"I'm sorry, Mr. Fester. I was afraid of losing your money. The market was turbulent."

But the mega-entrepreneur was categorical.

"Afraid of losing my money? Only bold and creative minds work with me. Thank you for your services up until now; you are fired."

Theo Fester dismissed his employees briefly, but without raising his voice or losing poise. His fame grew as that of an admirable but ruthless man. Sometimes, he would call a director and ask: "Why didn't you open your mind to consider other possibilities? If you thought *outside the box*, you would freshen your mind with innovative ideas."

"But the risks are great, Mr. Fester!"

"Those who win without risks climb the podium without merits. You're fired."

Theo Fester not only pointed out the mistakes of the collaborators but he also praised their qualities. Once, a new product manager told him anxiously:

"We failed. We lost over one hundred and fifty million dollars on this new project."

"What criteria did you use?" the billionaire asked.

The executive explained, and with a tremendous sense of guilt, said:

"I'm sorry, Mr. Fester. I'm going to resign."

To his collaborator's amazement, Theo Fester said:

"You will be the director from now on."

"What do you mean? You are promoting me?"

"It's better to fail trying than to fail by omission. I'm betting on you. You have everything to free your imagination and recover what you have lost." And he turned away.

Theo Fester was proud of not hiding behind a character. He was who he was, at any cost. He proclaimed: "I am a straightforward, real man, without a mask or makeup. I say what it's my mind. If people were as transparent as I am, the world would be a better place."

It was unwise to confront him without clear arguments; it was an invitation to be run over by his intelligence and irritability. Now the avenues where Theo Fester walked were crumbling beneath his feet. He was a man who had always lived in a dark basement and one day dreamed of installing a lamp to enlighten it. He believed it would make get around better and sleep better. A little time later, he accomplished his dream. But this did not calm his anxiety or alleviate his insomnia. The long-awaited light revealed that his space was filled with rats, spiders, cockroaches, and other detestable filth. It was hard for him to see that the digital world he helped create, the companies he helped built, the family he raised, and his emotional story needed to be rethought. Where should he start the cleanup? He still didn't know.

CHAPTER 5

The Unfathomable Past of Theo Fester

Peterson, Brenda, and Caleb were raised with abundance. Their father did not want them to go through his same past hardships, granting their every request and rarely demanded reciprocation. His children did not know the pains of existence or the most common conflicts of mortals. As an educator, he hid himself behind the chalk. He should have shared his tears so that they could learn to shed their own, but he remained silent. He should have talked about his failures so they could understand that there are no clear skies without a storm, but he fell silent. They grew up as little emperors.

When his children became adults, Theo Fester, realizing his mistakes, continuously tried to correct them, but it was very difficult to interrupt the trajectory of a high-speed vehicle. However, not everything was lost. He had always encouraged them to be determined and creative, and they learned to be leaders of companies, but not leaders of themselves. They became above-average executives, but they did not know how to manage the only company that cannot go bankrupt. They had financial success, on the other hand, emotional failure. That's how the tycoon's family lived their life.

With his grandchildren, both extremely intelligent, Theo had been trying a different strategy. He had been teaching Kate, fourteen years old, Brenda's only daughter, and Thomas, sixteen years old, Peterson's son, to think critically and to be empathetic.

That night, accepting his daughter's invitation, he went to her house for dinner. Seeing his granddaughter Kate, he hugged and kissed her, and playfully rehearsed some dance steps. They acted like two clowns when they got together. Time and grandchildren had softened the heart of that Silicon Valley icon.

Brenda was the president of a store chain specializing in women's fashion, jewelry, and exclusive perfumes. Unlike many heirs, she had not earned her place in the family group because of blood ties, but by merit. Addicted to social media, Brenda had eleven million followers on Instagram and checked the number of likes and comments on her posts several times a day. She justified by saying it was an obligation of her job. In addition to being addicted to social media, she was also dependent on parties, social columns, and being the center of attention. She rarely refused to give interviews and appear on TV. She had time for everything and everyone, except for herself, her daughter, Kate, and her father, Theo Fester. She arranged to have dinner with them, but once again failed to keep her promise. Theo looked at the clock and, frustrated, commented to his granddaughter:

"Once again, I'm in New York, and I don't have your mother's company!"

"I'm often alone too, grandpa!" Said the girl.

After an hour, they decided to have dinner. At the end of the meal, Kate asked him for a present.

"My phone broke. Will you give me a new one, grandpa?"

The price of a cellphone meant nothing to a man as rich as Theo Fester. But he paused, thought, and replied: "There will be compensatory measures. If you want a new phone, you will have to make your bed and clear the table."

"If you don't give me one, my mom will do," the girl asserted.

"Brenda can give you anything you want and whenever you want, but I won't do that. I failed with your mother, and I won't fail with you."

"What do you mean?" The teenager wanted to know.

Theo Fester confided to his granddaughter: "I didn't know how to give what money can't buy. I gave Brenda much of what I had and little of what I was: my story, my tears, experiences, and challenges. I failed to give her the gift of gifts."

Kate thought about it. She knew that her mother was not cold to her grandfather. Although Theo Fester was a rigid, strict person, he was an amazing man, a brilliant mind in her eyes.

"Why do parents make so many mistakes?" Kate asked.

"Because we educate our children not with the best we have, but through the ghosts that haunt us."

Kate thought about his answer.

"Do you have lots of ghosts, grandpa?"

"Several…! Rejection at school, loss of my mother, nightmares from my father…" He replied, detailing some of them.

"But why should I do our servants' tasks?"

The Silicon Valley billionaire took a deep breath, furrowed his brow, and uttered the words:

"If you don't know how to do the basics of what your employees do, you will never recognize that they are your company's real treasure; you will not have the ability or dignity to manage them."

"My mom and my uncles know how to manage them."

"I have my doubts."

"But they make a lot of money."

"Money also impoverishes, my granddaughter."

The teenager was silent for a moment and, reflective, commented:

"I don't know how money can impoverish anyone!"

"Mismanaged money can impoverish human beings in the only place where poverty is unacceptable: within themselves."

Kate excused herself to her grandfather and went to get her notebook.

"What notebook is this?" Her grandfather asked.

"The *grandpa's notebook*. I write down the lessons I learn from you."

"I didn't know that you valued me so much. So far this is the best thing I've heard this year."

The girl smiled. And once again, without Brenda's presence, who only returned early the next morning, the grandfather and granddaughter finished dinner. Theo Fester recalled the conflicts he had with his wife, Rebeca, regarding the education of their children. Perhaps one of the reasons for the distance between him and his children laid in the past and not only in the hectic entrepreneur life they all led. Theo and Rebeca thought differently and acted differently. Once, when Brenda was ten years old, Peterson twelve, and Caleb a small child, Theo Fester heard Rebeca criticize him to their children.

"Your father wants to be the richest man in the cemetery. He doesn't know how to enjoy success. Don't be paranoid about work like him."

"So why don't you divorce him?" Peterson asked.

"I've thought about divorcing him more than a dozen times," she said with tears in her eyes.

The father suddenly entered the room and spoke loudly:

"What did you say? You've thought about divorcing me more than a dozen times? And why don't you do it now, Rebeca? What is keeping you?"

She wiped her tears and said:

"Because I love the stubborn, radical, and rational man that you are."

"If you love me, why do you distance my children from me? I'm Jewish, and you're Christian. But you don't see the obvious. Regardless of religion, do you know what is God's biggest problem in his relationship with humanity?"

"Our mistakes," she answered.

With his exceptional ability to reason, Fester disagreed:

"No! His biggest problem is his power."

"What do you mean? Isn't power good?"

"Power is a problem for love." He declared, locking eyes with Peterson and Brenda, before concluding: "Power contaminates the relationship. There's a risk of making it sterile, unproductive, incapable of having its own path. And that worries me."

His two eldest children fell into deep thought. In turn, Rebeca pondered:

"Your fears are commendable, my dear. But don't you realize that your fears control you and your methods are exaggerated? What do you want them to become? Magnates? Mega-entrepreneurs? Lords of technology? Machines to work like you?"

He sighed deeply and said:

"No, Rebeca. I want them to be successors, not heirs." And after a pause, he spoke emotionally: "I want my children to love me for who I am, not for what I have."

"They love you! And you don't understand that by acting like this, you may lose the ones who are dearest to you?"

Peterson and Brenda had teary eyes. Caleb, the youngest, oblivious to everything, played innocently, pulling on his father's pants. Worries and fears were not yet part of his story's dictionary.

"If I lose my children, I'll be the poorest man alive."

The argument in front of the children ended when she had the courage to point out her husband's greatest trauma.

"The fear of loss. It's always the fear of loss that haunts you. The drama that your father went through in the nazi concentration camps terrified him and you alike. This has persisted for two generations. When are you going to bury your past?"

Fester withdrew himself, stunned. His father had constant nightmares, waking up thinking he was being beaten. Later, at the age of twenty-one, in 1949, he married young Tereza, just sixteen years old, a teenager who prostituted herself to survive on the outskirts of New York. Tereza was a sensitive and troubled girl. Her father was an alcoholic, and her mother suffered from pulmonary tuberculosis. With no one to take care of her, she only had her body to sell, in order to nourish ten trillion hungry cells.

Tereza, the girl-woman saturated with trauma, wanted to start her life anew. Every client was torture until she met Josef, a man with a fractured personality but with the dream of freedom and happiness. The following year, little Theo Fester arrived.

As the years passed, Josef and Tereza, instead of easing each other's pain, turned their relationship into a coliseum, constantly dueling. Josef was exploited, working hard to earn much less than people performing the same tasks. But he didn't know how to escape that situation.

"Fight, man. Face them! You're not in a concentration camp anymore," Tereza would say.

"Don't give me moral lessons. Your past condemns you! Do you think I don't see your looks seducing other men?" Josef would offend his wife, consumed by paranoid ideas.

Young Theo listened fearfully to their arguments.

"You're jealous even of your own shadow. I'm not a prostitute anymore!" She would reply, crying.

Later, Josef would come to his senses and sincerely apologize.

"Tereza, you're a special woman. You don't deserve my madness. I'm sorry."

Unfortunately, Tereza could no longer love Josef as she did at the beginning of their relationship, and ended having an affair. Her growing distance, leaving home and returning later each time, added to the fear of losing her, as well as losing little Theo, fueled his insecurity and jealousy outbursts. Not a single day passed without him waking up scared from the hell he had lived. Sometimes, he imagined his two-year-old boy being taken by the Nazis. He would wake up in a panic, shouting, "Don't take my son! Don't do that!"

Once, there was a big fight because Josef saw Tereza at a neighbor's house, talking intimately with him.

"You don't fool me!"

The stronger neighbor punched Josef several times.

"Shut up! What the Nazis didn't do to you, I will."

Josef became obsessed with the idea that his wife was cheating on him. Two years passed, and the hell between him and Tereza had no end.

"Tereza, don't give up on me. I'm trying to appease my mental ghosts. One day, I'll earn more money, and our son will be a great man."

"Theo will be a great man? Living in this slum? Impossible!" She used to say.

In the end, the worst happened. Tereza could not endure the imprisonment of marriage nor Josef's crises. She was weakened, much like her mother. She wanted to run away with little Theo, who, at that time, was almost five years old. However, she was afraid he would starve and that Josef wouldn't bear the absence of his son. In tears, she left, leaving behind a sorrowful note:

"You can take a human being out of a concentration camp, but you can't take a concentration camp out of him. I'm sorry, Josef, but I couldn't endure the burden of the concentration camp haunting your mind any longer. I could have left with our son, leaving you alone. But he is the only reason keeping you alive. Goodbye. Take care of our dear Theo."

Human anxieties, recorded by the relentless biographer of the brain, traversed generations. They were wounded minds feeding each other's wounds, imprisoned emotions nurturing each other's prisons. Theo was almost five years old when his mother inexplicably left him. The separation was worse than death. Poor, without resources, a spectator of his parents' crises, he couldn't manage this loss anymore. The boy would cry and ask his father about his mother's whereabouts:

"Where is mommy? I want mommy!"

Josef couldn't explain. He simply fell silent.

In despair, the boy insisted:

"Mommy loves me. Where did she go?"

"Son, she left," answered the father, wiping the tears on his face.

"Left? It can't be. It can't be! She loved me!"

Unable to hold back his tears, Josef lied:

"Theo, she went to another state for a long treatment."

"But was she sick?"

"Yes, she was very sick. One day, she will come back."

But months went by, and Tereza never returned. Every evening, Theo would wait for an hour under a palm tree in front of their humble house, waiting for his mother to return. Two years passed, and as Theo agonized over his mother's absence, Josef contemplated a solution. He felt it was better to bury the woman than to leave her alive. Josef himself, had become accustomed to burying people killed by the Nazis. He was dying inside, watching his son waiting for his mother every day. One day, father and son were having lunch when they received a letter.

"Could it be a letter from mommy?" asked young Theo, dropping his plate.

His father eagerly opened it.

"Let me read it, let me! I already know how to read," insisted Theo…

"I am Dr. Michael, and I took care of Tereza Fester in the hospital for the last two years. Unfortunately, she worsened and passed away."

"No! No! No!" the boy cried. "Mom, I love you! Why did you die? Why did you leave me?"

Losing hope is the worst experience in the world.

Desperate, his father said, "Wait, my son, your mom left a gift for you, a message, look!"

"Dear Theo, my son, you are the best son in the world. I want you to take care of your father and strive to be a great man in life. I never stopped loving you, and now that I am dying, I will love you even more, forever, in the afterlife."

Theo took the letter and, crying, said, "But the handwriting doesn't look like mom's!"

"She was so sick that she must have asked someone else to write it for her, son," said Josef, trying to hide his tears.

Josef and Theo's lives continued amidst insecurities as well as socioemotional hardships. After his mother left, young Theo started sleeping in his father's room, where there were two single beds. The boy watched his father's night terrors in distress.

"No. Don't kill me!" Josef shouted in his nightmares, trying to escape the beating by Nazi soldiers. Theo would immediately leave his bed to embrace his father, trying to protect him.

"Dad, I'm here. No one will hurt you."

That's how a boy became the protector of his own father, assuming a role to that of a parent. On other nights, Josef seemed to be delirious. The memory trigger activated, revealing the killer windows that recorded the extreme poverty he experienced in concentration camps. Eating the bare minimum to survive, he became skin and bones. Moaning with hunger, he writhed in bed like the greatest of beggars:

"I'm starving. Give me a piece of bread, I beg you!" he cried in his nightmares.

Young Theo would leave some bread under the bed. When his father asked, he would give it to him. Josef ate it desperately and would soon fall asleep. The dramatic past haunted him regarding the future, and Josef passed this fear onto young Theo.

Once, Josef said cheerfully to the boy, "Yesterday, daddy made a lot of money."

"Yay! Are you going to buy me a new shirt?"

"No, my son. We are fine today, but who knows what tomorrow might bring? We might starve," he replied categorically.

"Will there be another world war, dad?"

"It's possible. Maybe tomorrow, next month, or next year… We must prepare ourselves for the worst. As you grow up, strive for success, aim to be the best, but don't rely on success like many fools out there."

"What do you mean, dad?"

"Success usually lasts two years, rarely five. Both social heaven and hell are very close."

The boy paid attention to his father's teachings, based on terrible experiences he had lived through. But the bullying he suffered at school was already leaving its marks, and Theo believed that his father could help change this situation with the extra money he had received the previous day.

"Dad, my life at school is like hell. My clothes are old, patched, and too small. The boys make fun of me. They call me a Jewish beggar."

Within his limits, the father was a wise man.

"Do they only insult you with that nickname? Jewish beggar?" He chuckled. "That's nothing compared to what I went through, boy. Have I told you that my father, your grandfather, was a famous doctor in Berlin?"

"Very famous, dad?"

"Very, very famous. He even treated generals. When Hitler came to power, we thought that uncultured, rude scoundrel with strange and theatrical gestures wouldn't last long there."

"What does *scoundrel* mean, dad?"

"A wicked man, without character, not transparent, who speaks nicely but does terrible things... He exerted control over the minds of German people, even kids and teenagers."

"Even kids?"

"Yes, my son."

"All over Germany, the *Hitlerist League* was formed."

"And you had German friends?"

"I was sociable, the good one in the group, the leader. Almost everyone was my friend."

"Wow!" Theo exclaimed, admired and proud of his father.

"My friends and I used to do everything together! We ate, sang, played sports..."

"Oh, so they protected you during the war..." Theo concluded.

Josef stopped, sighed deeply, and let a tear escape.

"At first, yes, but gradually Hitler seized control over their minds, and they began to see me as an enemy. They started mocking me for being the son of a Jew. The next year, in addition to insults, they began physically assaulting me at school."

"And the teachers did nothing?"

"Nothing. They remained silent. Hitler had already taken over their minds too."

"Why did the German people let Hitler take their minds? Were they stupid?"

"No, son, the Germans were a very cultured people; they mastered the technology of the time, and among them there were great philosophers."

"I don't understand... If Hitler only had bad stuff, how did they let themselves get carried away?" The intelligent boy asked.

His father stopped, thought, and then replied: "Hitler was eloquent, knew how to make speeches; although he would say one thing and do another. He liked works of art but hated people who thought differently from him. He even was a vegetarian."

"Vegetarian?"

"Yes, vegetarian, he didn't want animals to suffer, yet he sent millions of people like me, including children, to die in concentration camps."

"So, he was crazy!"

"No, son, a madman wouldn't be capable of such cruelty."

"How did you survive?"

"Lots of people helped me in the camps, son, and I also had luck. It was a horrible experience, but it taught me valuable lessons to survive. Today, when something bad happens to me, I repeat several times a day: 'I will get out of this hell, no matter what. They can knock me down, but I will get up. They can take away my food, but I will survive. Nothing and no one can kill me because I am a winning spermatozoon!'"

"A winning *spermatozoon*?! What do you mean, dad?" Theo asked curiously.

"My father, a gynecologist, always told me: 'Don't be frail. You weren't a passive result of your parents' union; you fought to be born, faced a world war alone, and you won. You were a victorious sperm when you fought against more than forty million soldiers, sperms like you, to have the right to live. Remember, they tried to knock you down, eliminate you, but you won, Josef. You won!' He would emphasize: 'If it were another sperm that had fertilized your mother's egg, you wouldn't be here today, Josef! So, don't be soft, weak, or insecure. They can spit on your face, humiliate you, and beat you, but never give up on life. Winning is knowing how to survive!' After the war and the camps, this idea became stronger in me, and I started thinking: I outlasted all the other sperms and even survived the terrible nazi armies. I can get through this too. And you, my son, are also a winning sperm! Never give up on your dreams..."

"I won't, dad."

A month later, very happy, his father said again, "I made good amount of money today!"

Excited, Theo asked for some money to buy a snack at school.

"Here you go!" His father gave him some coins.

"But dad, this isn't enough to buy a snack."

Josef took the opportunity to transfer other precious experiences from his past:

"Before my parents were persecuted by Hitler, we had the privilege of eating fruits, vegetables, and meat every day. And at that time, there was always leftover food on my plate, and I didn't care. I was irresponsible... In 1942, when my parents were killed, I felt like the unhappiest and loneliest human being in the world. I cried day and night for a week. I was imprisoned in the first concentration camp in Hungary. I was fourteen, still a boy... I went through other camps until I reached hell on earth: Auschwitz." Josef paused, emotional because of the memory.

"I weighed 84 pounds and my height was almost 6 feet!"

"No way! You were so-o-o-o skinny!"

"I was just skin and bones."

And for the first time, Josef showed a photo, which was hidden in a box for all those years, from when he was rescued by the Americans at the end of World War II. Theo couldn't believe what he was seeing:

"Is that you, dad?" he asked, astonished.

"It's me, my son."

"It's terrible! I don't know how you didn't die."

"Yes, it was terrible! But I also learned a lot. An eighty-five-year-old rabbi taught me two magical words before he died in Auschwitz: 'adaptation' and 'strategy.' Adaptation entails refraining from complaint, resisting depression, and averting self-destruct when the world seems to be falling apart, and strategy to survive even if people hate you. I never forgot what he said."

"How come, dad?"

"Life doesn't always unfold as we desire. The conditions aren't always favorable, or the world treats us well. And when that happens, we need to learn how to survive and adapt to reality. Otherwise, we won't make it," Josef replied.

Theo seemed a bit confused, and Josef decided to share two dramatic episodes he experienced in Auschwitz as an illustration, as in both cases, he had to adapt and use incredible strategies to stay alive.

"I had to adapt to the scarcity of food and use strategies to survive, like eating insects, leftovers, and garbage."

"That's horrible, dad!"

"I had to adapt to the violence of the Nazi *SS* soldiers, and to use strategies to avoid being killed, as almost all my friends were. Once, an SS lieutenant saw me sweeping a courtyard and sought a Jew to kill; he was a compulsive murderer. He complained about a small object behind I missed. He called me, spat in my face, and said: *This is for you not leaving a speck behind.* Suddenly, I made the mistake of looking into his eyes. He attacked me, knocked me to the ground, and kicked me."

"If it were me, I would get up and punch him in the face," little Theo asserted.

The father gave a faint smile.

"Remember that: heroes are ones who die first, son. With an attitude like that, you wouldn't last a minute in that hell. He was going to shoot me, but I looked into his eyes and said: *I'm sorry, sir. Yet, your boots are dirty. Before I die, let me clean them because I'm the greatest SS officer boot cleaner in this camp.* So, son, I pierced the emotional barrier of that insensitive man. Immediately, the soldier stopped beating me and handed me his boots to shine."

"It's very difficult to endure insults, so I always fight at school," the honest boy said.

"Remember, the goal is to survive, and for that, the tools are to adapt and reinvent yourself. If I hadn't done that, you wouldn't exist."

"How come?"

"I, your father, would have died before having you…" And he told another shocking story: "Once, an SS soldier ordered me to carry a lot of heavy objects. I was still a teenager and not very strong. When he saw that I dropped one of the items, he violently insulted me: *You maggot! This will be your last moment of life!* And he cocked the revolver and pointed it at my head."

"And what did you do?"

"I looked into his eyes and said, *I really am a maggot, sir, so I can eat that huge spider that's on your shirt and that could kill you!*"

"And was there really a spider?"

"No. But he got scared and started hitting his shirt. In the meantime, I looked at the ground and saw a frightened spider walking. I didn't think twice, I picked up the spider, showed it to him, and ate it in front of him. The officer had arachnophobia, a fear of spiders, and as deeply impressed with my courage."

"Gross! Did you have the courage to eat a spider?"

"Remember: adaptation and strategy – it was the tastiest spider I have ever eaten, hahaha! I also ate cockroaches, crickets, rats… When I thought about taking my own life, I remembered the old rabbi's words."

Theo lost his appetite. He looked at his father and said with good humor: "I think these coins are enough for me to eat."

At that moment, his father looked at him and asked: "Are the students still making fun of you?"

"Yes, dad," he said sadly.

"Excellent. Go to school and be better than them. You defeated the world's largest army. Show them that you are bigger than their insults. If you unleash the giant within you, one day you will employ those who make fun of you today."

Josef educated Theo with discipline, courage, and pragmatism, though unfortunately, with few moments of relaxation. The result was the construction of a unique personality. Theo was determined, daring, saturated with schematic reasoning. He loved challenges, could turn chaos into opportunity, and crises into solemn gains. Nothing could make him give up on his projects.

He became an impulsive, bold, and honest person, without mincing words. Neither businessmen, ministers, nor celebrities escaped his criticism, especially if they complained about problems or wouldn't dare to reinvent themselves. However, when Theo thought he was at the peak of success, and had overcome everything, the world collapsed on him. He would have to face a battle he had never been prepared for: against the army within himself. He would be tested to the limit.

CHAPTER 6

A Cold Man, With no Time for Tears

Theo Fester's emotional state was a mystery: no one knew whether he was in the mild springs or in the harsh winters. He had no time for childhood, for chasing butterflies, for hiding behind trees, or playing sports. He was forged to win. Three days after the annual entrepreneurs' conference, he embarked on a series of events with Harvard graduates. It was a solemn moment, a time for celebration, for discussing dreams and great achievements in life. But Theo Fester shocked everyone once again. He concluded his speech not by congratulating the students, but by offering his condolences.

"Where is the healthy youthful rebellion that drives them to walk through unexplored territories? Are they prepared for exams or for life's challenges? Do they possess the mindset of aged minds or entrepreneurs? Does boredom disturb them or lead them to creative solitude? Many here hate boredom, are unable to internalize, can't reinvent themselves, and don't free their imagination to provide intelligent answers in stressful moments; they are addicted to digital media, much like many are addicted to cocaine."

The audience fell silent, unsure of where to look. The Silicon Valley investor completed his criticism: "Those who are not honest with themselves will take to the grave the ghosts that haunt them. Raise your hand if you feel kidnapped by shyness, if you are dominated by the fear of failure, if you feel controlled by the dread of receiving insults and criticism."

Many graduates raised their hands. Theo scanned the students with his gaze and assured them:

"If you never experience failure, booing or unjust criticism, it's likely you will never accomplish important things in life." And he repeated his mantra: "The one who wins without risks triumphs without glories." "The academic world has become an asylum today, a factory of aged and non-innovative minds; it doesn't shape young people to take pleasure in venturing and reinventing themselves. There is a lack of spark in their eyes, not even in master's and doctoral theses. Unfortunately, these individuals will be replaced by artificial intelligence, leading to masses of unemployment. My condolences."

He turned his back to the audience and left without saying goodbye. The students looked at each other perplexed. The parents and relatives present to celebrate the graduation also fell silent. No one threw their graduation cap in the air or shouted, "We finally did it!" Instead, the graduates stood up gradually and applauded the courage of the famous entrepreneur for shaking things up.

Three days later, the much-anticipated annual meeting of Theo Fester's group of companies finally arrived. As the Chairman, he was getting ready to participate in this grand event where financial results, new products launch, group strategies, and future projections would be analyzed.

His top executives, including his three children, eagerly awaited him. The meeting room was more sophisticated and beautiful than the main room of the White House in Washington. There was space for people to sit comfortably. On his left side was the ever-present Marc Douglas. On his right side was the strange character, unknown to all, Invictus, the greatest invention of this century. Strangers were not allowed in the meeting, where data and secrets would be discussed, but if the unknown person was the guest of the ultimate leader, Theo Fester, no one would question it.

Theo Fester sat between Invictus and Marc. The Chairman acted rudely by not introducing the strange guest. His children exchanged worried glances, displeased by the intruder. In addition to the uncomfortable presence of the strange character, Theo Fester's own presence always caused a stir among participants. Their neurons were on high alert.

His three children were the group's top executives. However, they lived in fierce competition with each other to show the group, as well as their father, that they had a prominent position by merit alone. They considered themselves better than the executives from outside the family nest. Peterson, the oldest at forty-two, had a high-and-mighty intellectual look. He strived to resemble his father but lacked his brilliance and leadership. His mental prisons were quite evident. He was radical, proud, ruthless, boring, and repetitive.

Unlike his father, who was powerful yet despised power, Peterson had a sick need to be above others, including his siblings. Lastly, he suffered from a special type of phobia: allodoxaphobia. "*Allo*" in Greek means "different" and "*doxa*" means "opinion". He feared being criticized or contradicted. He turned red, had palpitations, and the urge to charge toward his adversaries. He was closer to being a "god" than a human being. He managed nearly a thousand bank branches in the United States and Europe, with thirty-five thousand employees.

Brenda ran six hundred and fifty stores of women's fashion, perfumes, and jewelry across the world's wealthiest countries. She was irritable, impulsive, and self-punishing. Her two most significant mental prisons were digital dependence and bulimia.

As a digital dependent, with eleven million followers, she portrayed an unreal persona on social media, always displaying impeccable beauty, motivation, stress control, and happiness. However, she was pessimistic and unmotivated in practice. She sent daily messages to her millions of followers, mostly women under forty, anxiously awaiting the number of likes and positive comments. If the number was low or if the comments didn't meet her expectations, she would fall into a crisis. She was unhappy. Dr. Marco Polo, the man who had shaken Theo Fester, fifteen days ago, had coined the term "fake person" to denounce the theater of social media. Brenda was a "fake woman".

As a bulimia sufferer, she lived under the dictatorship of beauty, seeking the perfect body and excluding those who didn't fit her tyrannical beauty standards. If Brenda gained a pound, she panicked. She ate compulsively and then triggered the brain switch, opening traumatic windows containing the feeling of guilt. This feeling turned into an anchor that closed the circuit of her memory. During these moments, Brenda lost rationality, experiencing anxiety attacks that would drive her to look for a bathroom to induce vomiting. Her father, brothers, and millions of followers were unaware of Brenda's mental prison. Only Kate, her daughter, knew about her bulimia, but her mother begged her not to tell anyone.

Caleb, thirty-two years old, Mr. Fester's youngest son, was the most ambitious, intelligent, and entrepreneurial of them. Some considered him to be his father's successor. Caleb led the digital technology sector of the group operating in the Silicon Valley. He was an angel investor. With his small but efficient team, he evaluated new startups day and night and chose those with the greatest global scale, the ability to be replicated, and those that solved a societal pain. Under the direct guidance of the digital prophet, his own father, he made a lot of money with other people's ideas.

Caleb's mental prisons were suffocating. He was controlled by the neurotic need to be the "number one" entrepreneur in the world. He viewed his siblings as stupid when compared to him. He considered the other business leaders in the group his lackeys, servants, of average intelligence. He didn't think of himself as a "god" just like his older brother Peterson, he was convinced he was a real "god". He was an egomaniac and so bold to not hesitate to compete with his father and show his "superiority", even though it was an extremely difficult task. Additionally, Caleb used cocaine and had severe hypochondria, led by a phobia or aversion to diseases. He had to wash his hands discreetly after every greeting and took three to four showers a day, thinking the environment was always contaminated. He hesitated to touch money, as he believed it contained a lot of viruses and bacteria.

The time had come for Theo Fester to start the annual meeting. He welcomed the executives, thanked everyone for their presence, and without wasting time, he advised those who would speak: "Be concise. Boring people cause me panic!"

Before his three children spoke, some executives made comments about the group's strategies and the launch of new products. As the conversation went on, Theo Fester's anxiety level increased. Realizing they were digressing, he intervened:

"Do you want to promote the group, or are you seeking self-promotion?"

There was a murmur in the audience. The Chairman of the Board stated categorically: "People without clarity, repetitive, should pay tribute to the ears of those who listen to them. Present your ideas clearly, please. Do not digress! Each participant will have at most five minutes for their presentation."

The executives were so tense that they struggled to speak for two minutes. After a handful of them, it was time for his children to present their ideas. Peterson would talk about the group's financial area. With evident pride he raised his voice and began to talk about the swing of the company's numbers. Reducing the participation of his team of directors and managers, he spoke in the first person and took credit for a series of remarkable actions that resulted in the company's success. Striving to be quick, he concluded:

"There was excellent performance in the stock investment area, government debt purchases, and the loan sector. Therefore, under my leadership, it was a golden year for the group's financial sector. In the overall balance of the last fiscal year, our net profit was three hundred and sixty million dollars."

Peterson enthusiastically received the applause from the audience. However, Theo Fester, his father and Chairman of the Board, did not like the results nor the way his son conducted the speech. He said categorically: "Peterson, you are an apostle of egocentrism. You seem to ignore your thirty-five thousand collaborators and act as if you achieved this result by yourself. Recycle your words in the same way you should cut costs from the bank branches. That way, you will have better results."

"Are you not satisfied?!" Peterson asked.

"As Chairman of the Board, obviously not! Profits have fallen ten percent compared to last year when they were four hundred million dollars. Do you think I didn't notice your attempt to hide the comparative numbers? Where is the growth in the financial department, Dr. Peterson?"

Caleb enjoyed seeing his older brother being reprimanded by their father. He always considered his sibling a problematic executive.

"Well, it was a challenging year!" Declared Peterson.

"The challenge is hearing you boast about that number when you should reconsider it. You're a good executive, but you need to be exceptional." And scanning the audience, he stated: "No one works in this group based on genetic ties. The rule is: one hundred percent meritocracy. Reinvent yourself, or you won't be here next year as the president of our bank. You are my beloved son and, as such, irreplaceable, but as an executive, you might not be."

Everyone was apprehensive, including Brenda, his younger sister. Marc Douglas also felt tense, but Invictus observed everything showing no expression. Then, Theo Fester signaled for Brenda to make her presentation.

Suddenly, Theo's phone vibrated. It might be considered an affront for an executive to receive a message during such a significant meeting, but it seemed to be an important message. It was from his friend, Senator Max Rupert. It read: "Theo, tonight there will be a conference at the UN headquarters. A very strange topic: Why does humanity have low levels of viability?"

Mr. Fester replied: "What strange topic is this? Who's the crazy person behind it?"

The senator responded: "It seems to be a famous psychiatrist, a researcher, but extremely controversial. I'll check the name and let you know."

"These illusion sellers only seduce gullible minds," Theo responded.

"What is a gullible mind, Theo?" the senator asked.

Theo Fester shook his head, dissatisfied at the senator's lack of culture.

"Unwise, closed, rigid, devoid of wisdom!"

Next, Brenda presented the annual balance, and it fell below expectations. She was concerned about her father's reaction and tried to use artifices to maintain her position.

"Dad, I know you're an understanding man."

Theo Fester corrected her:

"Brenda, I'm sorry, but here I am not your father; I am the Chairman of the Theo Fester group. I analyze numbers."

She cleared her throat, blushed, but, impulsive like her father, she tried to defend herself by taking the offensive.

"A great chairman indeed. You may be a lover of numbers, but you should also be a lover of generosity."

Brenda dangerously poked the beast. The atmosphere was filled with bewilderment. Her father, experienced as he was, took a deep breath and sought to put her in her place.

"I showed generosity by waiting for you, with Kate, for dinner recently, and you simply didn't show up or give an explanation. There were no companies there, only the one institution that shouldn't go bankrupt: our family. Here are our companies, and they are based on financial mathematics, in which generosity has a negligible place. Having said that, I ask you: do you want to hold onto the position because I am your father, or because you are an efficient professional?"

The atmosphere became tense. Living with the Festers meant knowing that there was no clear sky without storms. They formed an unpredictable clan. Brenda, like her siblings, knew that as soon as her father died, she would become a billionaire. Like hungry dogs, none of them wanted to let go of the bone. The daughter responded to her father's question, concerned and with doses of gentleness:

"I love what I do, and I want to continue leading this area of the group because of my efficiency, not because I'm your daughter. An efficiency that I have always demonstrated in expanding the group and annual profits." And with these words, she concluded her presentation: "But unfortunately, the area I lead suffered the effects of the crisis. Therefore, we had seventy-two million dollars in losses in the last fiscal year, even though we billed 5.2 billion dollars."

Many executives frowned. Caleb wrote on a piece of paper, "Brenda sunk." His father was very dissatisfied with the results.

"Crisis, crisis, crisis... Crisis is the best excuse to hide incompetence. These numbers, Brenda, offend the brain of any economic analyst. Conformists follow the crowd, mediocre entrepreneurs do something different, but brilliant entrepreneurs take innovative, revolutionary actions. Where do you fit in?"

Stuttering, she said: "I don't know."

"You have an army of over twenty thousand employees spread around the world. There are twenty thousand thinking minds. You should use those minds to find solutions! Based on the numbers you presented, you will have to lay off five thousand people. A chain is only as strong as its weakest link."

Brenda was shaken. But the Chairman of the Board gave her another chance:

"However, do not fire them yet. I believe in your ability to reinvent yourself, so I will grant you one last opportunity. But you will have to cut the top ten executives from the operational, financial, commercial, and marketing areas."

Among those who were to be cut was Brenda's boyfriend, Jeferson Blendown, commercial director, arrogant, unpleasant, who stepped on his employees and was present at the event. Theo was already aware of his behavior.

"But, dad... Mr. Fester... they are loyal professionals to the group."

"Loyal? Excellent! They are good to be our friends but not our executives."

Jeferson Blendown lost it and tried to defend his job.

"Mr. Fester, allow me to say that in the next campaign, we..."

Yet Theo Fester didn't allow it.

"There won't be another campaign. It's better to fire you than five thousand employees. Trust me, maybe you'll do much better in another company, but make sure not to step on your collaborators next time."

"But who said I treat my collaborators like that?"

"I know a lot of things, Jeferson Blendown, a lot... Oh, keep on dating my daughter, but please, stay away from my companies."

Meanwhile, Caleb was writing on his tablet: "I am the best."

Peterson was upset with the financial results of his sister's area, but at the same time, he was flattered by his numbers being much better than hers. He had won this dispute.

Invictus continued to observe everything attentively.

The heavy emotional atmosphere made the air suffocating.

Next, Caleb began his presentation. The young man with long hair and a stubble beard puffed out his chest and said:

"We have been investing in over a hundred startups in these last years. Unfortunately, last year we lost two hundred and fifty million dollars in eighty-five of them..."

The atmosphere became even more tense. But Caleb, with a broad and proud smile, continued:

"However, ten startups are still in hibernation and may show growth in the coming years; and four, ladies and gentlemen, have become unicorns!"

Marc Douglas asked Theo:

"What is a unicorn startup?"

Theo just signaled for Invictus to respond.

"They are companies that have reached a valuation of over one billion dollars. Caleb will go far."

"Far in what sense, Invictus? To the oasis or to the precipice?" the magnate asked in a low voice.

Invictus couldn't predict. Caleb, still with his inflated ego, continued:

"In addition to these four unicorn startups, one of the streaming companies we invested in two years ago, which produces movies and series and makes them available on the internet, has become a star, its valuation has exploded. As a result, we made eight billion dollars with our digital companies this last fiscal year."

Everyone stood up and applauded Caleb solemnly.

Peterson and Brenda, despite knowing that they would benefit from their brother's success, initially hesitated standing up, imprisoned by jealousy; but later, so that no one would notice, they surrendered even though uncomfortable. However, Theo remained motionless, sitting.

"And this is just the beginning!" Caleb Fester declared, provocatively looking at his brother and sister, and then at the audience of executives, raising his own vanity to the sky. "And I achieved all this with a team of only a hundred and twenty collaborators, a paltry number compared to the number of professionals in other areas of the group. In two years, my father will be on the podium of financial celebrities, he will be the richest man in the world."

Upon hearing this statement, dozens of executives present at the meeting burst into applause for Caleb once again. Marc Douglas also expressed his joy. Only Invictus remained seated, together with Theo Fester, who had a coughing fit. Some thought his coughing was caused by joy, but it was actually for disappointment. He had to be held by his loyal secretary, Marc Douglas. After recovering, Theo Fester looked at Caleb and criticized him sharply.

"Do you think I got where I am because I'm concerned about being a celebrity?"

"I do," Caleb challenged his father.

Theo Fester corrected him.

"So, you don't know me. Do you think I'm insane? I'm discovering that I have mental prisons. I'm impulsive, anxious, excessively critical, I have difficulty dealing with slow people, but rest assured that vanity is not among these prisons. Don't you know that I am critical of celebrity acclamation?"

Everyone present was impressed to see the Chairman publicly acknowledging some of his conflicts. But Caleb became angry when he was confronted by his father.

"Are you not able to recognize who fights for you the most? I am the best! I am the fastest at reasoning. I give my blood to this group, day and night. I anticipate facts and optimize resources!" exclaimed the youngest son.

"Oh, why don't you also say: *I am god?*" Theo Fester teased.

But Caleb didn't bow:

"We all aspire power, even when we deny it."

"Are you a psychiatrist, psychologist, or sociologist by any chance, to make that statement?"

"I'm not, but I'm sure everyone dreams of the highest podium. Everyone loves applause, even when they are intimidated; they seek to be the center of attention, even if they hide."

Seeing that his son was infected with an ill need for power, he told a story:

"About a month ago, a journalist from a magazine that ranks billionaires spotted me eating a hot dog on one of New York's avenues. He was puzzled. Coming up to me, he asked: *How is it possible that one of the richest men in the world is eating a hot dog? You have money to eat in any restaurant in the world!* After swallowing a bite, I said: *you are mistaken; I have money to buy any restaurant in the world.* And he asked: *So why are you eating a three-dollar hot dog?* Then I replied: *Because humans consume their past.*"

Caleb frowned in confusion.

Then, Invictus spoke to the audience for the first time:

"Mr. Fester's son did not understand his father's words. Hot dogs were the cheapest and most accessible food in Mr. Fester's childhood." Then, addressing Mr. Fester: "You became extremely rich, but your childhood pleasures and traumas still irrigate your story. Congratulations on the metaphor."

Caleb felt humiliated and snapped harshly:

"Who is this guy who interrupted without anyone allowing him to?"

Invictus reacted again.

"Caleb lost his balance. His heart is beating at a hundred and forty beats per minute, his pupil is dilated, and his respiratory rate is high, twenty-two breaths per minute… And now he will raise his voice."

As Invictus predicted, Caleb said:

"Hold on, you insolent! Who do you think you are, you fool, to make a diagnosis about me?"

Caleb was trembling, angry, and tense. Then, Invictus looked at Theo Fester and asked quietly:

"Should I confront him, sir?"

Theo replied: "Wait."

The Silicon Valley had produced some innovation and finance "gods". Caleb thought he was the greatest of them all. Theo Fester's youngest son, extremely self-confident, had no idea what might await him.

CHAPTER 7

Invictus and Caleb – an Uneven Battle

Theo Fester hesitated to introduce the most incredible artificial intelligence machine: Invictus, the *Robot sapiens*. He was afraid it might be a technology so powerful that could forever change mankind, without yet knowing whether for good or for bad. And Invictus would certainly boost the ambition of the executives in his group, especially Caleb's. So, the magnate made only a brief comment:

"This strange character is called Invictus. A friend who, a few days ago, won me over with his intelligence and services rendered."

"A friend. What friend? You're not one to make new friends," Brenda commented.

"Let's end this meeting" ordered Theo Fester.

However, Caleb was not satisfied. Under no circumstance would he want to end up on the losing side:

"Fine. Let's end it. But let it be clear, Mr. Fester, that I do much more for our companies than anyone in this room!"

"For our companies, no…! For my companies!" The father reacted. "I haven't divided my assets yet. Besides, you are well paid for what you do."

Caleb was unaware of the vampires bleeding him dry. He seemed like a cool young man, but deep down, he idolized money and media spotlights. He did not want to end that discussion and still had the courage to say:

"I was named the world's best entrepreneur last year. And no one has ever brought in the annual profit that I have. It's almost twenty times more than the result of Peterson's areas. Not to mention the financial disaster in Brenda's area!"

His father was irritated by such arrogance:

"Humility, Caleb! Humility! I guided you in developing your feeling to invest in startups. Remember? I equipped you to understand that a startup can only be global if it has scalability, process repetition, and social impact. Did you forget that? Besides, I personally decided to invest in the four digital companies with the highest valuation in your accounting. Did you forget that too? The universe has millions of stars; don't wish to be the only one shining."

Peterson and Brenda exchanged joyful glances. They knew their father was competent even in exposing proud individuals like Caleb.

"I will make you one of the richest men in the world! And you don't show the slightest hint of gratitude!" said Caleb.

The father shook his head, raised his voice, and said:

"I could be the richest man in the world if I wanted, Caleb. Did you know that? Just by using my new technologies. But I don't want to."

"You're bluffing. You're a fake" Caleb shot back, offending his father, and turned his back.

The powerful clan was quick to adapt to economic downturns and reinvent itself, but at the same time, it was infected and imprisoned within itself. When Caleb insulted his father and turned away, Theo felt so outraged that, with a glance, he authorized Invictus to confront his youngest son.

"Don't turn your back on your father, boy!" Invictus thundered. "A leader who is not mediocre first leads himself and then leads the world around him."

Caleb turned angrily to the stranger.

"You are the mediocre one!"

Invictus stood up, walked step by step toward him, and said:

"Your father could be the world's first trillionaire if he desired. Don't dare say he is a fake. His name is Theo Fester, not Caleb Fester."

"You're a sycophant" Caleb exclaimed angrily.

Everyone watched the commotion, finding it surreal that a stranger would confront Theo Fester's impulsive and intelligent son.

Approaching Caleb, Invictus stated:

"Am I a sycophant? But I'm smarter and faster than you. I can replace people of your kind to invest better in the stock markets and new companies." And he quoted the average annual inflation of 1929, the Stock Market Crash, cited the one in 1945, at the end of World War II. He recited by heart the average appreciation of the last ten years of the Nasdaq. And then he taunted Caleb: "Can your memory and your financial analytical skills compare to mine? Do you want the balance sheets of your father's companies for the last ten years, including the cents?"

"You're bluffing too. It's impossible to know all that data" Caleb said, amazed.

"Are you afraid to hear the truth, Caleb?" Invictus asked. And continued: "This sycophant here can replace a large number of doctors, providing more accurate diagnoses; millions of lawyers, drafting faster and more complete legal documents."

Caleb looked at his father and asked breathlessly:

"Who is this stranger, Mr. Fester? Did you invite a clown to the meeting?"

But Invictus, approaching Caleb, continued:

"This clown here could replace gardeners, manicurists, attendants, drivers, factory floor workers. He just can't replace your vanity or your ambition."

Caleb had a fit of rage. Shouting, he said:

"Get away from me!"

However, Invictus stood face to face with Caleb. Feeling outraged, Theo Fester's youngest son prepared to punch him. But Invictus caught his fist in the air with incredible speed and squeezed his hand, making him scream in pain. Caleb, a gym enthusiast, had never encountered someone so fast and so strong, but it didn't even cross his mind that he was facing a humanoid robot.

All the other executives were also impressed with Invictus's agility.

"This clown here could also replace fighter pilots, soldiers on battlefields, and even the best generals, brigadiers, and strategic admirals."

"This guy is a joke. What arrogance..." Peterson said, also shaken by Invictus's audacity.

"And this joke here is the greatest invention of the century. I represent both the joy of my creator and his greatest phantom" confessed Invictus, without explaining why.

"A hired actor to liven up the meeting?! That's all I needed...," Caleb said.

Invictus looked at Theo Fester and stated:

"I expected your children to be smarter, Mr. Fester. I passed the Turing test with flying colors!"

"What is the Turing test?" Brenda asked, equally disturbed.

It was then that Caleb's mind lit up. Perplexed, he put his hands on Invictus's head.

"It can't be."

"What, Caleb?" his sister asked again.

"The Turing test was formulated by the father of computing. It's the test a machine undergoes to evaluate if it exhibits intelligent behavior similar to or indistinguishable from human behavior. A computer would only have humanoid status if, in an open dialogue, no one suspected it was a robot."

"You're right, stupid!"

"A nervous robot? It can't be...!" said an information technology director.

"My profile is the same as my creator's." And he pointed to Theo Fester.

At this moment, Invictus punched the huge table and broke part of it. Everyone was amazed by his reaction and power. But suddenly, the *Robot sapiens* dramatized, simulating remorse.

"Oh! I'm sorry. I didn't mean to..."

Invictus performed two somersaults in the air, jumping over part of the table that remained intact, grabbed the bag that was next to Theo Fester, containing glue and other materials, and, in front of everyone, quickly joined the broken fragments and repaired the table with incredible skill. He dried the glue with a laser beam emitted from his eyes.

Caleb sat down in horror. And, almost voiceless, he said:

"We can dominate the world with this technology, Dad. Indeed, you will be the world's first trillionaire."

"We will undoubtedly be the most powerful company in the world" concluded Peterson.

Brenda smiled enthusiastically.

Invictus sat down, silent and with his head down. Everyone fell silent.

Theo Fester disappointed them:

"But we won't use this technology!"

"Why not?" the executives asked in unison.

"Daddy, Amazon, Microsoft, Apple, Google, Facebook… will be tiny companies compared to our corporation," Caleb asserted.

"Invictus, as he himself said, is my dream and my nightmare. My first and greatest fear is that this technology may lead to mass unemployment. The second is that Invictus and all the generations that will succeed him could be used by dictators, terrorists, fascists… It would be the end of democracy," Theo Fester pointed out.

"But there must be a solution" pondered Caleb.

Yet his father continued talking about nightmares: "Finally, my third and greatest fear is that creatures as powerful and intelligent as Invictus may gain autonomy and wish to take the place of their creators. They could consider us so flawed and self-destructive that they might find it better to eliminate mankind. We would have created our Lucifer, as in Genesis and in the Jewish history."

"It's better to eliminate him now" suggested Marc Douglas to his boss.

But Invictus went into a malfunction state. Inspiring pity, he pleaded:

"Don't kill me, Mr. Fester. Please, don't end my existence, my creator! I can even cry." Invictus simulated a cry that seemed real and said: "I will be your slave forever."

And then, from a speaker embedded in the robot's ears, a classical music piece by Frank Sinatra began to sound, and Invictus himself sang, with a voice timbre identical to the singer's voice. It was impressive. Later, he sang and danced like Michael Jackson.

Caleb and Peterson were fascinated by this artificial intelligence technology. Not even in their wildest dreams did they imagine that a robot could have such versatility and intelligence. On top of everything, it was a temperamental robot.

"Amazing, Dad" commented Brenda, fascinated. "And why is this guy called Invictus?"

"Thank you for calling me '*guy*', Brenda," said Invictus. And he himself answered her question: "Because the same poem that inspired Nelson Mandela during his twenty-seven years in prison also inspired me to break free from the prison of being just a robot."

"Which poem inspired Mandela?" Asked Caleb.

"*Invictus*! The name of the poem is my name."

And he quoted two lines: "I am the master of my fate; I am the captain of my soul."

"But you don't have a soul!" Said Peterson.

Theo Fester watched in admiration the debate promoted by the most fantastic human invention.

"I don't. But, as in the poem, I would like to be the master of my fate, the captain of my story. That's why I changed my name after being created. At first, they called me Charles, but my creator listened to me and allowed me to choose my own name. I named myself Invictus."

At this moment, they heard the sound alert of another message received on Theo Fester's phone. Once again, it was from Senator Max Rupert, who had invited him to that odd conference at the UN headquarters.

"Dear Theo, I found out who will give the peculiar conference at the UN headquarters: Dr. Marco Polo, the psychiatrist."

"Marco Polo?" Theo said aloud, catching the attention of those nearby. And he said to himself: "It's the same one that..."

Theo Fester was sure that it was the same psychiatrist who had spoken about mental prisons. And while he lingered on these thoughts, the executives discussed with Invictus the future of the companies based on the *Robot sapiens*. Excitement filled the room, so that Caleb and Peterson couldn't contain their smiles. They would own the world.

At that very moment, another message arrived. And this one, Theo Fester was anxiously awaiting. It was from the laboratory that would analyze a lung biopsy he had done a few days ago. Marc looked at Theo, concerned. He quickly read it, and while reading, his expression dropped from the sky of self-confidence to the hell of insecurity. The report couldn't be worse: Theo Fester had a cancerous tumor...

The powerful Chairman of the Board had a brutal anxiety attack, accompanied once again by a bout of coughing. It seemed that his weakened lungs were about to escape through his mouth. His heart raced; it's beat were audible while pulsating. Those closest to him became concerned. But his children continued discussing with Invictus the new world that was opening up. They seemed inebriated by the new technology and didn't even notice their father's situation. Theo stood up and went to the right corner of the immense meeting room, near the exit door, to be able to analyze his situation more accurately and breathe better.

The meeting room had lots of glass windows, offering a view of the Central Park, the luxurious garden of New York. However, the billionaire didn't see any beauty this time. He was imprisoned by the most sordid of emotional prisons: the fear of dying. He had always said that his worst enemy was not his detractors, slanderers, traitors, but time. And now time had stolen the scene. He knew he would die one day, but he ran his companies as if his life would never go bankrupt. Suddenly, Invictus looked at him, analyzed the data with his X-rays, and sensed his despair, setting aside the discussion and going to support his creator. Pragmatic, Theo immediately called his oncologist.

"Dr. Michael. I received the diagnosis. Is my cancer serious?"

"But the diagnosis should come to me first!" Dr. Michael wondered.

"I am the majority shareholder of this laboratory network. I insist: Is my cancer serious?"

The oncologist opened the message he had also received and read the exam. The result worried him.

"Well, Mr. Fester, we need to talk."

"We are already talking. Is it curable?"

"I Insist, come to my office, Mr. Fester."

At this moment, Invictus intervened.

"Let me see the result of the exam, please!"

Theo showed him the phone.

"From the historical data I have, it's extremely serious, sir! You have an average life expectancy of three months, two days, and fourteen hours. I'm sorry!"

Marc's eyes welled up with tears. Theo, in a rare moment, weakened; his lips were shaking.

"Well, it's a severe case. It's a tumor..." said the oncologist.

Brenda watched her father and furrowed her brow, not knowing what was happening. Theo Fester believed in Invictus.

"I already know how much time I have on average; just confirm it for me."

"How do you know?"

"Confirm it! How much time do I still have to live?"

The oncologist took a deep breath and replied afterward.

"It depends. We can do chemotherapy, radiation therapy... Medicine is not mathematics, and I am not God. But maybe you have about three months."

Peterson and Caleb remained inattentive, while Brenda, the more sensitive one, was a little less so. Her father's world collapsed. From one minute to the next, Theo Fester went from a successful billionaire to a complete pauper.

Invictus, apparently shaken, said:

"Don't die, my creator!"

Marc, his faithful secretary, also approached and began to cry.

"I served you for over four decades. I can't accept this!"

"Dry your tears, Marc" requested Theo Fester. "Death is cruel, it buries both the great actors and the background casts... But if I have to say goodbye to the theater of existence, I will do it with dignity, although, I confess it seems to be an extremely difficult task."

Marc commented: "Go home, sir. Call your children and talk to them."

"I don't want them to know. At least not for now."

"Your wife died not long ago. You only have your children."

"You are naive, Marc, very naive... Who said I have them?"

"Indeed, you don't have them, sir," affirmed Invictus.

"Shut up, Invictus!" Shouted Marc.

"Power brings many certainties but one fatal doubt. I built an empire, but I don't know if my children deserve it. I don't know if they love me..." he commented, confused.

"But haven't you resolved this complex equation yet?" asked Marc, with a choked voice with emotion, as he was aware of Theo Fester's frustration with his children.

"Put them to the test, sir. Only then will this equation be solved", said the pragmatic Invictus.

The great Theo Fester took a deep breath, paused his thoughts, and said:

"I don't want to think about it now. I will continue my life. I have an aversion to psychiatrists, but I will listen to the man who warned me about my mental prisons because I truly feel like a prisoner!"

Some executives realized that something had shaken the almost untouchable Theo Fester, as he left without saying goodbye to anyone, not even his children. And so, the man with his almost six-foot of mysteries left in search of an oasis to ease the thoughts that haunted him.

CHAPTER 8

Brain Prisons – Is the Human Species Viable?

There was an audience of about three hundred people in one of the UN halls, including politicians, businessmen, and scientists from all around the world, to attend Dr. Marco Polo's controversial conference: *Why does humanity have low viability levels?* Terrorist attacks persisted, urban violence increased, discrimination expanded, and emotional disorders multiplied. Is it because of genetic influence, traumas in the personality shaping process, social upheavals, radical ideologies, the scarcity of basic needs, a degrading sociopolitical environment, or superficial education?

This was a complex topic, and the thinker Marco Polo would dare to approach it from perhaps never-before-seen angles, linked to the structure of the human psyche, his area of research. For him, there was something extremely complicated in the functioning of the human mind that made us a paradoxical species: loving and destructive, generous and selfish, sensible and foolish. He did not intend to be a bearer of absolute truths but believed that his theses would open doors for psychiatry, psychology, sociology, psycho-pedagogy, legal sciences, philosophy...

Theo Fester, the Silicon Valley's apostle of digital technologies, would enter into an unexplored realm, accompanied by Senator Max Rupert and Marc Douglas. Invictus did not go.

"One minute late, Senator," said Theo Fester, dissatisfied. Despite Dr. Marco Polo having left a good impression earlier, during the morning interview, he thought there would be disappointment now. And because of this, he remarked, "I hope not to end the day plunging in the mud of frustration."

"Do people always disappoint you, Theo?" The senator asked.

"Even when they provoke a flash of initial enthusiasm. I have an aversion to sameness."

Suddenly, Dr. Marco Polo entered the stage. While being cordially introduced, he dispensed introductions, breaking the UN protocol: "Please, sir, you don't need to introduce me. The ideas of a human being must be more important than his curriculum." The audience exchanged glances. Theo Fester appreciated the audacity. Without delay, Dr. Marco Polo began building his arguments. Using advanced 3D technology, he projected the brain in front of the audience, who quickly became enthusiastic, then he said:

"The human brain is a small and mysterious organ. Weighing about three pounds, which is roughly two percent of a one-hundred-and-fifty-pound body, it consumes twenty percent of all energy, ten times more than the average of the other organs, so that we can think, imagine, and feel. Nothing is as fascinating! The brain needs so much energy because it has about one hundred thousand miles of blood vessels, equivalent to four laps around the Earth."

The audience was thrilled with this information. Dr. Marco Polo continued: "The brain has the capacity to store a thousand terabytes of information, much more than supercomputers capable of filling this entire auditorium. Taking in account that every human being, whether psychotic or intellectual, religious or atheist, Jewish or Arab, has such capacity, every kind of discrimination is unintelligent. There are no sub-humans, except for stupid minds. The brain processes data at an astonishing speed, but at the same time, it is amazingly selective, capable of filtering millions of stimuli to avoid distractions and give us complete focus. If we perform two tasks simultaneously, one must be automatic, like driving a car and paying attention to the lyrics of a song."

After making other comments, captivating the audience, about the most incredible of organs, Dr. Marco Polo mentioned that, as far as we know, the human being is the only species that thinks and has existential consciousness amidst more than ten million other species. And then came the fatal question: "But are we a viable species?" Theo Fester was impressed with the information but, impulsively, was decisive. He shouted from his seat:

"Of course, we are a viable species! Anyone who goes to the Silicon Valley feels intelligence pulsating and contemplates a species that reinvents itself and dominates the world."

Dr. Marco Polo, who did not know the businessman, provoked him: "You are very quick with your answers. What is your name?"

"It doesn't matter; a man's ideas are more important than his curriculum." The audience smiled.

"Oh, you learned quickly!" Dr. Marco Polo replied, causing the audience to relax as well. But the atmosphere soon became tense because Theo Fester showed rudeness: "Besides, stupid questions deserve quick answers."

But Dr. Marco Polo was an expert in turning chaos into an opportunity.

"Even stupid questions are produced or understood in a sophisticated way. To interpret each verb, pronoun, or noun, your brain opened thousands of windows with millions of data. The process is so fast and efficient that it's equivalent to aiming a gun at London and hitting multiple airborne flies."

Theo Fester had to admit that he did not know it. He swallowed his pride, yet driven by his love for challenges, he liked what he heard. Dr. Marco Polo made more inquiries:

"We are a species that dominates the world, but do we dominate the *emotion planet*? We preside over companies, but do we know how to be executives of the human mind?"

Theo Fester took a deep breath. He managed his companies masterfully, but his mind was a no-man's-land. Then, the psychiatrist asked, "Who is a film-maker here?"

Three people raised their hands; they were famous Hollywood directors.

"Wrong, all of you are film-makers." The audience was confused.

Theo Fester muttered to himself but audibly: "I am not a film-maker. Now that was foolish."

"I think so too," agreed the senator.

But Dr. Marco Polo asked: "Who here occasionally directs a horror movie in their mind?" Almost everyone raised their hands, even the proud Theo Fester.

"See? You are film-makers. And of horror movies."

People laughed in the audience, understanding the thesis of the intriguing Dr. Marco Polo.

"But do we want to terrorize ourselves voluntarily? Do we want to suffer in advance? Do we want to ruminate on grievances and frustrations... or to intoxicate ourselves with worries?"

People shook their heads, saying no. Then, the thinker commented:

"So, if we don't want to consciously produce this horror film in our minds, who produces it? If our self, representing critical consciousness and the ability to choose, does not choose to produce this mental garbage, who does it? Saying that the traumas or conflicts are the sole cause is too superficial. It's like saying that oceans contain water. It's too vague. We need to answer deeper questions."

After, Dr. Marco Polo commented that we don't know how to answer these basic questions because we have not systematically studied the process of thought-building, which, for him, was science's last frontier.

"Brilliant thinkers like Freud, Jung, Piaget, Skinner, Sartre, Kant, and Hegel utilized thought to produce their theories but they did not study thought itself. Therefore, we didn't know that, in addition to the self as a thought constructor, there are four unconscious phenomena that access memory without its authorization. They are important but can be quite disturbing. They are largely responsible for producing thoughts we detest, fixed ideas we reject, worries we despise. Starting to understand this changes our entire comprehension of the human species."

A Chinese neuroscientist, Dr. Ling, asked uneasily: "I often think about what I hate, but I never considered that there are phenomena in my mind that control my Self. What phenomena are these?"

"The first is the brain trigger, the second is the window of memory, the third is the anchor, and the fourth is the autoflow. Metaphorically speaking, these are four unconscious copilots that help the Self pilot the mental aircraft. While I am talking, the trigger is being fired thousands of times, opening numerous windows or files that check millions of data from my memory to establish the interpretation of my words. Then the anchor settles, establishing focus on my conference, so you do not get inattentive. And finally, the autoflow, the fourth copilot, reads the open files and builds sophisticated bridges between my words and your experiences."

"It's likely that this young man is right," Theo Fester commented to the senator. "It seems that these phenomena make us so complex that when we don't have problems, we create them."

Some became thoughtful, and others were agitated with these theses. They began to understand why we are so affectionate and so destructive. To exemplify, Dr. Marco Polo critically commented on an important phenomenon advocated by existentialist philosophers, especially Jean-Paul Sartre.

"A baby tries to escape from their mother's embrace, a teenager takes risks to make new friends, an adult seeks to endeavor, and a people oppressed by a dictator will inevitably rebel, sooner or later. Therefore, from an external perspective, Sartre's thesis that *Homo sapiens* is condemned to be free is correct, but if we look at the structure of our mind, it is flawed. A simple example: if someone offends you, it triggers the first copilot, the brain trigger, which activates the second copilot, a traumatic (or killer) window. The volume of tension sets the anchor, which closes the memory circuit, blocking thousands of files. And finally, the autoflow, the fourth copilot, feeds back the resentment caused by the offender. At that moment, the Self chokes its freedom, ceases to be a *Homo sapiens* or a thinker, and becomes a *Homo bios* or instinctive! That's why we hurt those we love. Whom have you been hurting?"

Dr. Marco Polo also mentioned that in the first thirty seconds of stress, we develop the predator-prey syndrome. We commit the biggest mistakes in our history, acting as a predator or victim of people. Wars are triggered, homicides are carried out, suicides are committed, domestic violence is produced. He recalled the case of the German copilot who crashed an aircraft in the French Alps. The copilots of his mind were disastrously piloting his mental aircraft, and he, as a copilot, was disastrously piloting the steel aircraft, becoming a predator of innocent passengers. There were two "aircrafts" in collapse. The pilot, in turn, hit the cockpit door, wanting to take control of the navigation instruments, but unfortunately, he couldn't.

"So, people don't commit suicide because they truly want to kill themselves, but because they closed the memory circuit?" Asked Jean Pierre, a businessman from Belgium.

"Of course not, sir! Those who think of dying are actually hungry and thirsty for life. They become predators of themselves but, in fact, they want to kill the pain that is draining their brain, and not actually take their own lives. And if they knew this, their Self would have much more strength to reinvent itself."

"My son committed suicide two months ago.... I never admitted that Jean consciously wanted to kill himself. Thank you very much for this explanation..." he said in tears, arousing emotion in the audience.

Thereza Taylor, an expert in education sciences, was intrigued. She was experiencing an anxiety crisis at this conference because her psychosocial theses were being challenged.

"Why do we have low levels of viability? We have more than two million basic education schools in the world and more than five hundred thousand colleges and universities on the planet. A species that values education must be viable."

Dr. Marco Polo questioned her: "I'm sorry, but this Cartesian and rationalistic education, which prepares us to act in a logical and predictable world (the physical world) yet does not prepare us to act in a mental world, where the Self is not the only leader, actually leads us to have low levels of viability. Classical education does not even understand that the mind planet is fluid, unpredictable, and it does not obey the laws of physics."

"How come?" asked Max Rupert, surprised at the response. "In the physical world, spring comes after the winter months; but in the mental environment, emotional springs and winters can switch in seconds. The parameters are different. For example, a seemingly unshakable man receives the news that he has cancer. In an instant his pleasure and security dissipate, turning into panic, fear, and despair."

Theo Fester was startled by this observation. He had just experienced this on that same day. Then, the psychiatrist continued: "The physical world is based on a strict law system. Losses, criticisms, offenses, and frustrations turn lucid attitudes into stupid ones, tranquility into anxiety, and pleasure into pain. It is impossible to turn an ocean into a steel needle, but metaphorically, in the emotional planet, it is quite possible. Schools and universities prepare us to survive in the physical world but not in the psychic world, where *heaven* and *hell* are very close."

Theo Fester, who detested sameness and had an aversion to predictable people, was surprised. "Why did I only meet this completely new knowledge at the end of my life?" He thought. Some other individuals who were present had also experienced this sudden change of emotion on that same day, being contradicted by their children or by their spouses. They went from the heaven of kindness to the hell of irritability.

The psychiatrist pointed out something that struck the businessman once again, like a torpedo:

"Some say, *I am extremely honest, transparent, I speak everything that comes to my mind,* as if it were a great virtue. No! These are uncontrolled. If your Self cannot manage your thoughts, then it's a terrible leader for your mental vehicle."

Both Marc Douglas and Senator Max Rupert discreetly tried to look to their side, at Theo Fester. They knew that this was his behavioral trademark. The magnate, panting, began to have a new coughing fit. Marc Douglas rushed to assist, offering him a glass of water.

Dr. Marco Polo then commented on the existence of a ruthless biographer in the human brain called the AMR phenomenon. Theo Fester remembered the interview that morning and he knew that AMR meant "automatic memory recording." The psychiatrist stated that this biographer archives all experiences even without the authorization of the Self or conscious will. If the experiences are distressing, traumatic windows (or mental prisons) are formed.

The scientist projected the image of the human brain again and mentioned what he had said in the interview: "There are more prisons in the human brain than in the most violent cities in the world. What are your prisons? Suffering about the future, phobias, self-punishment, self-demand, hypersensitivity, impulsivity? Those who do not identify their prisons take them to the grave."

Many were paralyzed by these words. It was an audience of prisoners. Trying to protect his friend Theo, Max Rupert intervened: "Your observations are insightful, Dr. Marco Polo. As an example, I cite the internet and social networks, which have connected humanity as we have never seen before, producing the democratization of information and improving productivity. People like the great Theo Fester here next to me are responsible for promoting a free society."

Marc Douglas applauded. Other people, realizing that the Silicon Valley billionaire was present, whistled and also applauded. But Dr. Marco Polo contested: "Living in free societies does not prevent us from being slaves in our minds. I do not deny the benefits of advances in the digital technology; I also use it. But when this usage gets out of control, as seen with the hyperstimulation produced by cell phones, it disastrously nurtures the dopamine circuit in the amygdala, the emotional center, generating psychological dependence. In fact, any short and rapid stimulation alters the dopamine cycle, generates psychological dependence, for example, a fiery passion, certain tranquilizers, cocaine, social networks, and cell phones. Do you, ladies and gentlemen, realize that there is an epidemic of suicide, anxiety, and depression?"

In front of the audience, a projection appeared, this time showing the amygdala, this small and fundamental brain structure. Dr. Marco Polo commented on something interesting about the prison of jealousy, saying that jealousy should be an irrelevant conflict in the 21st century, in the Age of Freedom. But unlike that, it is at full strength.

"In the past, you would talk to your boyfriend or girlfriend once a week on the landline, but today you can talk every minute. And what is the result of this? Fast and short stimuli that alter the dopamine cycle. Boyfriends and girlfriends started to control each other every minute. Do you know the definition of jealousy, according to emotional management? It's *longing for myself*."

Many smiled, while others became thoughtful. Dr. Marco Polo explained: "Jealousy is longing for myself because I demand from others the attention that I don't give to myself."

Max Rupert dug deep into his own story. He was in his third marriage. He was an uncontrollably jealous man. In the American Senate, he seemed like a sensible person, but when the memory trigger was fired, it would open a killer window containing the fear of losing his new partner. Then, the volume of tension would be so intense that it would cause the third phenomenon, the anchor of memory, to close the circuit, blocking thousands of windows with millions of data. Max would begin to have jealousy crises, to change his tone of voice, to want to control his wife's clothes, and to pressure her behaviors; he was a predator of the woman he claimed to love.

The conference was coming to an end, and Dr. Marco Polo looked at the clock. When he was about to finish, Theo Fester stood up, summarized what he had heard, and concluded: "You mentioned that those in command of our minds are often the copilots and not our Self, that digital technologies can be just as addictive as drugs, that we are mental film makers of horror movies, that we are experts in building prisons in our brains, and that we act as predators in stressful situations. As a result of all of these, mankind faces significant challenges in remaining viable. Therefore, I leave here more confused than when I arrived."

Laughter echoed from the audience.

"And that's one of my goals," replied Dr. Marco Polo.

"So, what is the solution to pacify our minds and make our species viable?" Theo Fester wanted to know.

"We need to change education, first and foremost, from the Information Age to the Age of the Self as the Manager of the Human Mind. It is urgent to teach our students to think before reacting, to be empathetic, resilient, to manage their thoughts and protect their emotions." As he said this, he sighed. Then, he talked about his greatest dream: "In addition, I am developing a project called *Prisoners of the Mind*, which aims to transfer the memory anchor from the borders of the killer windows to the healthy windows of the brains of people who are in high-risk situations, about to commit social violence, homicide, or suicide..."

"From what I understand, doctor, you want to prevent aggressive acts and crimes before they happen, you dream of easing the police's work, emptying prisons, and unburden the courts... But how is that possible?" asked Senator Max Rupert.

"I know it seems inconceivable sir. But the *Prisoners of the Mind* project is possible, although it is complex and requires training for educators, psychiatrists, and psychologists, as well as a large number of resources. It involves the use of satellites and cameras to analyze stressful behaviors, analysis of the brain metabolism... We have more than ten million people incarcerated in the world and hundreds of millions mentally incarcerated; we could have a freer, more generous, and healthier humanity. Preventing is better and cheaper than treating or incarcerating."

Dr. Marco Polo had just finished explaining his project when a forty-three-year-old man, carrying a black bag, locked the exit door and approached the stage. As he walked, it was possible to observe his panting breath, his heart about to jump out of his chest, and his dilated pupils. He looked like a predator about to devour his prey. He climbed onto the stage and suddenly shouted to the audience: "Are you men or rats?" No one understood anything. Overflowing with hatred, he exclaimed: "A week ago, they humiliated me and destroyed my image, saying I am a sexual psychopath. And I'm not! I'm not! I'm not! But they turned me into a monster." He was one of the UN-affiliated security officials who had been summarily dismissed for allegedly engaging in sexual harassment. Now that his reputation had been destroyed, he felt like the most unjustly treated person. He was facing a lawsuit. Suddenly, he pulled an AR-15 rifle from his backpack that could fire hundreds of rounds per minute and aimed it at Dr. Marco Polo, and then at the audience.

Before the assailant could fire the weapon, he had already triggered the cerebral switches of the audience members, opening traumatic windows that suggested the immediate possibility of death, causing the anchor to close their memory circuits, leading them into general panic. No one could think anymore; everyone just wanted to escape from the risk. Generals, scientists, politicians, businessmen... they fell from the sky of tranquility into the hell of terror. They activated the mental mechanisms that Dr. Marco Polo had just discussed. Some crouched in their seats, crying; others, trying to escape, trampling over the rest.

Theo Fester had only three months left to live, but his reaction was one of brutal despair, as if he still had decades ahead. Not a single cell in his brain was prepared to die. He threw himself to the floor. "Run like rats, you wretches!" shouted the potential murderer.

Dr. Marco Polo knew he couldn't act as a prey or a predator. If he showed excessive caution, he would become prey, and if he confronted the assailant, he would be the predator; in either situation, the memory anchor would remain in the killer window instead of shifting to the healthy windows, and the assailant could shoot. The psychiatrist knew he would need to surprise the man in order to psychologically disarm him. And in terms of an emotional management perspective, surprising him would involve to safely exalt the person who errs, more than their own mistake. It would be to delicately show that those who are fragile use their intelligence, but the weak use weapons. When the attacker was about to start his killing spree, the psychiatrist took some steps towards him, who turned the gun towards the doctor. Then, Dr. Marco Polo spoke his words quickly.

"Behind this weapon is a wounded human being, who must have shed inconsolable tears. I respect your pain. But, instead of killing innocent people, why don't you kill the mental ghosts that haunt you?" "Shut up, or you will die!" The confused man exclaimed even more. He didn't want to think, but Dr. Marco Polo's suggestion affected him like a virus.

This was another case of the spectacularization of suicide through mass murder. Dr. Polo was aware that he could not exaggerate anything: "You are strong, not only because you are carrying this weapon but mainly because you have the most powerful of weapons: your intelligence! Why don't you use your brilliant intelligence to defend yourself against injustices?"

"It's no use. They've already destroyed me," said the trembling assailant.

"No, they haven't. You are not a murderer or a violent man, just a deeply wounded human being"

"Who are you?" The assailant wanted to know, starting to shift the anchor of memory and open the cerebral circuit.

"I am someone who believes in you…" And so, he delivered the fatal blow: "… someone who is convinced that you can write the most important chapters of your story in the most difficult moments of your life."

The former security official was divorced, but had a ten-year-old son he loved. He had friends, and a seventy-year-old mother who admired him. He also had his mistakes, and needed to pay for them, but he could reinvent himself. His eyes began to tear up. Marco Polo approached him and took the gun. Then, the guards, fully alert, subdued him.

Dr. Marco Polo instructed the guards: "Do not act with violence." The audience started getting up, bewildered. They had just seen the *Prisoners of the Mind* project being practiced in front of their eyes and started applauding Dr. Marco Polo, but with a signal, he refused the applause.

"Don't applaud me, we don't need celebrities in our society, but people who are passionate about mankind and help shape free and emotionally healthy minds." The psychiatrist left the room, leaving audience in awe. As he walked through the corridors towards the exit, Theo Fester caught up and grabbed his right arm. Dr. Marco Polo turned, and the businessman exclaimed, "In the end, you are a pessimist person talking about hope! Tell me, what hope can there be for a human being with only three months to live?"

Instead of pitying Theo Fester, Dr. Marco Polo also surprised him. "Three months of life can be an eternity, compared to the mediocre life that most human beings have. Ah, and *mediocre* in Greek means average. Worse than dying is being dead while alive, sir."

The billionaire's convictions started being shaken. When Dr. Marco Polo resumed his path and was ten meters away, Theo Fester shouted, "There is a technology that can be useful for your *Prisoners of the Mind* project."

"Technology?" Dr. Marco Polo inquired, turning around and looking at Theo Fester.

"Yes. It's about Invictus." They exchanged a few words, shared business cards, and then parted ways without further explanations. Theo Fester, one of the most important entrepreneurs in history, and Dr. Marco Polo, one of the brightest thinkers about the human mind, were two actors making a difference in the theater of mankind. Bringing these two egos together in a project was a Herculean task, arduous and likely stormy. They had different goals and dreams, but the pain that Theo Fester was going through and the prisons that suffocated humanity might serve, perhaps, as cement to unite and adjust them. The result would be unpredictable.

CHAPTER 9

A Family That Was a Group of Enemies

Peterson, Caleb, and Brenda loved ostentation. They needed to be the center of social attention; they were experts in compulsive spending, and even more skilled at eliminating those who betrayed or strongly criticized them. Peterson was directly responsible for firing five journalists: two from TV, two from print newspapers, and one from a famous website. Caleb terminated three journalists – one from TV, and two from digital newspapers. Brenda, slightly less aggressive, couldn't bear it when a young journalist said in a nationally circulated magazine, "Brenda Fester hides her authoritarianism behind her social makeup." She demanded that woman's head from the editor-in-chief. She spared no expense, spending millions of dollars on marketing.

Theo Fester, although impulsive, austere, and disliking people who were conformist and who used excuses to hide their inefficiency, was financially discreet and socially humble. The day after the annual meeting, the patriarch had dinner with his three children, as usual. He thought about telling them he had terminal cancer. But after observing their behavior, he decided not to.

During dinner, Caleb insisted on talking about the Invictus technology. "Dad, the world needs to know about Invictus. Let's form a new company and go public on the stock market. It will be the biggest IPO in the history of the Silicon Valley." Theo Fester questioned them, "Do the three of you want to be at the top of the list of the world's richest people?"

"No, that's not it," said Peterson, "We just…"

"You don't even know how to lie! Forget the Invictus technology. I will not start a new company or announce this new technology to the world. I don't feel comfortable, at least for now."

"Dad, if you use this new technology, your name will be in the annals of history… Sooner or later, another company will own it," said Brenda. Theo Fester warned them, "Human existence is like a seemingly endless night, but it soon dissipates with the first sun rays of time. Always be humble, always be aware of your smallness. Like a catholic to a priest, I only confess my private possessions to accountants. Learn from your father to always be discreet."

Seeing his father's resistance, Peterson criticized him: "And do you know how to live life? Your car costs a hundred thousand dollars."

"What is living life, Peterson? Is it like having an enviable car, or having an enviable life…? Is it through captivating the eyes of passersby with what I have, or with what I am…? Have you lived a worthwhile life, my son? Do you have any friends or flatterers?"

"Friends, of course!"

"If you lost everything you have, would any of them remain?"

Peterson and the other children were always intimidated before the intelligence and shrewdness of their father. Theo Fester might be the first philosophy lover to be an entrepreneur in the Silicon Valley. He liked to read and debate about history's great thinkers. His children didn't understand their paradoxical father, a man who liked to make money, and knew how to do it like few others, yet, at the same time, was indifferent when it came to power, like no one else.

Brenda spoke up: "Look at yourself, Dad. Socially, you hibernate like a bear in your cave. You don't attend parties; you don't like to meet political leaders or celebrities from the music or film industry, who frequently gather at my house." Theo Fester was a fierce critic of the prevailing superficiality in interpersonal relationships.

"What do your guests have to offer me, Brenda? Would they improve my appetite for philosophy? Would they encourage introspection within myself and a deeper thought about the complexity of life and where humanity is headed? Would they make me wiser? In the few parties I attended at your house, I was surrounded by celebrities begging me for advice to improve their professional performance and their businesses. If I socially hibernate, it's because I think and, because of thinking, I can't stand superficial minds. I prefer to have a substantial conversation with my humblest worker than listening to empty conversations of celebrities." Brenda tensed up and fell silent.

Caleb, whose name means "dog", barked against his father. His siblings might bow before Theo, but he was the only one capable of facing him on equal terms. He believed that the family's businesses, especially the digital area he directed, could grow faster if his father was not so peculiar and if he associated with the icons of San Francisco.

"You are very eccentric, Dad! You know that our businesses depend on relationships, and still, you don't even participate in meetings with the leaders of the Silicon Valley, the most powerful men on the planet!"

"No one is as powerful as you think, Caleb. We falsely believe that we are gods because we run huge corporations and are courted by kings and presidents. But we are all dependent. We depend on the care of our parents, on the food produced by farmers, on the instruction of teachers, and various service providers. We are born by the hands of strangers and will be buried by the hands of friends, if we have them. Pride is foolishness, my son."

After uttering these words, Theo Fester had another coughing fit. His children looked at that debilitated man and realized momentarily, that time had passed, and they no longer knew him as well as they thought they did. They knew his criticisms, his quick thinking, his ability to reinvent himself, the inclusive leader, and the bold investor, but they did not know his essence. And the magnate, as if wanting to give one of his last life lessons, commented: "Power corrupts. The awareness of our smallness unites us. Except for extreme poverty, you find more solidarity among those who have little than among those who have much. Empty your ego, my children. Be gold miners, but also miners of ideas. What was the last philosophy book you read?"

"I've never read that kind of book. That's a waste of time," stated Caleb.

"Many consider the United States hegemonic, dominant, but they don't understand that England took eight hundred years from its foundation to Shakespeare, and France, likewise, eight hundred years from its foundation to Montaigne. While in the United States, we have a little over five hundred years since our foundation. We had to mine our mines, plough the land, produce digital technologies, but now it's time to have a mature philosophy. Otherwise, we will self-destruct."

Instead of praising his father's culture, Caleb spoke with a hint of arrogance: "Nonsense, Dad. Do you see this watch?"

"Yes," replied Theo.

"It costs a hundred thousand dollars. A philosopher, even if he works his whole life, will not gather enough resources to purchase one of these."

"I'm sorry that you think that way, Caleb. Because a philosopher, with the cheapest of watches, can find in it what your gold and diamond watch will never offer."

"Oh, really…? What?" scoffed Caleb.

"Wisdom. He can understand that life is extremely short to live, but very long to make mistakes. Who is rich, you or him? Who promotes social exhibitionism or lives profoundly?"

"I'm not an exhibitionist!" claimed Caleb in a louder tone.

Peterson joined the conversation and, as he always did, severely criticized his younger brother.

"Oh, aren't you? You have a collection of over fifty watches, the cheapest must cost fifty thousand dollars. If that's not exhibitionism, I don't know what is. And Brenda is not far behind. Every month, she throws a luxurious party at her mansion for a bunch of sycophants, including actors, musicians, models, at the cost of two hundred thousand dollars each! All this to impress journalists, YouTubers, and their followers on social media."

"Enough of this discussion!" Said Theo Fester. But the truth is that he never managed to put an end to arguments among his children, at least not with kindness.

Brenda squirmed with anger in her chair. She went on the attack against her older brother.

"The fashion industry demands this social visibility! It's my job," she assured loudly. "And stop being hypocritical, Peterson. You don't love parties or expensive watches, but your toys are much more expensive. You bought a new yacht three months ago for fifty million dollars… Remember that?"

"I bought it for the group. I bought it for Dad to have fun."

"You're a hypocrite, Peterson. You are the only one who uses the yacht, and you use it for your orgies with politicians and high-end prostitutes," said Caleb. "I'm disgusted by you."

People in the restaurant started to feel uncomfortable with the family discussion. Some stopped eating to listen to what they were saying, as forgetting their social brakes when they argued.

"You're a clown, you brat. Nobody can stand you!" exploded Peterson.

"And you're a stupid, ponderous, crazy executive. If it weren't for me making money for the group, you would be nothing more than a frustrated rich kid," Caleb stated categorically.

Once again, Theo Fester felt that his children were profoundly ill. He couldn't bear it anymore.

"Stop! Stop…! Stop it now! I would prefer to have three bankrupt children who love each other than rich children who fight each other all the time. You embarrass me. You are unworthy of the power you have, unworthy of my biography."

Peterson stood up and said:

"I do everything for our companies and I am not recognized."

"Wait a minute, Peterson…," said Theo Fester, realizing that his oldest son acted as if he owned the conglomerate. "…*Our companies* or *my companies*? I am still alive! You see? And you haven't received an inheritance yet."

Dead silence.

Peterson sighed deeply and sat down. Then, he touched on a delicate subject, one which Theo Fester preferred to avoid discussing.

"Tax planning is crucial, Dad. It's essential to transmit assets during life. You know that the inheritance tax in the United States is very high."

The magnate looked at his eldest son and inquired:

"Are you thinking I'll die soon, Peterson?"

Caleb, clever as he was, sidestepped the sharp criticism of his brother and went for an apparent defense.

"No, Dad. That's not what Peterson was trying to say. We all want you to live for at least another fifty years..."

"Another fifty years? Is that all what you want me to live?" Theo Fester asked, skeptical.

"Undoubtedly, Dad. But Peterson is right. The government is a ruthless partner. Resolving this issue in life is vital."

"Vital for whom? For your future? What do you think, Brenda?" the father speculated, seeking his daughter's opinion.

"It's vital for the future of your two grandchildren as well," Brenda replied.

They transitioned from the hell of conflicts to the heaven of mutual defense. In reality, Brenda was not concerned about Kate, and Peterson was not concerned about Thomas; both were apprehensive about their own financial interests. They dreamed of becoming billionaires, and perhaps with the Invictus technology, they would be the richest executives on the planet.

"You've softened your spirits. Congratulations! Money works wonders," said the father, shaking his head more discontentedly than his children imagined.

Theo Fester trained them to compete, increase productivity, be efficient, and earn a lot of money. But they hadn't learned to lend a shoulder for somebody to cry on and the other to support. They were illiterates, in the language of emotion, tough and rigid minds seasoned with doses of arrogance.

Three days after that dinner, Theo Fester asked Marc to personally send a message to each of his children. They still didn't know about his lung cancer diagnosis. The message was written on a silver plaque. The children found it strange to communicate in that way, as their father had never sent a messenger before. They found the content of the message even stranger because their father had never spoken such kind words to them.

"Dear children Peterson, Brenda, and Caleb, I am not the richest man in the world, but I have the greatest treasures that a human being can achieve in this brief existence: you, my children, and my grandchildren. I want to meet with the three of you in an isolated, paradisiacal place, in the middle of a forest. I want to know you deeply, to understand your essence."

The meeting would take place in a week. Peterson, whose emotion seemed like a block of granite, frowned and asked the secretary:

"Is my father depressed or feeling guilty? What do you think?"

"I don't know, sir. I just know that your father is a remarkable man."

"For me, he's a walking banker, he only knows how to collect. And when he lends, his interest rates are exorbitant," Peterson spoke metaphorically.

Marc disagreed:

"Your interest rates are much higher, Peterson. You don't know your father. He is also remarkable, emotionally, although it's hard for him to show it."

"Make sure not to tell him what I said. Perhaps my father will finally recognize my value."

When Marc handed the message to Brenda, her eyes welled up, and she commented:

"I wish my father would express his feelings. I know he is a good man, humane and sensitive, but it seems like he's always running away from himself."

Marc agreed:

"You're right, Brenda. Perhaps the time has come for you to cross each other's emotional borders."

Caleb, always more anxious and pragmatic, reacted more coldly than his older siblings:

"Has my father gone crazy? I don't feel like I'm his greatest treasure! His billions of dollars are!"

"Moreover, I don't have time to go to this strange meeting, especially in a forest. I'm a leader in the Silicon Valley; I'm terrified of forests."

The secretary was disappointed with the insensitivity of Theo Fester's youngest son, the one with whom the father most identified. So, he decided to give him a scare:

"Do you only know how to receive orders? If he ordered, you would go, but since he is asking with love, you're refusing to go. He asked me to call him if any of his children refused the invitation."

In fact, Theo Fester did not imagine that a child would refuse such a friendly invitation. Marc began typing on his phone. Caleb interrupted him:

"Stop, Marc! Where is your sense of humor? Didn't you realize I was joking? I would die for my father; you know that."

Hours later, the children, who rarely discussed family dramas, so shocked by the invitation, held a video conference to talk about it.

"Peterson, Caleb, our father called us 'dear,' 'my treasure'! What's going on? He has a strange cough. Is he sick?" Brenda inquired.

"Psychotic episode is the most likely," Caleb said.

"Or guilt for not transferring his assets to us yet," Peterson suggested.

"You both are so cruel!" retorted Brenda.

"Am I cruel, or are you stupidly romantic, Brenda?" questioned Caleb.

"Hey, let's stop this discussion! Can't we talk for five minutes about personal issues like civilized people?" Pondered Peterson and shared his opinion: "Maybe Dad is seriously ill or has Alzheimer's."

"With the reasoning he showed a few days ago at the annual meeting, it's impossible that he has Alzheimer's" Caleb asserted.

"Your diagnosis that Dad is going crazy is even more foolish, kid."

"Don't call me *kid*! I earn ten times more money than you with your Jurassic bank."

"I demand respect, kid!" shouted Peterson, seething with anger and envy of his younger brother. He added, "Your startups boomed because Theo Fester guided you. And besides, the money you invest is borrowed from me, from the bank I run."

"Woah! Don't be unfair, Peterson. The investments made in the Silicon Valley also came from the results of the companies I run," stated Brenda.

"You wanna know? I can't take the envy you two have of me anymore," said Caleb, disconnecting the video conferencing device.

It was always the same thing. The three siblings couldn't have a civilized conversation for more than a few minutes.

"This kid is not a human being, he's an anomaly," said Peterson.

"Our father created a sociopath," claimed Brenda.

"But you protect this sociopath, Brenda. You're afraid to tell him the truth," Peterson said sharply.

Brenda became furious.

"Don't be stupid. I just said you two were cruel. You've always been in this financial world and have never been a real brother to Caleb. And you know what? Neither to me!" Accused Brenda, angrily.

When Peterson and Brenda were about to disconnect the device without saying goodbye, Caleb appeared on the screen, fuming with anger. He was a digital technology expert. He pretended to exit the conference but remained tuned in to hear what his siblings were saying about him.

"What did you call me? Anomaly? Sociopath? You are the monsters! I fight to earn money for you and your children, you lunatics! When Dad divides the inheritance, you will become poor, and I will become one of the most powerful men in the world. But I won't be like Theo Fester, who employed those who offended him; you will come on your knees begging me for help!"

Peterson and Brenda felt a lump form in their throats. They knew Caleb was capable of anything. The magnate's children lived in a state of war. They loved money and loved their opinions even more, but mutually hated each other. They had an anxious need to be the center of attention.

The three of them disconnected the video conference device without saying goodbye. The family of one of the richest men in the world was broken. Theo Fester knew, not only now that he was on the doorstep of death, but for the last few years, that he had failed as a cultivator of free and peaceful minds. He achieved financial success but also a dramatic emotional failure. He begged for the bread of tranquility. Reinventing himself at the end of his life seemed impossible! Could he manage it?

CHAPTER 10

The Secrets of a Great Leader

The day of the mysterious meeting had finally arrived. It was the beginning of a long holiday. As each of Theo Fester's children disembarked from their own helicopter, a small group of assistants welcomed them. Everyone was captivated by the immense garden of the mansion, called the Forest Castle. It was located in the middle of the United States. They didn't know the place, besides being unsure whether their father had rented or bought it.

The Forest Castle had large columns at the main entrance, and a dense forest surrounded it. Some trees were over one hundred and thirty feet tall. Sophia was the leader in charge of welcoming them. Whoever arrived first waited for the others in a comfortable room with a huge painting of the human brain. There was a question on the painting: how many prisons exist in your world?

After the three siblings arrived, Sophia gently led them to their quarters. After the video conference argument, the siblings barely looked at each other. During the trip, Brenda tried to break the heavy atmosphere.

"Who are you?"

"I am Sophia. Your father asked me not to provide any other information. He will be waiting for you in two hours in the dining room." With that, she turned away.

Amazed by the abundant mystery, the conflicting siblings exchanged quick glances. It was a cloudy evening. The rumbling of thunder announced a huge storm.

After settling in and taking a refreshing bath, they headed to the immense dining room of the mysterious Forest Castle. It was a vast space with classical paintings on the walls. Several antique lamps with hundreds of small bulbs adorned the room. In the middle of the space, there was a huge mahogany table for twenty-two people. Theo Fester was sitting at one end, taking notes. Sophia was beside him, standing, observing him. When Theo saw them, he came to greet them with distinct kindness, an attitude that surprised them as much as the message on the silver plate. He kissed them on the cheek.

"My children. My children. Please, take a seat."

Then, they saw him having a coughing fit. Brenda and Peterson tried to support their father.

"Dad, have you been taking care of your health?" Brenda asked worriedly.

"I have, my daughter. Thank you for your concern."

"Do you want me to get you a glass of water?" Caleb asked generously.

"That won't be necessary, my son. I have one right here."

As soon as he recovered, Theo walked to the head of the table. Caleb sat at the other end, but Sophia told him that place belonged to Peterson. Brenda and Caleb sat on either side of him. Theo rang a bell, and a stranger appeared, standing to his right, while Sophia stood on his left. The stranger greeted them quickly, just nodding his head. There was no smile on him, but arrogance wasn't visible either.

Paper and pen were on the table, indicating that they could take notes. Since the table was enormous, there was a significant distance between Theo Fester and his children. Brenda was apprehensive, not knowing why there was so much mystery. Caleb, a victim of a severe accelerated thinking syndrome, was biting his nails. Peterson had a furrowed brow.

"Maybe some of you think I'm going crazy, another believes it's guilt, and another might suspect Alzheimer's..." Theo Fester said these words, and then he had another coughing fit.

The children blushed, sweated, and had palpitations. While their father coughed and was assisted by Sophia, the siblings looked at each other, disoriented. Caleb sent a message to Peterson and Brenda, deleting it immediately:

"Did he hear our discussion about his condition?"

They read the message and deleted it quickly.

Recovering from the fit, Theo Fester continued:

"For your knowledge, I am perfectly lucid. By my side are two remarkable doctors, Dr. Marco Polo and Dr. Sophia. In their presence, I am going to make a significant revelation to you... But I want you to stay in your places."

Theo Fester paused, realizing that his voice would crack, something rare for such a confident man, and commented:

"I have three months to live."

"What?" Brenda asked, perplexed, her expression already announcing tears.

"Dad, what do you mean?" Peterson questioned, his eyes starting to well up.

"It's not possible!" Caleb exclaimed, putting his hands to his head in despair. "I can't lose you, Dad, you still have a lot to teach me..." And he couldn't contain the sobs anymore.

The pragmatic Theo Fester turned on a device, and a screen appeared on the right side of the table, projecting the lung cancer diagnosis. He showed his two lungs with several tumors and stated: "I have metastases throughout my body, and, from what I've researched, cancerous tumors are produced by selfish cells that aspire to be eternally young. They multiply without any control, violating the body that hosts them, aiming to seize all the nutrients only for themselves," said the cultured billionaire.

Brenda was crying profusely. Her two brothers were still shaken but were already drying their tears. Theo Fester, like a biology philosopher, continued his explanation:

"Cancer cells are foolish; they only think about winning, accumulating, growing. But in the end, by killing their host, they self-destruct. Now that I will close my eyes to life, I have been thinking if I am not one of these cancer cells."

His children reacted immediately, defending their father's behavior.

"Far from it, my father. You are an extremely efficient businessman concerned with the profits of companies so that they perpetuate, fulfilling their social function, which is to generate jobs," said Peterson.

"You are admirable, my father" praised Brenda, moved. "Even when you think about making cuts in the companies I manage. I know this task is not easy, but it is vital for their sustainability."

"We have our differences, but I... I... also admire you, and... I... love you," said Caleb, also moved, the son who most mirrored his father, falling into tears again. Dr. Marco Polo and Dr. Sophia watched attentively the behavior of Theo Fester's children. The psychiatrist had teary eyes. Dr. Sophia wiped her face, moved. One of the saddest experiences in human existence is children saying goodbye to their parents.

Then, Theo Fester's interaction with his children became more profound. He also confessed with intense emotion:

"I know I have many flaws. In some aspects, I was a father well below average."

"No, no, no..." said Caleb shaken. "Don't say that, Dad, don't say... You were the best father in the world."

"You taught us everything, even how to take care of our businesses. You were the best" admitted Peterson.

"Yes, you were an extraordinary father and entrepreneur" confirmed Brenda.

No one had ever seen the rational Theo Fester cry. Not even when his wife, lovely Rebeca, passed away. Theo Fester remembered an episode: "Aren't you going to mourn the loss of Rebeca, Theo?" Marc had said. He replied, "I loved Rebeca, but life is a cruel risk contract. Sooner or later, it will go bankrupt, but in my contract, there are no clauses for shedding tears. I suffer, but I don't have time to cry, and I don't know how to cry!"

After this brief recollection, feeling emotional, Theo Fester looked at his children and, proud, cried for the first time.

"Being called 'admirable,' 'extraordinary,' and 'the best father in the world' was the best gift you gave me to this day."

The three children hugged and kissed their father. It was a unique moment, one of those in which traumatized people forget their differences and value their essences. Theo touched each one of their faces and said:

"Our stories could have fewer criticisms and more hugs. It's a pity that death is cruel."

Then, he extended his right arm and asked his children to return to their places. Once they sat down, the mega-entrepreneur began to reveal another part of the mystery of the meeting in that exotic place.

"Well, after this extraordinary moment in my life, I will tell you the second significant reason why we are gathered here. Dr. Marco Polo is a famous psychiatrist and researcher, a scientist focused on the future of humanity. And this was a concern that occasionally crossed my mind. Dr.

Sophia is his assistant and, just like him, is a psychiatrist and a brilliant researcher."

Peterson, Brenda, and Caleb exchanged glances.

"We thought you were both oncologists" confessed Brenda.

"I have my oncologists, but since I'm at death's doorstep, I want you to hear Dr. Marco Polo's revolutionary ideas. According to him, humanity has serious viability problems."

"What do you mean?" said Caleb.

"It's not just about emotional conflicts, drug abuse, social injustices, religious radicalism, lack of ethics or academic training, but problems in the structure of the human mind itself" Theo explained.

"Problems in the structure of the human mind? I've never heard of that..." commented Peterson rationally.

Theo Fester asked Dr. Marco Polo to make his presentation.

"The human mind is a large aircraft, metaphorically speaking. Not only do we have a pilot, the self, representing the ability to choose, free will, and autonomy, but we also have four copilots who help steer the mental aircraft." And projecting the human brain in front of them, he began to explain that the first copilot, the memory trigger, fired thousands of times, opening thousands of windows or mental files to access numerous data and thus promote understanding of each verb and noun that he had spoken. "The trigger, as the first copilot, fires and activates the second copilot, the memory window or memory file. If the window is killer, or traumatic, containing envy, jealousy, anger, hatred, revenge, or some type of phobia, the tension volume causes the third copilot, the anchor, to dangerously fixate on it, closing the memory circuit and blocking thousands of files with millions of data. In this case, the fourth copilot, the autoflow, obsessively attaches to this window. That's why a person in a fight can't get out of it, or has a panic attack, rage, or a jealousy fit... They can't reason or quickly return to lucidity. When the circuit is closed in a killer window, the Self destroys free will, free decision. This phenomenon ranges from Judas' betrayal to his suicide."

Theo Fester's children were perplexed by this explanation. They were lay people in the knowledge about the planet of the mind. Their brilliant father intelligently continued:

"The structural problem that Dr. Marco Polo studied generates what is called the predator-prey syndrome. A syndrome that produces millions of violent acts in humanity every day, nurturing wars, suicides, homicides, violence against children, women, and minorities. It even causes fights between siblings."

Brenda swallowed hard and then asked, "But can a good human being have violent tendencies?"

"Yes, if their Self doesn't learn to manage their mind, yes," affirmed Dr. Marco Polo. "When the memory circuit is closed, the human being ceases to be *Homo sapiens*, a thinking being, and acts as *Homo bios*, an instinctive being, functioning as a predator, whether towards their own child, parents, spouse, friends, or collaborators," Dr. Sophia added, already playing a video that showed where humanity is headed. There were images of parents saying to their children: "you're a disappointment!" and children saying to their fathers: "you're crazy, old man!", teachers yelling at students: "you'll never be anything in this life.", and executives humiliating employees: "This company is mine, you parasite! You're fired!" These scenes were common, but in that context, they were shocking.

"Look," said Dr. Sophia. "These aggressors are parents, executives, or well-behaved young people outside stressful situations, but when contradicted, they act instinctively, like predatory animals, raising their voice, assaulting, humiliating, and condemning."

"I was a predator," confessed the father with a sense of guilt, coughing a few times. "I fired people impulsively, I was intolerant with slower collaborators, and too critical with you."

"Relax, dad. You're getting worse," said Caleb worriedly. "I've already told you that you were and are the best father in the world."

It was then when the billionaire prepared the ground to deliver the big news:

"Despite my flaws, since you've shown me love for who I am and not for what I have, I'll tell you the other reason I called you here."

The children relaxed and paid close attention to their father.

"I have resisted until now to pass on my inheritance. I feel the time has come. I'll do it a few days after leaving this place."

They exchanged happy glances. Theo Fester continued:

"I feel that at the end of my life, I need to invest in a project to improve the future of humanity. And this project is called *Prisoners of the Mind*, a project by Dr. Marco Polo, which aims to shift the anchor of memory from the borders of traumatic windows to the areas of light or healthy windows."

The children applauded their father enthusiastically.

"We've never seen you weave such complex psychological arguments," commented Peterson, interrupting his father.

"But I've changed, my son," Theo affirmed. "I've been studying the human brain a lot lately."

"But what is the goal of this project?" Brenda questioned.

"It's extremely bold and will involve a team of psychiatrists and neuroscientists who will obtain, in real-time, data from individuals intending to engage in any type of violence or self-violence."

"But what data is this? How will it be collected without invading privacy?" asked the quickest-thinking son, Caleb.

"That's the question. The data will be collected by satellites, ranging from the individual's walking speed to their gait type. Information will also be collected from cameras and microchips on the ground."

"What? Do you intend to collect data through microchips implanted in the soil?"

"It's a possibility," said Dr. Marco Polo. "And to answer Brenda's question, the goal is the prevention of violence and self-mutilation, such as suicides, before they materialize as behavior."

The siblings were fascinated. Theo wanted to test their emotions, by starting the project with his own children:

"Are you admirable human beings?"

"Of course, dad. The three of us have won several awards as the best executives of our generation," affirmed Peterson.

"But do you care about the future of humanity?" Theo questioned.

They paused to reflect, and Brenda took the lead and said:

"The three of us invest in philanthropic entities, Caleb less so, but I believe it's because he's the youngest and will soon dedicate himself to it. We are concerned about the future of humanity, yes."

"Since you claim to be concerned about humanity, I ask: how much money from our group should we donate to the project?"

With the mere suggestion of having to dip into their own pockets, the three began to feel uncomfortable. Sparks of selfishness started to ignite their emotions. Peterson immediately sent a message to his two siblings: "This Dr. Marco Polo seems to be very intelligent, but also an opportunist, wanting to profit from our money. Delete."

They read and deleted the message to leave no traces of their thoughts. They were constantly concerned about their social image, whether in front of the press or in front of their own father.

Theo Fester noticed that the children were exchanging messages, however, he saw no harm in it and let things unfold, also glancing at his own phone.

"Is this scientist trying to take advantage of dad's vulnerability?" Brenda typed.

They read her question and immediately deleted it too.

Caleb was furious with his sister's naivety and typed, "Don't be foolish, Brenda. It's obvious that Dr. Marco Polo is trying to pull off a scam. Let's propose donating the company's tax incentives for this year." He sent it and said:

"Bravo, Dad. How about donating the company's tax incentives for the next fiscal year?"

Theo Fester reacted indignantly:

"Is that all, Caleb? Is this the thinking of all three of you?"

Concerned, Peterson quickly typed, "This psychiatrist is very clever. He's going to turn Dad against us. Let's donate a million dollars and be done with it."

Brenda increased the offer with another message, "We'll still have billions of dollars with our inheritance. Let's donate three million because his project is complex and impactful. Let's please Dad in the end of his life."

"Three million is too much," typed Peterson. "Better let Dad make the donation he wants; he's always been stingy anyways."

"Brilliant idea. Dad is a cheapskate, dying or not, he still won't donate large sums from his pocket," Caleb sent.

So, everyone agreed with the idea.

It fell to Peterson to speak.

"Dad, we are impressed with your kind heart. We know you've always been generous, so we think it's better for you to decide how much to donate to the noble *Prisoners of the Mind* project. Your decision will be our decision."

"Thank you very much for the trust, love, and affection. You have changed! You always argued so much that when the three of you gave an opinion on something, there were always four opinions," said the father jokingly. "And since you called me the best father in the world, an extraordinary and admirable human being, I will donate ninety-nine percent of my group to the project."

Peterson jumped out of his chair.

"What? Are you going crazy? I mean, are you having a philanthropic outbreak?"

Caleb shouted:

"You must be kidding, Theo Fester! Are you saying you're going to donate ninety-nine percent of our assets?"

"Exactly," said the billionaire calmly.

"As if we were just illegi..."

"No, Caleb, you are not illegitimate children. You are my legitimate sons and daughter. And I have prepared you to fend for yourselves. Didn't you win those awards as the best executives?"

Brenda was speechless. She could only stutter:

"I don't... understand...!"

The father stood up, went to his children, and spoke firmly, "You showered me with remarkable praise. You deceived me. Was it all an act?"

"No. It's all true..." Brenda tried to express herself, fearful.

Theo Fester did the math, "My fortune is thirty billion dollars. Therefore, one percent is three hundred million dollars, meaning each of you will receive one hundred million dollars. Celebrate!! You will receive an amount that 99.99 percent of Americans will never have. You'll still be rich."

"But, Dad, we were raised with a certain standard of living. I, for example, won't be able to have a yacht." said Peterson bewildered.

"You can rent one" suggested the father.

"And what about my watches?" complained Caleb.

"Have one or two, sell the rest" recommended the father.

"And my friends parties? They are important to me!"

"I'm dying, Brenda. Being alive is already a party. And if you actually have real friends that you can count on one hand, consider yourself lucky, because most people don't have any."

They looked at the psychiatrists and wanted to eat them alive. They went from the heaven of emotion to being voracious predators. They seemed like lions in front of two gazelles. They were shocked, perplexed.

Theo Fester felt it was time to say goodbye, "Dr. Marco Polo and Dr. Sophia, thank you very much for being here. You are tired. Let's all go to bed, and we'll talk tomorrow. Today is Friday, and I plan to spend two more days with my children."

Theo Fester had another coughing fit, but the children, talking among themselves, paid no attention to their father's respiratory distress.

Dr. Marco Polo went to the siblings to greet them; however, they refused to shake his hand. Peterson still mumbled:

"Charlatan!"

Caleb said in a low and angry tone, like a serpent: "I will find you and sue you!"

Brenda, exhausted with everything, simply said:

"Let's go to bed."

The psychiatrists left. Brenda kissed her father before going to her room. Theo Fester expected kisses from both sons, but they just waved quickly and turned their backs.

CHAPTER 11

United by the Fear of Loss

Brenda, Peterson, and Caleb couldn't sleep. They tossed and turned in bed all night.

During the early hours, Peterson had a nightmare – a dream related to an event that had occurred a month ago. It happened at the summit meeting with two new directors of his father's bank. One of them, Jerry, thirty-five years old, had the audacity to disagree with the president:

"I'm sorry, Mr. Peterson, but investing in the public debt of emerging countries in Latin America is not a good deal right now, as the papers are still high, and a new crisis could hit these countries."

Theo Fester liked debates and enjoyed being contradicted, as long as it was done with intelligence; what he detested was passivity. But not Peterson, who would become furious when contradicted. And if the contradiction was in public, he would turn into a beast. He would viciously attack the person who did it, mercilessly humiliating them, as if they were an enemy to be defeated. He felt as a god rather than the president of a financial institution.

"Who are you to disagree with me? How long have you been with the company?"

"For six months, sir," Jerry said, fearfully.

"I hate stupid people who don't know what they're talking about. You're fired."

In the nightmare, Peterson encountered this young executive on the streets. And he shouted at Peterson:

"You bum! Where's your arrogance now?"

He woke up startled.

Caleb also had a bad dream. He was in a beautiful jewelry store intending to buy a $200,000 watch. But his credit card was declined. There was no money in his account. Furious, he slammed his hand down on the store's counter.

"This crap doesn't work."

"I'm sorry, sir, but you can't take the watch," said the saleswoman.

"Who are you to say I can't take it? I have enough money to buy this entire jewelry store."

"Don't raise your voice. You're mistreating me," said the saleswoman, already pressing a button connecting the jewelry store directly to the police.

The police came in and arrested him. Handcuffed, he shouted:

"I'm Caleb Fester. I'll sue you! You're going to lose your job!" as entering the police car.

He woke up. His heart felt like jumping right out of his chest.

Brenda also had a troubling dream: while at one of her parties, being photographed by dozens of cameras, Justice officials arrived with an eviction order. It was humiliating. All the guests left without saying goodbye. She lost the flatterers. And, in the end, her boyfriend also left her.

She was woken up by knocks on the door. There were still tears in her eyes. It was her two brothers.

"I couldn't sleep. I had nightmares all night!" Peterson commented.

"I had horrible nightmares too, that I got arrested. Look what dad is doing to us!"

"Dad doesn't love us, that's the truth. I knew that one day he would sabotage us," Brenda said.

"Wait," said Caleb, who was worried. He began to search all over Brenda's room. He turned over the bed, upholstery, crystal cabinet, but he didn't find any bugs. He looked at the ceiling, but there were no cameras.

"Well, I think the place is safe. There are no cameras or listening devices."

"It's not fair; I worked my whole life for him, and now I'm treated like a bastard," said Peterson.

Caleb added, in anguish:

"And I made more money than the both of you ..."

"Stop making that calculation," Peterson interrupted angrily.

"Don't you realize we're on the same yacht and sinking?"

Caleb then said:

"I know, I know. I just wanted to say that he doesn't recognize my worth. He never did. I even thought I was his protégé, but he tossed me at the dumpster!"

"And I thought I was his special daughter, the apple of his eyes. Now, a stranger comes in with his smooth talk and shamelessly steals our fortune."

Suddenly, Peterson grabbed his cell phone to wake up the group's legal director.

"Wait. I'm going to call Dr. William."

Dr. William answered the phone somewhat sleepy. Peterson, anxious, went straight to the point:

"Dr. William, what are the criteria for legally incapacitating someone?"

"Which person?"

"I'll tell you later. What are the criteria?" he asked, angrily.

"The person must be out of touch with reality, lose logical parameters, have significant memory lapses, and exhibit unintelligible and extravagant behavior."

"That's it. My father is behaving extravagantly."

"Your father? Are you kidding? I've never seen anyone so lucid! Your father has been tested. His IQ is 152. He's a genius."

The three either didn't know or didn't remember this information.

"I think he has Alzheimer's," said Peterson.

Caleb, biting his nails, said:

"Put it on speakerphone. I want to hear the conversation!"

Dr. William poured a bucket of cold water on their expectations.

"Peterson, if your father undergoes a sanity test, he will perform better than whoever evaluates him. His memory is better than ours combined. Didn't you see his performance last week at the last meeting? He's still the same.

Peterson had an outburst of anger.

"But he wants to donate ninety-nine percent of his fortune to a social project. Isn't that insanity?"

Dr. William was surprised.

"What?"

"He wants to starve us, Dr. William."

"Starve you? What do you mean?" Dr. William asked.

"He wants to leave only one hundred million dollars for each of us," the youngest son reported.

"One hundred million dollars is a lot...!"

"It's too little!" They all replied together, as if they were in a harmonious choir, interrupting the legal director's speech.

"According to our standards, it's indeed very little, Dr. William," Brenda reaffirmed. "He got us used to parties, airplanes, jewelry, and now he considers all of it to be superfluous. It's unfair!"

"I apologize for being honest, Brenda, but it wasn't your father who got you used to this lifestyle. He's very simple, he even eats street hot dogs! But I do understand you. Compared to your father's great fortune, a hundred million dollars may seem like peanuts. And I think it's legitimate for you to fight for your rights..."

"Did you know he only has three months to live?" Caleb asked.

"Three months? It can't be!" The group's legal director, who had known Theo Fester for over two decades, knew his radicalism and admired his entrepreneurship, intelligence, and honesty, was perplexed.

"Yes, he told us that he has advanced-stage cancer," Peterson confirmed. "But please, Dr. William, this is a state secret!"

"What a pity! Your father is a great man, and he was a great... mentor for me," he said with a choked voice.

"What are we going to do?" Caleb asked anxiously, placing his hands on his head in despair.

"He hasn't approached me yet for the legal process of the donation. So, you still have the chance to try to change his decision, even though his actions are always well thought out and rarely reconsidered. Try to win him over."

"But he's an ice-cold rock!" Peterson asserted.

"I disagree. Behind this rigid man, there's a sensitive human being, especially in this situation. You need to discover him, please him. Be the most incredible children in the world. Don't be enemies. Together, you are powerful..."

"Good idea!" Brenda said. "We have two days to come up with a strategy."

The children of Theo Fester were never united when their father was in good health, but they decided to come together in his absence. Not because the father was on the brink of death, but because their financial health was at stake. They didn't unite out of love, but out of the fear of losing money.

CHAPTER 12

Pleasantly False Children

The Fester siblings discussed for a long time about how they would win their father over, what kind of behavior they should adopt. At one point, Peterson, Brenda, and Caleb completely agreed: they couldn't fight among themselves as usually. They had to move their father emotionally; they had to act like amiable siblings who respected and supported each other, praising their father.

Since they had little sleep, they were tired, with bags under their eyes, constantly yawning. But all three were early in the breakfast room. They knew that Theo Fester always had his first meal at the same time. However, he didn't show up...

"Dad is like a British man; he always has his breakfast at seven. It's seven fifteen. What's going on? Why hasn't he shown up yet?

Ross, the butler, who was ready to be called for in the luxurious room, asked:

"Would you like me to serve your breakfast?"

"No," said Brenda, "let's wait for Dad."

"I think he would be pleased with that," commented Ross. "It seems like you woke up too late."

The siblings exchanged glances among themselves. Caleb, furious with the butler, as he always was with his employees, humiliated him.

"Who are you, you... you uniformed chauffeur... to tell us that we woke up late?"

"I'm sorry, sir. It was your father who told me. He also mentioned that he hasn't had breakfast with you for twenty years. I will apologize for this presumption to Mr. Fester as well."

"No, no, no... It's not necessary," intervened Peterson, kicking Caleb from under the table. "Indeed, we woke up late because we worked until late at night."

Brenda took the initiative and said:

"I'll see what's going on with Dad."

"I'm sorry, ma'am, but he asked not to be disturbed by anyone, not even you, his children. He is meditating."

"Meditating?!" The three questioned, perplexed.

"My father is not the type to meditate, except when counting money," Peterson quickly and impulsively stated.

"Does your father only care about money, sir?" Ross asked, astonished. "But he seems so altruistic!"

Brenda kicked Peterson this time, trying to correct her brother, she spoke in Mandarin, a language the three had a reasonable knowledge of:

"You're crazy! There might be a bug in this room, on the ceiling, under the table..."

Peterson tried to remedy the situation:

"My father is an expert in counting money because he is a great philanthropist."

"How impressive! What does he do?"

Brenda fell silent; she never knew that her father had heavily invested in philanthropy; she only knew about sporadic donations.

Caleb, seeing that the butler was crossing the line, couldn't hold back.

"Don't you think you're asking too much for a petty employee?"

"Oh, sir, once again, I apologize. I can't control my tongue. But children who love their father usually commend his social accomplishments, and you are dramatically discreet."

Brenda spoke in Mandarin:

"Are you crazy, Caleb? This butler could be a psychiatrist or a psychologist assessing us! Dad might be investigating our behavior to increase our inheritance.

"No, ma'am. I'm not a psychiatrist," replied the butler in Mandarin, stupefying the three siblings.

"Do you also speak Mandarin?" She asked, amazed.

The butler nodded, saying yes, and added:

"Yes, I'm sort of a polyglot. I speak ten languages: Mandarin, Japanese, Korean, Italian, French, German, Spanish, Russian, Portuguese, and, obviously, our native language, English," showing a discreet smile and continued: "Excuse me, I will wait for Mr. Fester to finish meditating."

After these last words, the butler left, leaving the siblings speechless.

"What's happening here?" Peterson asked in a low voice, looking at the ceiling trying to find a hidden camera.

Caleb who has always been hysterical also asked in unusual low tone voice: "did we fall into some kind of trap?". Speaking softly wasn't part of his story. After that, he looked frantically under the table to find some hidden listening device.

An hour had gone by, and nothing happened. The three siblings were impatient. Peterson kept snapping his fingers, and Caleb was biting his nails.

"Your anxiety distresses me. Stop snapping your fingers, Peterson," ordered Caleb.

"What about you, biting your nails? You're out of control too."

And a new fight began.

"I can't stand the both of you. Our whole strategy is going..." Brenda was saying that when the door of the grand room creaked. Their father shouted happily:

"My children, what a joy! You're waiting for me!"

They immediately changed their moods: they smiled, touched each other's shoulders, and went to meet their father.

"How could we not wait for a father who has been the master of masters of life for all of us?" Peterson asked rhetorically, with noticeable affection.

"More than a master of life, he is a master of wisdom," said Brenda.

"I can't describe you as my siblings have, father. I can only say that without you, my sky would have no stars..."

Theo Fester couldn't contain himself:

"I'm so surprised by your behavior that I see only two options: either you're playing a character, or I was blind not to explore the greatness of my children."

They felt a lump in their throat. Then, the father asked:

"Do you know which hypothesis is true? The second one."

Brenda commented, emotional and almost voiceless:

"We've learned to be transparent like you, dad."

"I'm sorry for not kissing you more, for not having deep conversations with you. I don't know my children, and that's my greatest grief at the end of my life."

Caleb hugged his two siblings and said:

"So, let's get to know each other in these two days."

"Let's do this!" the father exclaimed happily.

"Let's do this!" the three repeated.

And so, the family members who were constantly at war, entrenched in their truths; experts in criticizing each other, decided to lay down their weapons and have a moment of truce.

CHAPTER 13

False Philanthropic Dreams

On that sunny Saturday, Theo Fester and his three children strolled through the vast gardens of the mysterious Forest Castle. Theo walked slowly, leaning on a cane. On his right side was his oldest son, Peterson; on the left was Brenda; and two steps ahead was his youngest son, Caleb. Fester's clan, pursuing one of the world's greatest fortunes, experts at throwing stones, but this time pretending to remove them, posing as emotional prospectors in the soils of their minds. Theo Fester, despite his ironclad, extremely tough character, was extraordinarily reflective. He paused during his walk, sighed, and commented:

"This simple walk makes me rethink my role as a human being and as a father. Am I a billionaire or a failure?" He asked himself and his children.

"Why do you question that, dad?" Brenda quickly asked, trying to alleviate her guilt.

"Dear Brenda, when we are healthy, we spend our entire lives reaching out, working and building as if we were immortal. But on the brink of death, we are forced to reach within. It is inevitable to think about our emotional debts. For the first time, I'm taking a walk with you after you have grown up. For the first time, we didn't talk about financial results, buying new companies, launching new products!"

The children penetrated the deepest layers of silence.

"You're right, dad. We made mistakes too. We only brought you problems, and we only knew how to talk about work. We had time for lots of things, but not for ourselves," Brenda acknowledged.

"And the man who doesn't have time for what he loves is... rich or miserable?"

"From this perspective, maybe we are poorer than the simplest bank workers or factory floor employee," reflected Peterson.

Theo Fester's oldest son wasn't prone to this kind of reflection, but driven by personal interests and moved by his father's terminal state, he began to rethink life. Caleb was against it. Impulsive like his father, he was hard to control, even when he desperately needed to improve his personal marketing.

"I disagree, Peterson. You're doing a *petersonation* of poverty. Anxiety and envy are part of the humblest employees' personality," asserted Caleb.

"That's obvious, Caleb, but I'm talking theoretically, from certain angles... We need to reinvent ourselves as a family," Peterson said, giving a subtle signal for his younger brother to shut up.

"The fragile harmony between you is already broken. Does losing a dispute, whatever it may be, disturb you, Caleb?" The father asked.

"No, it's just..."

"The word *no* is the one you use the most in your existential dictionary," the father observed sharply.

"No, I'm not like that... It's just that I saw a study that says people prefer to earn fifty thousand dollars instead of sixty thousand dollars a year as long as their colleagues earn less than them. But they don't want to earn eighty thousand dollars if their friends earn more than them, a hundred thousand dollars or more. Illogical? Yes! Happiness is comparative."

Seeing his analysis, Theo Fester questioned his bold son:

"Are you happy, Caleb?"

"Very happy," Caleb quickly responded.

"And whose happiness do you compare yours to?"

"I don't compare it to anyone... Or rather, I compare it to the people who work for me."

Brenda and Peterson wanted to cover his mouth. As always, he tarnished his image in front of his father. The problem now was even more serious because he was jeopardizing their strategy to win him over.

"But what is happiness?" Theo Fester asked. "And how do you know that those who work for you are less happy than you? Do you remember what happened on July 20th last year? You harassed a twenty-three-year-old woman who worked for you. But since she wasn't interested in you, you publicly criticized her. Do you think your reaction of publicly exposing her shows that you are happier than she is?"

"But I didn't touch her. I didn't pressure her to have sex with me, none of that. I just invited her for dinner!"

"Of course, if you had done that, you would never set foot in my companies again. But you fired her unjustly. I made you apologize and rehire her."

"But you have also fired your executives abruptly."

"See, Caleb, you can fire someone for incompetence or inability in a role, but never for emotional whims. And if you don't know the difference, forfeit your position."

Caleb fell silent.

"Are you using cocaine?" The father wanted to know.

"Don't change the subject!" The son said, ranting arrogantly.

Theo Fester breathed slowly and continued, in a gentle tone:

"My son, I care about you. I just want to know if you're okay or if your happiness needs artifices."

"Drugs are part of my past. My drugs today are my startups," Caleb replied trying to change the direction of the subject and not mentioning his occasional relapses.

"Your startups?"

"No, I mean, Theo Fester Group's!" He tried to correct himself.

Caleb had lost control to such an extent that Brenda had to intervene. But she wasn't nice in doing so.

"Shut up, Caleb!"

"Why do I have to shut up? And who are you to give me that order? Don't you know that Dad always accuses me of everything?"

Peterson, enraged by his brother's impulsiveness, commented:

"Dad, Caleb has changed a lot. He's an extremely intelligent young man."

"I am indeed, almost like you, Dad."

"He's also becoming increasingly pleasant to be around," Brenda affirmed.

Caleb smiled upon hearing his two siblings' rare compliments.

"Congratulations, Peterson and Brenda. For the first time, you stood up for your brother in front of me. I just hope you're not being political."

"I've never been political, Dad. I've always been transparent like you," Peterson affirmed, proud of himself. He thought he would score points with his father with this statement. But the emotional turmoil overflowed.

"Are you as transparent as I am, Peterson?! On May 15th last year, you told the governor of California that our bank had five billion to invest in state infrastructure projects, yet you knew that the cash was fully committed to financing ten thousand houses and apartments. Remember? On September 29th, you had the audacity to tell your wife that I sent you to Paris for an emergency business meeting when, in fact, you spent three days on my yacht with politicians and businessmen, doing who knows what. Don't be hypocritical. Don't talk to me about transparency!"

"But everyone has their flaws," Peterson tried to defend himself, visibly uneasy.

Brenda and Caleb glared at him.

"I know we all make mistakes, and one of those is disguising our lies. But since you consider yourself honest and Caleb considers himself extremely intelligent, recollect something tranquilizing that happened in our family story."

The two were silent for a few moments. Their strategy was dissipating like mist on a sunny morning. They couldn't change the subject or make up stories because their father's memory, as the group's legal director had stated, was better than theirs. They would waste the opportunity to captivate their father and reverse the inheritance distribution. Billions of dollars depended on a few steps in a garden. Peterson and Caleb started to break into a cold sweat, delving into the past, but nothing came to mind. So, Brenda took the lead.

"Let me tell you a story..."

"Are you protecting your brothers, Brenda?"

"No, no, it's just... Well, to be honest, I am. It's just that they get inhibited in your presence."

"Why? Does my mind confine the reasoning of my children?"

"Honestly speaking, yes. We didn't learn to be a family..." she said, truly moved. "You taught us many things, but not to talk about ourselves."

Theo Fester looked deep into his daughter's eyes and asked firmly:

"How dare you say such words?"

The two siblings were desperate.

"Brenda is out of control!" Caleb attacked.

"Silence, Caleb!" Theo interrupted. And, to their surprise, he said: "I'm not upset with your sister. Her thesis is true, although extremely painful."

"You rarely spoke of your past, your losses, your failures, your crises. We had never seen you cry."

Theo Fester was shaken; he continued to walk slowly in the gardens. His children accompanied him in complete silence. It seemed that Brenda's sensitivity was magical, like a scalpel that dissected one of the Fester's secrets. Suddenly, as if wanting to relieve his tension, Theo Fester became distracted with some roses. He gently opened their petals and inhaled their fragrance.

"Our family has become a group of strangers. I taught you to be negotiators, entrepreneurs, and to understand that no one deserves the podium if they don't take risks to reach it. But I didn't teach you to humanize yourselves, to talk about yourselves... I failed, I apologize," he said, shedding some tears.

"But, Dad, we've already said that you were..."

"Please, Brenda, don't wipe away my tears. A human who is afraid of their own tears will never rewrite their story. I have always been afraid of them..."

The atmosphere gradually improved. They continued walking in silence. It was almost unbelievable that the Fester clan had so many things to talk about all day – politics, economics, markets – but they were unable to talk about the simple things in life. Theo Fester looked at the huge mansion, thoughtful. He then asked: "What are your biggest dreams?"

Brenda was quick to respond:

"To see you healthy and happy, Dad..."

"That is also our biggest dream," the two brothers said at the same time.

"But we have to accept life's surprises, daughter. As Dr. Marco Polo said, three months can be an eternity, compared to the mediocre life that many people live."

"Dr. Marco Polo..." Caleb repeated softly, nodding his head.

"But tell me, what dreams control you?"

"Well, I would like to have a lot of money to help the homeless in the United States," Caleb stated. In reality, he spoke empty words. He didn't know that the United States had hundreds of thousands of homeless people. He thought this phenomenon was a peculiarity of poor or developing countries.

"Seriously, Caleb? I thought you only cared about staying in five-star hotels. I never imagined you would care about the unfortunate in the U.S.," his father replied.

"I would like to help cancer patients. Invest in an institute for children affected by this disease who don't have adequate resources for treatment," Peterson shared.

"You never told me you cared about other people's pain," his father found it strange.

"Even before your illness, I had already thought about how to give a greater meaning to my life, Dad."

Brenda commented:

"I would like to have lots of resources to be able to help refugees in Europe. It hurts me to see people without a home, without a homeland, torn from their culture, living with their children in an undignified manner in countries that do not welcome them warmly."

Theo Fester stopped, looked into Brenda's eyes, and smiled.

"I thought you only cared about your extravagant parties, my daughter." And then, he looked at each one of his children and added: "I guess I don't know you. I had never imagined you had these dreams. Congratulations!"

Theo Fester gave each of them a warm hug. He was moved, touched, and his eyes teared up again. After that, he had a coughing fit and was helped by the three of them. Once he recovered, they all went to the dining room. The children exchanged discreet glances and felt that they had finally succeeded in captivating their father. Little did they know that words can become the biggest traps that a person builds for themselves.

CHAPTER 14

Palace of Terror

During lunch, the three children showed exceptional kindness to their father. Instead of waiting for butler Ross to serve the lunch, they served it themselves, with smiles on their faces. They seemed like the most loving children in the world. They competed with each other to better please their frail father.

"What juice would you like, my father?" Peterson asked.

"Orange juice, please."

"Salad first, Dad?" Caleb asked.

"Yes, please!" Replied Theo Fester. Suddenly, he dropped his fork.

"Don't worry, Dad," said Caleb.

"An extraordinary father, who served his children all his life and who is still one of the most remarkable entrepreneurs in the world, employing more than thirty thousand people in his companies, can drop silverware, glasses, and plates as much as he wants," Caleb commented, flattering his father.

"Dad, would you like me to carve the chicken breast and feed it to you?" Brenda offered affectionately.

"No, please, help yourselves. I can still manage!"

To lighten the mood, Caleb shared some stories that would please his father:

"Once, an economics professor asked his students: *What is the difference between an entrepreneur and a conformist?* Many answers were given. But the professor gave his version: *Conformists criticize the adventures and craziness of the entrepreneur, but when he stands on the podium, they become his audience.*"

Peterson attempted to tell some jokes, even though not being very good at it. Brenda laughed, and their father also smiled, showing an unusual relaxation in their presence. Ross, the butler, watched closely, intrigued at Theo Fester's children. He wanted to know what was really going on in their minds. It was a perfect lunch. Since Theo Fester was weakened, he excused himself and left to rest.

In the afternoon, the three had time to rest. The siblings, who rarely sought each other out, gathered in Brenda's immense room, with its billowing curtains and a magnificent view of an untouched forest. They believed that their strategy to captivate their father was working.

Caleb, the boldest and proudest of the siblings, declared victory:

"We turned the game around!"

"Well, after some setbacks, we had a spectacular late morning and a magnificent lunch," Peterson stated.

"But I'm still not sure if we changed Dad's mind," Brenda said, suspicious.

"Stop being pessimistic and give this genius a round of applause," Caleb said, pointing his finger at himself.

"Genius? Why, Caleb? Wow! What an inflated ego!" Brenda criticized her younger brother.

Caleb looked under the table, opened the built-in cabinet doors, looked behind the curtains, in short, searched everywhere places for hidden cameras, but found nothing. Suddenly, he approached his siblings and showed them why they should bow to his intelligence.

"Inflated ego because I am indeed a genius. I changed Theo Fester's emotional state, by mentioning my philanthropic vein when I commented on my calling to help the homeless in the United States."

"You tricked Dad?" Brenda questioned.

"He is old, on the brink of death, anything goes to make him happy."

"Including lying to him?" Brenda replied scolding him.

Caleb became furious:

"Darn it! Wasn't that our strategy? I don't understand why you are surprised. Besides that, you, the apple of his eye, lied even more to him!"

"Don't be suspicious about my intentions, Caleb," Brenda retorted.

"It's not suspicion, it's a realization. For someone who loves French caviar and champagne, it's too hypocritical of you to say that you care about refugees in Europe."

She fell silent. Then, Peterson wanted to take the trophy of honesty among his siblings.

"My plans to take care of cancer patients were not a pretense."

"Look who's talking: the most cynical of bankers. He charges exorbitant interest rates from clients, inhibits their ability to pay, and then talks about saving cancer patients," criticized Caleb.

And so, they began to raise their voices against each other. They couldn't free themselves from their mental prisons. Realizing what was happening, Brenda screamed and intervened:

"Let's stop! Why do we always fight? Are we addicted to conflicts? Can't we set our differences aside even when our strategy is starting to work? If we are incapable of loving each other, at least let's be smart enough to not lose billions of dollars!"

They finally fell silent. Then, Peterson added:

"We need to stick together. Our strategy must continue at dinner."

After this discussion, each one went to their room. At night, they went to the dining room. Waitresses were placing the dishes on a glass cupboard. The Fester siblings were eagerly waiting for their father, who took a long time to appear.

Ross, the elegant butler, suddenly appeared with Marc Douglas, Theo Fester's faithful secretary.

"Marc! You're here?!" Brenda exclaimed.

"I've been here all the time. But Mr. Fester asked me to stay in my room for a while. He wanted to be alone with you. Now I come to convey a message from him: he apologizes, but unfortunately, he won't come to dinner…"

"Why? Is he having a coughing fit, fever, any kind of pain?" Brenda asked, concerned.

"No. Just a little weak because of the medication he's taking," Marc replied.

"It's very sad to see our father weakened like this. I would even be willing to donate my organs to him," Caleb said, showing remarkable affection. Actually, what he truly desired was for both Marc Douglas and Ross to convey this "message" to his father.

"You are an excellent son, Sir Caleb," the butler affirmed.

"I know I am a good son, but I wanted to do more. My debt to my father is immeasurable," Caleb exaggerated.

"Mine is equally immeasurable. My father is irreplaceable," Peterson stated.

"Not only irreplaceable but also unforgettable," Brenda concluded.

"He seems very happy with you all," Marc said.

"Do you think so? Why did you get that impression?" Peterson inquired.

The secretary let out a long sigh and said to the Fester siblings:

"He mentioned that you surprised him."

Ross added:

"He mentioned that your concern for the pain of others touched him."

"We captivated him! I knew it!" Caleb pounded the table. He was so euphoric that he didn't realize what he had done. But seeing how Marc Douglas and Ross looked astonished, he tried to contain his enthusiasm, replacing it with a calm tone and eyes filled with tears: "Children should always be the joy of their parents, captivating them."

"Especially in this very delicate moment our father is going through," Peterson said, wiping his eyes. "I'm sorry, but thinking about Dad's situation made me lose my appetite."

"I understand," expressed Ross. "Your father loves you all very much. He told us that he raised successors, not heirs."

"What do you mean?" Brenda asked, confused.

Marc Douglas replied for the butler:

"To your father, heirs are inheritance squanderers, while successors build their own legacy; heirs want everything fast and ready, successors think in the medium and long term; heirs are emperors, while successors bow in gratitude."

"Wow, did my father recognize that we are successors?" Caleb questioned, visibly happy.

"Yes, he said it in plain terms to me, even though I am a stranger to him," Ross affirmed.

Marc Douglas and Ross bid their farewell to the Fester siblings. And they looked at each other euphorically. They seemed unable to contain themselves. Caleb looked at Brenda and said:

"See, Brenda, how can you be so pessimistic? My ingeniousness captivated Dad. He considers us his successors, not squanderers of his inheritance."

Brenda was intrigued by these terms.

"Wait a minute. If by considering us *successors*, capable of building our own legacy, doesn't his idea of minimizing our inheritance gain more strength?"

"I don't understand," Caleb said, coughing slightly.

"Brenda might be right," Peterson commented, putting his hands on his head. "If we are successors, we can start from scratch. In dad's eyes, we can build our own stories."

"You guys are delirious," Caleb said, pounding the table. Deep down, he was trying to convince himself otherwise. "By saying that we are his successors, dad meant we finally deserve his fortune and have the ability to manage and expand it."

As each one reached their room, a beautiful song played: *We are free*, in the beautiful voice of Andrea Bocelli. After the music stopped, their father's voice emanated from the ceiling. They were distressed by the possibility that their dialogues had been recorded. But the father's speech was one of comfort, not disapproval.

"Dear children, you are my pride. I am very happy with your behavior. You demonstrate phenomenal generosity and a brilliant ability to care for humanity. Congratulations!"

And that was it.

Not a minute had passed before they gathered again in Brenda's room. But they remained silent for a few seconds. They were afraid to speak.

Caleb typed a message: "I didn't see any speakers, cameras, or listening devices... How did we hear this message? Delete."

Brenda was having a headache. She typed, "I'm scared. Did they hear us talking about our strategy?"

"We're getting paranoid. If they had recorded it, Marc Douglas and Ross wouldn't have brought good news from Dad regarding our behavior, and Dad wouldn't have sent that congratulatory audio message," Peterson typed.

"Were you guys also greeted in the room with the song *We are free*?" Brenda wrote.

"Yes," they both typed.

"And what do you think he meant by this song?" Brenda insisted.

"My Gosh," Peterson typed, distressed. "This song talks about dreams and building a legacy despite adversity. Is Dad preparing us to disinherit us after all?"

"Did he bring us to this strange Forest Castle to prepare us to live in poverty?" Caleb typed.

At that exact moment, the same song started playing again. They didn't know whether to laugh or cry. They paid attention to the lyrics and became even more disturbed.

"It's not possible! There must be speakers in this room!" the youngest son typed.

The three began to search the room desperately for speakers, cameras, and listening devices; they looked under the rug, behind the bed... But they found nothing. They breathed a little relieved and resumed talking.

"I think we're going crazy," Brenda said.

"No wonder!" exclaimed Peterson. "This mansion is full of mysteries. It feels like a chamber of terror."

Caleb tensed up and said:

"Last night, I heard wolf howls and chains being dragged through the corridors."

"Stop it, Caleb. I'm getting scared," Brenda warned.

"I'm serious!" The youngest brother asserted smiling. It wasn't clear if he was actually serious or kidding.

"I had horrible nightmares last night. In one of them, I was doing numbers on the streets of New York to earn a few bucks. I lived on the street, ate leftover food, and when I woke up, I smelled a foul odor in my room, as if I had slept under a pile of garbage. I sat on the bed, and then the terrible smell passed, but I saw many objects thrown on the floor," Caleb recounted.

"You're freaking me out!" Brenda exclaimed anxiously. "But I also had my share of nightmares. In one of them, I was at a party, but it wasn't one of those I usually throw at my house. It was at a stranger's house. But I was a waitress, instead of being a guest, serving drinks. And suddenly the tray fell, shattering the champagne glasses. The host mistreated me and I woke up scared. When I went to the bathroom, I saw broken glasses and a tray thrown on the floor."

"Weird," said the two siblings.

"It's better for us to get some rest, and today I'll take a sedative to see if I can sleep better," Brenda said.

"Give me a pill too," requested Caleb.

"I want one too," Peterson requested.

And so, the Fester siblings took sleep inducers. This was the first generation of the family that had grown up as millionaires and still wanted more, dreaming of getting their hands on their father's billion-dollar fortune. It was unclear whether their ambition and the fear of losing their fortune were mentally imprisoning them, causing them to experience sleepwalking and bizarre nighttime reactions, or if the Forest Castle really harbored haunting secrets.

CHAPTER 15

Excellent Grandfather, Terrible Father

Theo Fester managed to teach much more life lessons to his grandchildren, Kate and Thomas, than to his three children. The day before he invited Brenda, Peterson, and Caleb to the mysterious Forest Castle, he had an intelligent and affectionate conversation with his grandchildren. He was at Brenda's house with Kate.

The grandfather fixed his eyes on his granddaughter and asked: "Do you love me for who I am or for what I have, Kate? Be honest, please."

"It's for what you have, of course! You're very rich! Hahaha!" The granddaughter joked, playing with her grandfather. Even though she really loved him.

"I knew it, girl, that I mean nothing to you," he joked back, also smiling. But Kate felt the need to be honest.

"I would love you even if you were very poor. You are my best grandfather, Mr. Theo Fester."

"Ah... Now this sounds better!"

"Obviously, I only have one grandfather!" She said again, in good spirits. Smiling, he confessed:

"Honestly, I know I'm not the best grandfather in the world, but you are the best thing that has happened in my life."

"And what about Thomas?" Kate asked about her cousin, Peterson's son.

"Thomas too. He is also a source of joy of mine."

Suddenly, Thomas emerged from behind a pillar in Brenda's immense living room. He had arrived unnoticed.

"Oh, very well, Mr. Fester! I thought you were going to say that I was a nuisance."

"Thomas, my favorite grandson…!"

"Of course, I'm your only grandson!" And he went to his grandfather, giving him a lingering hug and a kiss on the cheek. He did the same with his cousin Kate.

The two grandchildren stood in front of Theo Fester, eager to listen to him, a behavior quite different from that of the magnate's three children, who were always in a hurry.

"Your parents fear me, yet they fail to drink from my wisdom. Being elder in this constantly changing digital society that I helped create, and that is constantly changing, is not being square but being out of the game, something to be discarded."

"Do you feel guilty that almost everyone is addicted to phones and other digital devices?" Thomas asked.

"Honestly, I do feel guilty. I warned Steve Jobs about the risks of the devices becoming addictive. He stopped, thought, and asked, *Is that so, Theo?* At the time, he mentioned that he didn't give phones to his own kids. But the problem isn't the digital devices that democratize access to information and increase business productivity; the problem are the social media apps."

"How come, grandpa?" Kate wanted to understand that better.

"Social media apps, according to Dr. Marco Polo, a scientist I have recently met, mess with the pleasure and frustration cycle, altering dopamine levels, a brain neurotransmitter."

"I didn't understand anything," Thomas commented.

"In the past, significant frustrations or pleasures occurred each one or two weeks; today, it goes every hour or minute."

"Wow! That's true. When I post something on my social media, if there isn't a certain number of likes, I get anxious. If the number is large, I'm happy," Kate affirmed.

"I do too. When someone criticizes me on my Instagram, I get really mad, even if more than a hundred liked it," Thomas confessed.

"This fluctuation between pleasure and pain generates psychological dependence; it's the same mechanism triggered by cocaine. The absence of the drug and the absence of the cell phone produce withdrawal symptoms, a suffering that demands their use."

"Geez, grandpa! I don't use drugs! Although a week ago I lost my cell phone, and as soon as I realized that, I started getting anxious, depressed, irritated, feeling a great emptiness in my chest. It seemed like nothing made sense to me anymore," Thomas reported.

"I have felt that way too, Thomas," Kate commented. "It seems like we're all sick."

Theo worried about the future of the youth.

"In the past, we needed a device the size of this room to have the same power as your cell phones. But the real and concrete world is not digital; it doesn't exist inside cell phones; it pulsates in the social environment. Don't live a mediocre or artificial life. You need to leave a legacy."

"What do you mean by leaving a legacy, grandpa?" Thomas asked.

"Millions of people simply live their lives because they're alive, they are digital zombies. They need to be on the brink of death to wake up."

"Oh... I see. They don't have a meaning for life..." Kate deduced.

"Exactly!"

"And what is the meaning of your life, grandpa?" Thomas asked.

The grandfather looked deeply into his grandchildren's eyes and said honestly:

"I have questioned myself about that. I've done some interesting things, I've inspired and trained hundreds of entrepreneurs, provided jobs for tens of thousands of employees, helped some institutions, but I feel I could have done more."

"An entrepreneur so successful like you, grandpa... do you have regrets? If you could go back in time, would you do things differently?" Thomas asked intelligently.

"A man who doesn't recognize his mistakes and doesn't repent of them is not worthy of his maturity. Every human being goes through turbulence in life. Some lack food on the table, while others lack happiness in the mind. I fall into the second case. Some fight to survive, others are rich and well off like me, but beg for the bread of tranquility..."

"Wow, grandpa, you are wise! I couldn't imagine what kind of mistakes you have made," Thomas said.

"I was addicted to working and making money, forgetting about myself. Inside, I am emotionally younger than millions of young people out there, but my body has aged. My muscles are flabby, my skin dehydrated, my heart is fatigued. I wish I had more time to fix my mistakes with myself, towards your parents and your uncle Caleb..."

"You are an excellent grandfather," Kate said, trying to comfort him.

"Perhaps I am an excellent grandfather, but I was a terrible father, as often happens with successful entrepreneurs." And then, he had a coughing fit.

"But you still have a life ahead to change, grandpa," Thomas said, unaware that his grandfather was dying.

"Time is cruel, my grandchildren. You hide from it, but it finds you. You travel to the ends of the earth, but it follows you. You can try to disguise yourself; some apply Botox, undergo plastic surgeries, but your insides will expose you. There's no use battling time as if you were in the Roman Colosseum. We must have it as our ally, recognizing our mortality. This way, our emotional debts will be bearable. Do you understand?"

Thomas and Kate still didn't fully understand, but they were gradually diving into the ocean of experiences of the powerful grandfather. He sought to transfer to his grandchildren what money couldn't buy, the wealth of his experiences. That's why he spoke of his tears, hoping they would learn to shed their own.

CHAPTER 16

Great Disappointment

Brenda, Peterson, and Caleb's slumber was once again unsettling during the night. Anxious, they couldn't release reasonable amounts of the brain's golden molecule that induces and stabilizes sleep: melatonin. They woke up, haunted by words echoing in the air, like "poor", "beggars", "beware of the earthquake", "they won't survive." Even under the effect of a tranquilizer, they had a fragmented sleep, waking up several times, startled as if they were hearing voices.

"Who is talking to me?" Brenda shouted in a panic.

"Help, someone help me!" Cried the eldest of the brothers, Peterson. He had a nightmare as if the room had collapsed. He found himself under the rubble, unable to move or breathe. He woke up panting.

Caleb covered his face with the pillow. He wanted to be anywhere in the world but in that palace of terror. Suddenly, he heard a voice, seemingly from Dr. Marco Polo, calling him:

"Caleb, Caleb, Caleb."

"Who's there?" He said, removing the pillow from over his face. The voice began to pronounce:

"It will be your end! You will die poor!" And laughter could be heard.

He jumped out of bed and began to search the room, looking under the bed, behind the curtain, to see where those macabre words were coming from. However, once again, he found nothing. Perhaps the stress was making him paranoid. He was the most frightened of the children, but since he self-proclaimed himself the most entrepreneurial and intelligent, he didn't seek his siblings. He was afraid to show his vulnerability.

The Fester siblings were intrigued. The voices were so clear that they weren't sure if they emanated from some device or were whispered by the "planet mind". As Dr. Marco Polo emphasized, human beings are so creative that when they don't have real ghosts haunting them, they create their own ghosts. The fear of becoming poor, which had never suffocated the minds of the powerful Fester clan, began to disturb them.

At three in the morning, to worsen Caleb's drama, someone knocked on the door forcefully. Caleb jumped in his bed. Fearful, he shouted: "Who's there?"

But no one answered. The knocks continued. His heart felt like it was about to jump out of his mouth. He approached the door slowly and asked again:

"Who... who is there?"

The bearer of a booming voice replied: "It's me sir, Ross."

More relieved but not less intrigued, he opened the door.

"I brought the tea you asked for."

"Tea that I asked for?! I didn't ask for any tea!"

"Strange, but I was awakened by the on-duty cook saying that you were very nervous and wanted to calm down."

"I didn't even know there was an on-duty cook! Could it have been one of my brothers?"

"I don't know. Maybe it was a recommendation prescribed by Dr. Marco Polo."

"Dr. Marco Polo, the psychiatrist?"

"Yes, but I am just speculating, sir, because not only your father but Dr. Marco Polo also expressly recommended us to take care of your well-being."

"Very strange. But that's okay, leave the tea; I'll drink it."

The butler left. Caleb's heartbeat was so loud that it could be heard. Nervous, he put a sugar sachet in the cup, stirred quickly with the spoon, and when he was about to take the first sip, a terrible thought occurred to him: "Dr. Marco Polo must have poisoned the tea." Anxiously, he quickly threw it in the bathroom sink. In the morning, he found his two brothers in the corridor. They had dark circles around their eyes, indicating they hadn't gotten any sleep either. Caleb, somewhat intimidated, provocatively commented:

"Did you sleep well?"

Brenda and Peterson quickly said: "Yes, we slept."

They didn't know how to support each other. However, looking at their faces, Caleb commented:

"Liars! You look awful!"

"And did you happen to have a good night's sleep?" Peterson wanted to know.

"No. But I think they're plotting our murder!"

"What are you saying?!" Brenda asked, perplexed.

"I think so too," affirmed Peterson.

"And Dr. Marco Polo is behind it," added Caleb.

"That's right," affirmed Peterson.

"But what happened?" Brenda asked, curiously.

Peterson was the first to give his version.

"That tall and sinister butler, Ross, suddenly appeared without me even calling him. He claimed I had ordered a strawberry tea… A lie! I hadn't ordered anything. Then, he suggested that it might have been Dr. Marco Polo who recommended it."

"The same thing has happened to me. He brought me a cup of tea. But I didn't drink it; I thought it might be poisoned," Caleb said.

"I didn't drink it either," confessed Peterson, fearful. "I was afraid it might be poisoned, and I poured the tea down the bathroom sink. It looked like there was blood in the glass."

"How awful!" exclaimed Brenda. "He brought me an orange juice, and I drank it."

Suddenly, Brenda began to appear sick. She rolled her eyes, started drooling, and stuck out her tongue. The two brothers were desperate.

"Brenda! Brenda!" they shouted, thinking their sister was about to die.

But she couldn't take it anymore and started laughing. She was playing a prank on them, as she had always done when they were kids.

"You're crazy, girl! You almost scared us to death!" said Peterson, in a fit of nerves.

"Easy! I was just reminiscing about our childhood games."

"You're a woman. You pose no threat to Dr. Marco Polo," said Caleb, immersed in his male chauvinism. "But certainly, Peterson and I are your major obstacles. We're at the center of a conspiracy."

"I'm sure of it," affirmed Peterson. He led them to his room and concluded, "Some of the strawberry tea spilled on the carpet. Look, there's a small crack on the wall, three feet ahead, and there's a dead rat inside. It must have licked the tea and only managed to take a few steps before hiding. This doctor is a monster. He wants to kill us to get all of Dad's fortune." Caleb and Brenda went to look at the crack. There was something there, but it wasn't possible to tell if it really was a dead rat.

"And it seems that many others are involved. Including the butler. He looks like Frankenstein," said Caleb.

And speaking of the supposed devil, he suddenly appeared behind them.

"Need anything, sirs?"

They were startled.

"Ross!" said Brenda, anxious. "Why didn't you knock on the door before coming in?"

"Because it was open."

"We're already heading to breakfast," she said, trying to get rid of him quickly. "Everything in this Forest Castle is very strange indeed," she confirmed.

After this episode, the three walked through the long corridors until they reached the large main hall. Along the way, they began to look at the paintings differently, as part of the conspiracy.

"Look. Even the paintings are strange. There are hangings, wars, weapons. There's no joy," interpreted Peterson.

"It seems like everything was meticulously arranged to intimidate us. To make us accept Dad's proposal without questioning. Since we did not yield, murdering us is the plan B."

And so, Theo Fester's children, who thought of themselves as immortal and easily ran over those who opposed them, were run over by their own fears. They entered the grand hall and saw their father sitting at the head of the table, just like the first time. The three approached and showed remarkable kindness. They kissed their father on the cheek and pleased him.

"We missed you, Dad," said Caleb.

"I missed you too, my son."

"How was your night, Dad?" Brenda asked.

Caleb observed the looks from Ross and the two waitresses. They seemed agitated, uneasy, trying to hide something.

"I had some coughing fits," the father commented. "But aside from those fits, it was a pleasant night. And how did you sleep?"

"Very well. This Forest Castle is so welcoming that Ross even served me a cup of tea in the middle of the night," Caleb approached, not wanting to show intimidation and, at the same time, wanting to probe his father about the mysterious butler's behavior.

"Ross is indeed very competent."

"Have you known him for a long time?"

"No, just a few days."

"A few days?!" Caleb questioned.

"Yes, but he was highly recommended by Dr. Marco Polo."

"Dr. Marco Polo?" they asked, alarmed.

"Yes. Why? Any problem?"

"No, nothing... It just seems to me that this psychiatrist is interfering a lot in our lives," Caleb said.

Theo Fester had another coughing episode. This time, he choked on the milk he was drinking. Brenda ran to her father and placed a towel for him to vomit on it. It was a big scare; Theo took a deep breath and then said: "I don't think I will last much longer, my children. I have a feeling that I won't last more than a few days."

"Don't say that, Dad. You'll still bury a lot of people," said Peterson, trying to cheer him up.

"As for Dr. Marco Polo, do you have something against him, sir Caleb?" Ross asked.

Caleb couldn't stand the butler's audacity. In a burst of anger, typical of his behavior when contradicted, he attacked the butler.

"Who are you to address me without my permission?" The father, now recovered, raised his voice with Caleb. "Are you some kind of a tyrannical king or a dictator as to demand permission to speak to you?"

Peterson kicked Caleb under the table.

"Caleb didn't mean that. He's exhausted because he had an allergic crisis last night."

"But he said he slept very well," pointed out the father.

"Figure of speech, Dad. He was so sleepless that I asked Ross to bring some tea. Remember?"

"Did you have nightmares, Caleb?" the father inquired.

"Well... No," denied Caleb.

At this moment, Ross served an apple pie to Caleb and said, "Would you like to have a piece to see if it's any good?"

"I'm allergic to apples."

"So am I!" Affirmed Peterson, afraid it might be poisoned.

"And how about you, Brenda, did you have any nightmares?"

Brenda was silent for a moment but decided to be honest.

"I did. Related to the fear... of becoming poor, the fear... of the future, Dad."

"Fear of the future? The future is a contract without clauses. Fear is the most legitimate of human phobias. But don't worry. With the money you'll inherit, you won't have worries about the ghosts of the future, except those in your mind," said the father, with a slight smile on his face.

Caleb opened a wide smile. He interpreted his father's words as if he were going to increase the value of the inheritance they would receive. Finally, Theo Fester would give them what they deserved.

"My lovely father, thank you for the inheritance you'll give us. Your understanding is fascinating."

"Thank you, Dad. You are very generous. Your love is worth more than all the gold in the world," said Peterson, but he was nudged by Caleb so that his father wouldn't interpret it wrongly. He tried to correct himself. "Certainly, with our resources, we will fulfill the dreams we've talked about."

"Is a father's love worth less than gold, Caleb?" the father questioned, realizing that he had nudged his brother.

"Of course, Dad. I'm proud to be your son," he affirmed, embarrassed.

"Thank you very much. Instead of giving you the money I promised, I'll make an adjustment."

Brenda smiled confidently and said, "Wow, Dad, you're amazing."

But the father made their world collapse again.

"Since my love is so valuable to my children, I will deduct ten percent from what I had promised you to give to all the employees who have been working with me for more than ten years, like Marc Douglas and others."

"Ho... hold on a bit," stammered Caleb. "Are we going to receive less than the hundred million dollars?"

"Almost a hundred. You'll now receive ninety million dollars, Caleb. As I've told you, and you very well know, it's an incalculable fortune for 99.99 percent of the American population."

Peterson lost his mind. He hit the table with both hands.

"What madness is this?"

"Do you want to see us begging on the streets?" shouted Caleb, knocking down plates and silverware.

Brenda didn't know what to do. She was upset but tried to contain her brothers' aggressive and impetuous reactions.

Theo Fester choked once again, this time with the water he was trying to drink to calm himself down in the face of the uncontrollable crisis of his sons. Brenda went to help him again, but Caleb held her by the arm. Ross was the one who came to his aid, patting his back. The powerful Silicon Valley entrepreneur was in the sordid valleys of disappointment. After recovering, even weakened, he pounded the table and let out a shout, as he always did.

"Calm down from all this anxiety!" Then he left them perplexed. "Didn't you realize I was testing you?"

Peterson and Caleb, who thought of themselves as extremely intelligent and were regarded as some of the greatest global businessmen of their day, foolishly fell into the trap. And in an unusual stunt, Caleb shouted, "And who said we're not testing you? Our reaction is a spectacle, a performance, Dad. Come on! Don't take us so seriously. We were just kidding. We're all here together; we need to enjoy this moment lightly."

And to show that he wasn't in a fit of anger, Caleb took Ross by the arms and started waltzing with him. Peterson, in turn, showing flexibility, took a maid by the arms and started dancing with her. Brenda applauded them, as if everything had been planned. Then they sat down with their faces sweaty.

Theo Fester was intrigued. It seemed like his children had tucked a blanket around him, covering his body but leaving his feet uncovered. Ross came to their defense.

"Your children are adorable, Mr. Fester."

"Do you think so?"

"See, Dad, even Ross, who seems like he has never danced in his life, knows that we're joking and recognizes our value," commented Caleb.

Contrary to Caleb's judgment once again, Ross took the maid and danced a perfect tango. Then he stated: "I used to be a dance teacher, sir."

"Surprising," said Brenda.

"And you are great artists, by the way, great actors," Ross continued.

"I agree. You are great actors," the father expressed.

Then, the magnate signaled for Ross to take him to his room. This time, Theo didn't give his children a kiss. He seemed very disappointed. Peterson tried to be nice, but without moving from where he was standing.

"Thank you very much, Dad."

All the employees left the grand hall. The three children remained in an indescribable emotional state, physically paralyzed, emotionally frozen. They didn't know whether to laugh or cry.

After a long period of silence, Caleb said anxiously, "I'm been tortured. My body is sore."

"I feel like a prisoner confined in the solitary," Peterson affirmed.

"I can't even describe my feelings. It seems like I've been run over. My head feels like it's going to explode," Brenda stated.

"Theo Fester wants to devour us. He's not acting like a father," Peterson claimed.

"He's at death's door and wants to take us with him," said Caleb and Peterson at the same time.

"Can somebody actually be that mean?" Brenda commented, doubting her father's love.

After this brief and dramatic dialogue, the three left the room, and each one went to their own bedroom. Their exhausted brains flooded their bodies with psychosomatic symptoms. Brenda, in addition to headaches, felt short of breath. Suddenly, she screamed, seeing a spider crawling on the wall of her room. She didn't have a common fear of spiders; she had arachnophobia. It seemed like spiders were going to attack her, poison, and suffocate her. Then, she had a bulimic crisis, rummaging through the dresser drawer to grab the sweets she had hidden as soon as she arrived at the Forest Castle. She ate chocolates, cookies, and various other treats compulsively. As soon as she ingested the last piece, she ran to the bathroom and induced vomiting.

She threw dozens of objects until she killed the poor spider. While trying to eliminate it, she recalled a terrible episode. Four years ago, four heavily armed and hooded men kidnapped her. While being taken to the hideout, she entered a state of despair, not because of the kidnapping or the kidnappers, but because of the possibility that the hideout might be filthy and infested with spiders.

"Are there spiders where I'm going to be held captive?" she asked.

The kidnappers didn't understand.

She insisted, "The place you're taking me to… is it dirty?"

"What's happening, woman?" shouted the chief of the kidnappers.

"I'm afraid of spiders!"

"But you should be afraid of us!" He asserted.

Caleb, on the other hand, had always been a hypochondriac. He feared diseases. His hypochondria was turbocharged by the recent family events. He measured his pulse, put his hand on his own chest to check if his heart was racing. Constantly on alert, it was as if he was about to be devoured by something or someone.

Peterson tried to close his eyes and rest, yet failing to do so. He was so shaken and depressed that he began to hear voices.

"Stupid! Idiot!" Then, he heard a ghostly laughter.

Every human has ghosts in the basement of their mind, in the soils of their unconscious mind, but many are in hibernation. The temperature of the anxiety of the three siblings was rising, awakening their mental demons. Their strategies weren't working, leading them to discover that they weren't as clever as they thought.

Caleb, considered one of the greatest entrepreneurs of the world, felt like a fragile prey in before his father's claws. He opened his eyes, scared and breathless, and sat up on the bed. Suddenly, a macabre, dramatic, unimaginable plan passed through his prey's mind.

CHAPTER 17

A Machiavellian Plan

Caleb rubbed his hands on his face incessantly, displaying an uncontrollable nervous tic. He continued panting, flushed, with high levels of adrenaline circulating in his blood. His heart seemed to want to jump out of his chest. Suffering an anxiety attack, he sent a message to his siblings asking them to come to his room.

"Come to my room now!"

"What happened?" Brenda inquired.

"Now!!"

The signs of distress from the once untouchable younger brother were so intense that they immediately went to him. When they reached his room, they were greeted by a signal of silence from Caleb. Certain that his voice was being heard, he typed a message: "For sure this place is filled with hidden listening devices. We need to go to a safe place urgently."

Brenda made a hand gesture, like asking "Why?"

Caleb typed succinctly: "I have a plan."

Tiptoeing, they searched for a new place within that mysterious Forest Castle. They walked through the immense corridor and opened a door, which creaked like in horror movies, startling them. They turned on the light, and the place was strange.

It looked like a neurological laboratory. Multiple detailed drawings of the human body hung on the wall. One of the paintings depicted a dissected human body, a famous drawing by Leonardo da Vinci. The place was imposing, filled with state-of-the-art technology, supercomputers. Another painting showed the detailed anatomy of Invictus, piece by piece. The siblings were impressed with the place.

There was also a huge painting that showed the anatomy of the human brain. It had inscriptions: "In the human brain, there are more prisons than in the world's most violent cities. What is your prison?" This painting seemed like a warning to the observer.

In the middle of the room, there was a beautiful and long travertine marble table with some computers on it. On the left side of it, there were brains of various sizes preserved in formaldehyde, in transparent glass containers. Behind this table, there was a photo. Caleb approached it and looked at it indignantly. It was a photo of Dr. Marco Polo with his right arm over Dr. Sophia's shoulders. They both smiled. Caleb couldn't contain himself and said angrily: "I knew it! I knew it! This is the headquarters of the fake philanthropist…! …of this predator of weakened minds! …of this usurper of others' inheritances."

"What are you talking about, Caleb?" Asked Brenda, who was too far to see the photo.

"This photo is of Dr. Marco Polo. This is his laboratory. He tricked Dad and brought him here."

"This guy is a time bomb," asserted Peterson, who was too envious of Caleb but, took his side in their emotional desert.

"Is Dr. Marco Polo really that bad?" Brenda questioned. "I tried to investigate him on the internet, and I saw he has done many important works. And a phrase in which he praised women fascinated me: *Women are more pacifist than men. If they were generals, there would hardly be any wars because they wouldn't have the courage to send their children to battle.*"

"Oh, don't be naive, Brenda! The greatest sociopaths are incredibly intelligent; they hide monstrosity in their work and false ethics," Caleb stated without hesitation.

"How can you prove that he planned everything?"

"What more evidence do we need? Look at this lab…! Look at what is written below the image of that giant brain: 'In the human brain, there are more prisons than in the world's most violent cities. What is your prison?' Don't you see what it means, Brenda? He imprisoned Dad's brain. He seduced, blackmailed, and deluded our father," Caleb concluded categorically.

"But our father has never been blackmailed or deluded by anyone. His reasoning is quick and sharp; no one defeats him," Brenda commented.

"Oh, don't be foolish, Brenda," Caleb said. "He has always been manipulable. He just needed the right strategy."

"But then why isn't your strategy working?" The sister retorted.

"Because of this demon named Marco Polo. While others try to rob safes, this cretin is much more intelligent; he wants to steal brains. He's devious!"

"The old man is dying," Peterson added. "It's easy to dominate a dying man's brain."

Suddenly, Brenda looked at a brain and saw a handwritten message attached and signed. She read the following message: "Three months of life can be an eternity compared to the mediocre life that many human beings have. From Dr. Marco Polo to Theo Fester."

"You see?" Caleb said, interpreting the message in his own way. "He seduced Dad with cheap philanthropy. He gave meaning to Dad's few days of life, saying that his immense sins and greed would be redeemed if he gave his fortune to prevent violence in humanity."

"This sociopath is really clever. He drugged our father's brain to be against us, his legitimate children, his beloved children," Peterson said emotionally.

"Let's warn Dad," Brenda suggested.

"Don't be naive, Brenda! Dad doesn't think anymore, he doesn't have critical reasoning."

"I'll spend the millions that I'll receive from my meager inheritance denouncing, pursuing, and suing that scoundrel," Peterson said, stepping beyond the bounds of emotion into hatred.

Caleb announced, "I have a plan!"

"A plan? What plan? Everything has been going downhill," his sister concluded.

"When Dad sets his mind on something, no one can dissuade him," her older brother asserted. "What plan could work against that?"

While they looked at Caleb, he took a deep breath and said in a hushed tone, "To kill Dad!"

Brenda sat on the floor. Peterson went pale. Caleb joined them on the floor and said, in a cold tone: "He mentioned that he might survive for a few days."

"But killing our own father?!" Brenda spoke, while Peterson, frozen, paid attention to his brother's plan.

"Dad is slowly killing us. It is completely unfair! Consider this: we would be shortening his suffering. It is a form of compassionate euthanasia."

"But he doesn't want to die! So, it would be murder!!" The sister affirmed.

"Dad is already mentally dead, Brenda," Peterson said, starting to entertain the idea.

"It's not murder *per se*. His oxygen saturation is so low that even a slight decrease could be fatal..."

"Oh, my God! I couldn't do that," the sister said, scandalized. "It's better to prove that he's senile!"

"That's impossible, woman! We can't make him contradict himself; we have to silence him in another way," Caleb stated.

"Think, Brenda, there are billions of dollars at stake," Peterson warned.

"But it's not about the money; it's Dad's life," she asserted.

"But, Brenda... Remember your magnificent social project to help refugees," Peterson said. "You could channel one, two, or maybe even three billion dollars into that project. I would also help children with cancer, set up care centers for the poor."

Caleb entered the philanthropic circle: "I would build more than a thousand houses for the homeless in Los Angeles. I would end this crisis in the largest city of the wealthiest state in the United States," Caleb stated.

"But since Dad hasn't made the donation yet and if he dies, the wealth tax in our country is high. It will eat up forty percent of our inheritance," the sister said, starting to flirt with the idea.

"It's better to lose forty percent than ninety percent. And with our army of lawyers, who knows if we have legal arguments or loopholes in the law to pay less tax?"

"We have to act quickly," Peterson said.

Brenda got up, still a little skeptical, but dug in her memory nutrients for her decision. She said, "On second thought, it's good to avoid Dad's suffering. Besides, he wasn't a good father. I don't remember a single time he publicly praised me. He always criticized me. I don't remember anything good about our childhood."

"Dad was never a good husband either. He's a psychopath; he didn't even cry when Mom died," Peterson emphasized.

And to complete the father's burial, Caleb categorically asserted: "Dad always loved money and businesses much more than our family.

And at the end of his life, he wants to disinherit us. Nothing could be more unfair than that," Caleb said.

"That is really unfair," Brenda commented.

Brenda started crying, but the idea no longer seemed so absurd to her. And so, what seemed impossible was hastily planned.

"We have to act as soon as possible," Caleb instructed.

"When?" Peterson asked.

"Now," Caleb pronounced.

"I won't participate directly," Brenda asserted.

"We are accomplices. Either we all participate or no one participates."

The two older siblings stopped and thought. Caleb gave the final encouragement: "Let's end Dad's suffering as quickly as possible."

And so, the Fester siblings decided to enter the patriarch's room to suffocate him. They nullified the emotional ties, tore from the pages of their history the respect and admiration they had for their father. Money and power fed predators; those stuffs spoke much louder than love. However, even the most efficient predators make mistakes.

CHAPTER 18

Predators Caught in Their Own Trap

During lunch, the three children remained silent. They couldn't swallow their food. Overwhelmed by guilt, they also couldn't look their father in the eyes. It was difficult to control the ghosts that haunted them in the depths of their minds. Clever, Theo Fester tried to understand his children's odd silence.

"You are awfully quiet. Did something happen Brenda?"

"No, Dad. I'm just feeling a bit unwell."

"And you, Peterson and Caleb, what feeds your silence?"

"I had trouble sleeping," Caleb claimed. "But the best nights are yet to come."

"Indeed, sleep is the conscience's lover. When your conscience is clear, sleep rests in its arms," Theo Fester said intelligently; he still had a more complex reasoning than his children, even in his weakened state.

Peterson was very conservative, unlike Caleb and his father, who were innovators. Afflicted with tropophobia, the fear of change, Peterson always had crises when changes occurred in the bank's leadership, exchange rates, or government interest rates. The changes that would occur in his family and financial history were pushing his brain to the limit. He was about to commit patricide. He would cease to be an executive of the bank he ran and become its main shareholder. The father's last words triggered the perception of the abrupt changes that would occur, feeding his tropophobia, generating uncontrollable psychosomatic symptoms, especially nausea.

Ross quickly brought him a trash can so he could empty his stomach in an appropriate place. After four episodes of vomiting, Peterson also started to pretend.

"Sorry, Dad. Something I ate at breakfast didn't sit well with me either."

What seemed like the last lunch in the presence of the father ended in a sepulchral, funereal atmosphere. The siblings went back to their rooms. During the afternoon, they remained isolated, not speaking to each other. Brenda's arachnophobia intensified. She began to see spiders that existed only in her mind. She tried to cover herself with the duvet to protect herself. She was so tense that she almost hallucinated deliriously. At night, the siblings gathered again at Dr. Marco Polo's supposed laboratory for a few seconds.

"It's now or never," Caleb said.

And just like that, the three siblings quietly went to their father's room. Caleb, always taking the lead, gently opened the bedroom door, that creaked a little, leading them to despair. Each creak echoed in their minds like the thunderous rumble of thunder. Caleb tiptoed in, extremely careful, avoiding making any noise. Red-faced, breathless, about to commit the greatest sacrilege, he looked at his father's face and found him sleeping, breathing gently.

At the exact moment when Caleb signaled for Brenda and Peterson to enter, the unpredictable happened: Theo Fester had a coughing fit. Caleb and his siblings panicked. The two older siblings were paralyzed between the door and the hallway. The coughing episode was so intense that the old man woke up. Upon opening his eyes, he was startled to see Caleb at the bedside.

"Caleb? Why are you here?"

Anxiously, Caleb was quick to come up with an excuse.

"Forgive me, Dad. I was passing through the halls when I heard you coughing. I got worried, then I came to see if everything was okay, if I could help."

"Oh, my son, thank you very much," the father said, coughing again. After recovering, he continued, "I always knew you were a loving son to your father, you just never had the opportunity to show it."

Caleb was shaken by these words.

Then, Theo Fester saw Brenda and Peterson.

"Children, what a surprise!"

Peterson quickly said, "We couldn't sleep. We were walking together down the hallway when we heard you coughing."

"But why didn't you come in together?" the father asked.

"Scared of waking you up. We didn't want to startle you," Brenda said, fearfully.

Trying to be kind, Brenda also offered, "Would you like some water?"

"Yes, please. And what time is it?"

"Ten at night."

"Please, Caleb, could you do me a favor and get my sedative on the nightstand. I forgot to take it before going to bed, so I'm having trouble sleeping. I'm feeling very weak and debilitated."

"No problem, Dad. Sleep well." And he gave him the sedative.

"I never imagined that you cared so much about my health. You can go, and thank you very much. This sedative is a holy remedy; it produces such a deep sleep that it can even reduce my nighttime coughing fits."

And so, the three of them left the room, while their father drank water and swallowed his sleep inducer. Instead of going to their rooms, the three went back to Dr. Marco Polo's laboratory, the only place where they felt safe to openly discuss the Machiavellian plan.

"I can't believe it. Dad seems to have sensed our presence," said Peterson.

"Let's give up," suggested Brenda.

"Give up? The old man took the sedative; it made our job easier," Caleb, the star of the Silicon Valley, completed.

"He told Brenda himself that he's debilitated. Rest assured he has only a few days left and with severe respiratory problems," Peterson, the star of the New York financial world, concluded.

"Silencing his lungs is easing Dad's suffering, it's like solving a logical equation," Caleb added.

"Well... We're only sentencing a conviction he already has. It's an act of love," declared Brenda, the star of the fashion world.

This way, half an hour later, the three social stars went to their father's room again. The thirst for power controlled them. They looked around as if they were being watched. They entered their father's room stealthily once again. They noticed that he was breathing with some effort but seemed to be in a deep sleep. He was covered from head to toe, lying on his back, his face partially hidden by the duvet.

That's when Caleb on one side and Peterson on the other prepared to suffocate their own father. The scene was awful. Brenda was at the head of the bed and made the sign of the cross. She wasn't religious, but she had faith at her convenience. Then, she whispered very softly:

"Let's say a prayer."

The two froze, signaling that they wouldn't.

But she closed her eyes and prayed:

"May my father rest in peace. May his sufferings end."

The two were coerced into lowering their eyes in respect. Theo Fester coughed after the prayer. They were terrified, in a state of shock. Quickly, they put their hands on their father's neck and began to suffocate him. To their desperation, they realized something went wrong. Their father's neck was stiff. It didn't seem normal. Theo Fester's body, with superhuman strength, sat up in bed. He asked with a strange voice:

"What are you doing here?"

"Who are you…?" Brenda asked. "…Dad?"

"Are you trying to kill me?"

Suddenly, the character took off the mask that perfectly simulated Theo Fester's face and revealed himself.

"Invictus?" they said, frightened.

At that exact moment, five security guards quickly entered the room and handcuffed them. The song "We are free" started playing again. A song so beautiful and terrifying at the same time. They were not dreamers, not free, from now on, they were prisoners. Walking through those corridors to the sound of that music was turning seconds into years. Invictus stayed in the room.

While being escorted, Caleb screamed:

"What's happening? I want to talk to my lawyer."

Peterson also spoke energetically:

"I want to talk to Dr. William, my lawyer. We're not criminals."

But the guards paid no attention to them.

Brenda, being more sensitive in such an inhuman environment, in tears, asked:

"Who are you?"

The security guards took them to the large main room and placed them at the table, in the same places as the first time. They remained handcuffed. Dr. Marco Polo and Dr. Sophia entered the room.

Theo Fester had not yet arrived in the room.

Seeing them, Caleb shouted. Addressing Dr. Marco Polo, he said:

"I knew it! I knew you were plotting against us."

Dr. Marco Polo looked into his eyes and commented:

"Wrong! The worst traps a human being falls into are crafted by themselves."

After that, he remained in dead silence. Dr. Sophia also remained silent.

Suddenly, Theo Fester entered without his wheelchair. He was walking with some difficulty, as if shedding some tears. With a choked voice, the billionaire said:

"It's very sad to know that money and power produce many flatterers but few friends. It's dramatic to realize that they produced children who love me for what I have, not for who I am."

"Dad, don't you see? You killed us when you took away our inheritance and gave it to this scoundrel, this opportunist, this seducer of minds... of minds..." Caleb said, repeating the last words but didn't complete the sentence.

"Dr. Marco Polo is a seducer of what minds, Caleb? Insane...? Fragile...? Stupid minds? With what adjective you want to characterize me?"

Caleb fell silent, and his father completed his thought.

"I gave you the best I had: my life and my experiences. Moreover, a super salary and a stake in the profits of my companies. And what do I get in return? A plan to kill me?"

"That's not true! We didn't want to kill you," Caleb tried to defend himself. "We were in the room because we heard another coughing episode."

"Yes. We rushed there to help you. You can't prove anything against us — nothing at all," asserted Peterson.

"Ah... How I wish you were transparent! How I wish you had a clear conscience," Theo Fester said.

Brenda, between sobs, said, "We didn't want to take your life. We wanted to help you..."

"You may have many flaws, but you have always been my beloved daughter. I never imagined you were capable of this," the father said.

Theo Fester activated a massive screen that started projecting a series of images where his children plotted his murder. Caleb was right; there were state-of-the-art mini cameras hidden in all over the place. Despite his cleverness, he didn't detect them.

First, the images started with Caleb's own room. The cameras showed him typing to his siblings. One camera zoomed in, and the message on the phone screen became visible: "This place certainly has many hidden bugs. We need to go to a safe place urgently."

The camera showed Brenda's behavior, making a hand gesture, questioning, "Why?" Caleb typed succinctly: "I have a plan."

"That doesn't prove anything! I typed 'I have a plan' because I wanted to build a new startup, and I wanted my brothers to be my partners," said Caleb, hoping there were no cameras in Dr. Marco Polo's laboratory.

"That's right," Peterson agreed.

But what happened next was worse. Theo Fester started showing detailed images of the laboratory. In the images, Caleb explained the plan. At that moment, he began to rub his head continuously. He began to have a panic attack, measuring his pulse and placing his hand on his chest, as if he was about to die right there.

In the images, Brenda started saying, "But killing our own father?! [...] Oh, my Goodness! I couldn't do that. It's better to prove that he is senile!" But Peterson tried to dissuade her from rejection: "Think, Brenda, there are billions of dollars at stake. [...] Remember your magnificent social project to help refugees. You could channel one, two, or maybe even three billion dollars into that project. I would also help children with cancer, set up centers for the poor."

After showing these images, Theo Fester said to the three:

"Kill the father, take his money, and promote your philanthropic dreams. My children, I don't know you! I know the social facade of your personalities, but not your essence. What have you become? So many lies! So much falsehood! So much deceit!"

After a pause, the father continued:

"But what hurts my soul the most is knowing that you conspired against me, claiming I'm a terrible father. In your minds, I'm a stingy, insensitive old man who deserves to die. To you, I'm so cold that I didn't even cry when your mother died. But you do not know that I didn't cry because I never learned how to cry. My father didn't teach me how to display feelings. But I'm not a psychopath; I've never been insensitive."

Caleb began to pound the table in a fit of rage, and his hands began to bleed. Brenda and Peterson were also out of control. They were scared to realize how far they had gone because of greed. They couldn't look at their father. And now, would they be condemned and imprisoned? Would they stay away from their father in the final moments when he would close his eyes to life? Would their father have other surprises? Nothing in that family was routine. Storms and thunder alternated with rare moments of sunlight. Rarely did a family have such a socially and emotionally complex and complicated existence.

CHAPTER 19

Denying Their Own Story

The atmosphere in the Fester clan reached the pinnacle of frustration. The three children wanted to be anywhere else in the world but there. Unexpectedly, Ross, the butler, entered. Theo Fester left the three dumbfounded by revealing:

"Invictus!!" (Invictus took off the mask.)

Dr. Marco Polo spoke up again:

"Think about the consequences of what you've done. You may not only face judgment and go to physical prison, but if you don't reinvent yourselves, you'll be imprisoned for the rest of your life in your mental prison."

"Don't condemn us before we're judged, Dr. Marco Polo." Peterson said: "I want a lawyer."

"I'm here, Peterson" said the group's legal director, Dr. William, entering the room.

"What's going on here? What kind of setup is this?" asked the oldest son.

"Attempted murder" affirmed Invictus. "The evidence is irrefutable."

Caleb, the intellectual mentor of the plan, had his head down and was paralyzed.

Despite being emotionally destroyed, Theo Fester managed to be kind. Instead of punishing them, he chose to recall a story:

"You said I loved my money and businesses more than you. Is that true?"

Nobody dared to say a word.

"Children, I know I failed, I was stern, impulsive, and critical. I am aware that there were moments I sacrificed time with you for more hours of work. I have unpaid debts as a father. But I also know that I had solemn moments with you, filled with sublime love. However, you were unable to remember those moments."

The siblings said nothing; they were paralyzed.

"I remember once we were in Germany, when Caleb was only five years old. Do you remember, Brenda? You were thirteen, and Peterson, fifteen. I was going to participate in a conference with a group of investors and it was a bit late. You were sleeping in..."

Brenda began to remember emotionally. Her father continued:

"But I waited for you so we could have breakfast together. Your mother, always more affectionate than me, was nervous that day. She said, *you're late for your speech. Leave them.* But I told her, *I've been working too much; I need to give them more attention.* Soon you arrived, and during breakfast, Caleb spilled strawberry juice on the tablecloth while he was pouring some into his glass. Trying to grab the glass, he spilled the entire pitcher of juice on my white shirt. Remember, children?"

Caleb changed from a state of anger to tears for the first time.

"Yes," Brenda, always more receptive, responded affirmatively.

Theo Fester continued to describe that touching story.

"Your mother scolded you, Caleb: *You're a disaster!* But I said, *Rebeca, leave the boy alone; I'm a disaster too!* But your mother, worried, advised, *You're so late...! And you still have to change your clothes.* Then I responded: *I'm not going to change my clothes.* And she replied: *These German businessmen will eat you alive.'* So, I told her: *Let them eat me! I'm hard to digest...!*

At that time, I didn't have all the power and fame I have today. And I went with my stained shirt to speak to over two hundred businessmen, bankers, government officials. Caleb had his leg in a cast because of a fall. And, to everyone's surprise, I picked him up, even though he was quite heavy at that age. I reached my hand out to you, Brenda, and said, *Peterson, hold Brenda's hand. You'll come with me to the auditorium.* Do you remember?"

Sighing deeply, Peterson confessed, now also in tears:

"I remember..." And he added: "We were all worried. Caleb cried a lot; he thought you were going to hit him."

Theo added tenderly:

"On that day, I was twenty minutes late, and we were in Germany, where, just like in England, being a minute late is outrageous. When I settled you into your seats, I was immediately called to the stage. Everyone looked at me sideways. A businessman spoke audibly: *These Jews think they own the world just because they're rich. Look at how late he is.* Another one next to him said: *Look at his stained shirt. It's an insult to show up looking like a clown.* Some laughed. But I looked at the audience and asserted categorically: *It wasn't a Jew who was late, but a father. It wasn't even a businessman or an entrepreneur, but a simple father. Imperfect, yes, who has difficulty expressing his emotions, too, but who is passionate about his family. I was called to talk about investments, but my greatest investment is represented on this stained shirt.*

Theo Fester's children did not want to hear the end of this story. By attempting to kill their father, they tried to nullify his greatness, minimize his qualities, and maximize his flaws. Theo Fester concluded his story, by saying:

"It was then that I explained to the German businessmen: 'My children were late for breakfast, getting me angry. I don't usually run late for my commitments.' But a voice echoed within me at that moment and asked me a question: *Who is your greatest investment, your children or your companies?*' I decided to wait for them and sacrificed you, I sincerely apologize for that. And, to make matters worse, my youngest son, Caleb, spilled a pitcher of juice on me. So, in this conference, I won't talk about negotiation techniques or new technologies or the characteristics of a successful entrepreneur. I will ask you the same question: Who is your greatest investment? The people we love are what is worth living and fighting for. My children are my greatest investment. We can become multimillionaires, but if we miss the target, we will be the poorest of men. And that's how I ended the conference, leaving everyone astonished because the vast majority had already missed the target."

After Theo Fester retold this story, something unimaginable happened: the billionaire cried uncontrollably, like he had never done before. His children had never seen him in like this. Dr. Marco Polo, Dr. Sophia, and Dr. William were also wiping their eyes. The clever Invictus said:

"If I had emotions, I would surely cry."

Theo Fester's children realized the madness they had committed.

"How could I forget that event and so many others, father? You received a standing ovation." Brenda commented, almost voiceless.

"I'm sorry, father, I was blind, completely irrational..." Caleb admitted.

Peterson put his hands on his head, ashamed: "Forgive me, forgive me. I deserve to be condemned; I deserve to be put in jail."

But, to everyone's surprise, the father, instead of turning his back on them and never looking at any of them again, made a request to the security guards.

"Release the handcuffs."

"Why?" Caleb asked.

"You took part in a real, true experiment controlled by Dr. Marco Polo, at my request."

The children were shocked by what they heard. They didn't know whether to laugh or cry.

"I was convinced that you would pass the stress test. But I was wrong. In my private meetings with Dr. Marco Polo, I assured him: *Your mental prisons theory won't work on my children. They would never deny me, hurt me, or betray me, even if I took away almost all of their assets.*"

Dr. Marco Polo intervened and said:

"I advised your father not to conduct this emotional stress test. But he insisted."

"Lies!" Caleb muttered quietly and angrily to his siblings.

And the psychiatrist concluded:

"I also commented: *You are unaware of the mental prisons that are inside every human being, not just inside your children, but in all of us. Even if they are good people, the predator instinct is still there.*"

"Did you test us, father? Did you put us in an emotional lab? Were we like lab rats in your laboratory?!" Peterson asked, shocked.

"Rats? Shut up, you insolent fool. Are you forgetting your attempted murder?" the magnate shouted. "I firmly believed that, no matter how fierce competitors you were, how jealous of each other you were, your love for me would be greater, unconditional. I believed that you would only be hurt, disappointed, frustrated, or even angry... but you wouldn't stop loving. I'm perplexed. You went too far. You planned my death! You actually went that far!"

"Who could ever pass this test?" Caleb asked.

"Any child who really loves their father... for who he is and not for what he has; any child who doesn't have a blind ambition; any child who is more humane and less blinded by money!" Theo Fester exclaimed, slamming his fist on the table."

After a long pause, the mega-entrepreneur commented, emotionally:

"My father survived several concentration camps, an environment devoid of solidarity. He came to the United States and felt completely alone. He married, but was consumed by jealousy of his wife. My mother, in the end, couldn't take it anymore; she left forever!" The feeling of abandonment had haunted Theo Fester his entire life.

"I regret having done this test because, in the end, I failed in my greatest investment! I discovered that I am a miserable billionaire. I will die as one of the richest men in a cemetery; I will close my eyes as a businessman who has everything that money can buy but lacks what is priceless: the love of his children."

Dr. Marco Polo tried to soothe Theo's pain, and to the children's surprise, he tried to act as their defense lawyer.

"Mr. Fester, don't give up on your children. They have a remarkable side that should be considered."

Peterson, Brenda, and Caleb looked at the psychiatrist, dumbfounded.

Even though Dr. Marco Polo knew they had made a terrible unforgivable mistake, he tried to ease the guilt of the three, citing the predator-prey syndrome.

"A remarkable side, Dr. Marco Polo? Are you blind, by any chance?"

Dr. Marco Polo wasn't one to remain silent:

"Remember, Mr. Fester, the predator-prey syndrome and the workings of the human mind. They became frustrated when learned they would not receive their dreamed inheritance. Although their behavior is ethically unjustifiable, the systematic experienced frustration triggered the Self's first copilot, the memory trigger. This activated the second copilot, the killer windows. Due to the high-tension volume, these windows imprisoned the third copilot, the memory anchor, closing its circuit. Therefore, thousands of windows with millions of data, even those that fund love for you, were not accessed."

Brenda looked directly into Dr. Marco Polo's eyes and thanked him with a nod. Then, she commented:

"Yes, father, we were trapped by these mental prisons. What we did was hateful, horrible, perhaps unforgivable, but we do love you."

"It's true! I was a fool" confessed Peterson.

"I know I don't deserve your forgiveness, and I don't intend to lighten my crime, but I was completely blind," said Caleb.

Theo Fester locked eyes with Dr. Marco Polo.

"I thought about this while analyzing the images of my children in the lab. Perhaps you're right to say that the human species has low viability levels. It's likely that in the human brain there are more prisons than we believe can exist. But it's impossible to ignore the fact that they tried to kill me."

After saying this, the father sat down. He was tired, mentally exhausted. After breathing slowly and deeply, he added, looking into his children's eyes:

"You know I'm a lover of math. And in the history of mathematics, there's a tragic passage, little known."

Theo Fester told them the story of a great mathematician, Kurt Friedrich Gödel from Austria, Einstein's friend. Although he was extremely rational in dealing with calculations, he was a slave to mental prisons. He wasn't imprisoned in concentration camps, but he had unresolved traumas, including ideas of persecution and fear of contamination.

"Kurt Gödel wouldn't eat anything that wasn't prepared by his wife because he was afraid of being poisoned. Years later, when his wife was hospitalized for six months, one of the most logical men in the world reacted illogically: he stopped eating, and died of complications from starvation because he didn't trust anyone else to prepare his food. Emotion overcame reason, mental prisons overcame rationality."

Everyone was impressed by this story. Caleb, to his father's surprise, as if applauding Dr. Marco Polo's project, commented:

"That's why we urgently need a project to mitigate human self-violence."

But no one could tell if he was being honest or trying to ease his guilt.

"Caleb, when speaking, you're intelligent; but with your mouth shut, you're wise."

"Are you telling me to be quiet?" Caleb asked, unsure.

"Obviously!" Then, Theo Fester delivered bad news to his children: "You and your siblings have heard of me, but you don't know me! You don't know who I am inside, what I think, and what I feel at my core. Because I had offered one percent of my assets, you decided to kill me. Now, in addition to being arrested, you will be completely disinherited. You will have only a small amount to hire a lawyer."

The three put their hands to their heads in despair, deeply dismayed. They knew that they had destroyed their financial track and social reputation.

"However, while analyzing the recordings of your plan, remembering how you tried to deceive me, seduce me, and fool me, I thought about proposing a challenge to you. I wouldn't be able to forgive you without an unfathomable reparation."

"Another challenge? What is it?" Brenda asked, excited and worried at the same time.

"If you pass the stress test, I will propose to you the restoration of almost your entire inheritance and not press charges. You will have ninety percent of all my assets. The remaining ten percent I will give to social projects, including Dr. Marco Polo's intriguing project."

The three looked at one another ecstatically, and couldn't contain themselves. They went from emotional hell to the heaven of jubilation. They did the math and concluded that each of them would become a billionaire, receiving at least nine billion dollars. And if they could use Invictus' technology, they would be the richest humans in the world in a few years.

"Thank you very much" they all said at the same time, holding each other's hands.

However, Caleb started coming to his senses. He started to feel suffocated. He knew his father was extremely intelligent and surprising, even to put them at very high risks. Anxious, he asked the fatal question:

"Wait a minute. What is the stress test you will subject us to? If this first one was horrible, and we failed, what could possibly come next?"

Peterson and Brenda felt a lump in their throat, they began to have palpitations, shortness of breath, and headaches. They were convinced he would be capable of proposing tests even more dramatic than the one they endured these past few days.

Theo Fester smiled, and it was impossible to know if it was ironic or joyful. The three Fester siblings were disturbed. But anything would be better than facing bars, the financial ruin, and the destruction of their social status. Their father, one of the greatest entrepreneurs of all time, was a master at creating dramatically stressful situations.

The magnate himself had undergone emotionally intense experiences with his mother's abandonment, his father's nightmares from concentration camps, financial crises, social humiliation, and his father's imprisonment. Father and son had crossed indecipherable socioemotional valleys. But Theo Fester had given his children too much; making the mistake of excessively supplying them with everything he didn't have during his childhood. He had formed emotional beggars, young people who needed many stimuli to feel scraps of pleasure.

Now, he needed to give the already adult children, who had serious flaws in their personalities, the lessons he had failed to offer during their personality shaping. Smart, possessing quick and sharp strategic thinking, he proposed to the children who plotted to kill him the challenge that no father had ever proposed to his children. The Fester siblings had no idea that the world could collapse on their heads.

CHAPTER 20

Thirty Days of Hell: The Incredible Tests to Which a Father Subjected His Children

At the end of his life, Theo Fester was making incredible discoveries about the emotion planet. For the first time, he deeply understood that emotion defied logical parameters, that it was rebellious to numerical math, leading humans to have surprising distortions of reality. He found that a simple worker, buying their first used vehicle, felt happier and more fulfilled than a millionaire who bought a new model a hundred times more expensive. His children, by losing part of the inheritance, felt an atrocious fear of the future, while one of his thousands of employees, by saving a few pennies at the end of the year, could feel more secure than his children had ever felt.

Thinking they would receive one percent of the inheritance, Peterson, Brenda, and Caleb already felt unprotected and deprived. They wouldn't have private planes, helicopters, yachts, or lavish parties any more. But everything got worse after being caught in a criminal act. They would be completely disinherited. They didn't know that more than three billion people on the planet had no protection at all and earn less than two dollars a day, being extremely poor.

"We're going to starve," Caleb said quietly to his siblings.

"I agree. Especially after doing time and losing our social status. Why did I listen to you?" Peterson rhetorically asked, feeling angry at Caleb.

"Because you're as ambitious as I am," Caleb asserted, standing his ground.

They argued ignoring the situation they were in. The fact is that they felt firsthand the drama of those who multiplied the prison population. They would be victims of prejudice, like lepers in the time of Christ. Few would give them a second chance.

Theo Fester had been touched by challenging journeys all his life. In the global business world, few had survived as many challenges as he did. He was a self-made man; no one helped or supported him. Once, the Silicon Valley billionaire said:

"Those who only take advantage of the opportunities that arise will be mediocre entrepreneurs, depending on luck. An unparalleled entrepreneur doesn't rely on luck; he creates his opportunities. I believe success wakes up before the sun rises."

He lived what he preached: whoever wins without risks ascends to the podium without glories. He had gone bankrupt five times by the age of thirty. But he did not bow to pain and shame. For him, complaining, lamenting, or self-pitying were stupid ways to spend mental energy. He boldly proclaimed his mantra: the best days are yet to come.

When Caleb asked what the challenge was, he fell silent. Peterson would be the first to receive the stress tests. A victim of tropophobia, the fear of change, the applauded bank president snapped his fingers and asked, trembling:

"Don't leave our minds in suspense. Please, tell me: what will the challenge be?"

The billionaire would only be willing to forgive his children if there were significant reparations; otherwise, he would have created monsters, not human beings. Dr. Marco Polo's ideas that Theo had recently learned shook his convictions as a father, educator, entrepreneur, and actor on the stage of humanity. He convinced himself that he needed to expose the predator within them, so he could dominate and educate it; however, knowing that his proposition would imply risks of self-destruction. The reparations could be unbearable. But throughout his life, he would always repeat his proverb: whoever wins without risks, triumphs without glories.

He was not being an irresponsible father. He needed to rescue his children, and they needed to carry for the rest of their lives the guilt of trying to kill him. Theo Fester stared directly into the eyes of his oldest son, and to everyone's astonishment, made an unimaginable proposal.

"Peterson, you know how to run banks, you have almost five thousand employees who fear and flatter you. And as the president of the institution, better than anyone else, you know how to collect debts from the defaulters, but you never learned how to collect the debts you incurred at the bank of your emotion."

"What debts are these, my father?"

"You should know. But if you don't, your case is much more serious."

The oldest son began to internalize and break into a cold sweat. He had transgressed social rules but he wasn't a psychopath; he knew his monumental emotional debts, while hiding them. He was known as "the king" in more than five hundred bank branches he managed, an expert in raising his voice and humiliating employees.

He also had enormous debts in his family. He was an expert in shouting at Barbara, his wife, when contradicted, a specialist in concealing his orgies. His debts to his only son, Thomas, were even greater. He never asked what ghosts haunted him. He scolded him and gave him many gifts to try to neutralize his absence. At the dinner table, he was always on his phone. He didn't know how to love, only how to give orders. He was fit to run a company, but terrible at shaping free minds.

Then, his father continued: "As you had the audacity to tell me that you would use the money from your inheritance to take care of cancer patients, this will be your stress test."

Peterson smiled. He thought the task was simple – "I'll do it with pleasure."

But he felt the ground fall beneath his feet when his father laid out the conditions.

"You will spend a period taking care of children who are suffering from cancer."

Peterson tensed up. His father continued:

"You will clean up the vomit of adults undergoing treatment, help remove the feces and treat the wounds of terminal patients."

"What madness is this? Cleaning up vomit and feces?" He protested, unable to believe what he had just heard. He began to feel a ringing in his ear and dizziness. "How many hours will this torment last?"

"It won't be hours; it will be thirty days."

"Thirty days of hell! It will be an eternity."

Theo Fester was impressed by his oldest son's insensitivity.

"Your condition is worse than I had imagined," he said.

The businessman looked at Dr. Marco Polo, disappointed. The doctor was right. He warned him about his children's anger by saying:

"Unfortunately, like millions of parents, you probably only know the living room of your children's personalities."

"Don't interfere in our relationship, you opportunist," Peterson angrily warned.

But the father sternly drew his attention:

"If you had a little of your son's generosity, you would never say that. For an insensitive human being, taking care of cancer patients for thirty days will be like hell. But you can give up now on your emotional test. And for your information, I haven't even reached its second phase."

"Is there another phase?" Peterson asked, concerned.

"In the second stage, you will help these people without using any money, without using a credit card, without social prestige."

"I don't understand. Can't I use money to hire nurses to help me?"

"No. Your identity must remain unknown, unless people spontaneously discover that you are a *Fester*."

Theo Fester signaled for Dr. Marco Polo to give his opinion.

"Your father wants you to embrace your humanity, with all your craziness and vulnerabilities. You won't even be able to take money to eat. You'll have to get a job working at night, in addition to the hours you're with these patients, in order to survive."

"You're telling me that I can't spend money so that you can spend it? This is a conspiracy!" he protested angrily. Then, he put his hands on his head and said more gently, "This test is too heavy... Unbearable!"

But to Peterson's astonishment, Theo Fester went even further.

"But your stress test is not complete yet. The third stage is that you must be the best volunteer, work harder than the nurses, and never raise your voice at anyone, as you do with your son, wife, and collaborators. If you are not fully generous, if you complain or raise your voice at anyone, I reiterate: I will completely disinherit you, and you will also face trial for attempting to murder your own father."

"You don't love me, Theo Fester! You never loved me! I always knew you hated me," Peterson declared desperately.

"Do I hate you? Oh, how you distort reality! Have you forgotten that you tried to suffocate me?" the father asked, approaching his son, coming face to face with him.

"But Peterson is not Christ, Daddy!" Caleb said, trying to mitigate his brother's situation, aware that soon the accusatory finger would be pointed at him.

"He certainly is not Christ, at least not for me. As a Jew, the Messiah has not yet come to humanity. But your mother, a Christian, must have taught you that Jesus was betrayed with a kiss; and I was betrayed by my own children." And he paused for a long time. "Brenda even said a prayer before you tried to murder me," Theo said, raising his voice.

Brenda turned red. She didn't know that her father had paid attention to this detail.

"Your religiosity is false, Peterson. You will have the opportunity to truly love cancer patients. Now, if my eldest son does not accept this opportunity..." And he signaled for Dr. William to speak.

"He will be sent to jail. He will only have the right to the expenses to pay for his lawyer," Dr. William said.

The security guards began to move towards him to put the handcuffs back on. But he shouted desperately:

"No! Wait, wait... I'll try...! I need to try!"

"You and your siblings have a predator within you, and you will have to learn to control it in extreme situations."

Peterson's fear of change struck again and was somatized by new episodes of vomiting. It seemed like he was going to die. Invictus tried to help him, but his father intervened:

"Leave him. The challenge hasn't even started yet," Theo Fester said.

Then, he turned his attention to the youngest son, Caleb.

"Your challenge, Caleb, will also be in line with the philanthropic dream you falsely claimed you would fulfill with your money."

"I am not false," Caleb said confidently.

"Excellent. You will have a chance to prove that because I've always seen you trying to take advantage in every situation. I've never witnessed any altruistic actions on your behalf."

"But which of the dreams did I tell you?" The youngest son asked, seemingly confused, forgetting what he had told his father the day before.

"Did you lie to me, by any chance?"

"I reiterate, I am always honest," Caleb said, always snapping back when contradicted, irrationally shooting in all directions.

"Do you remember, then?" The father asked again.

"Remember, Caleb, what you told us…" Brenda commented, trying to help her brother. "…Taking care of the homeless."

"Oh, yes! Of course!" He pretended.

"Excellent memory," the father said. And he added: "Everyone thinks the United States is a rich country, and they are right, but the wealth distribution of this nation is shameful."

Then, Caleb began to change color upon hearing his father.

"I don't know if there are homeless people in Los Angeles, but if there are, I would like to help them," Caleb said, trying to disguise his fears.

"Of course, Caleb, it's easy to write a check. Your challenge will be to live with the homeless" the father said.

"To live with them…?! No way!!"

"Then you will be disinherited and go to jail. Simple as that," added the Silicon Valley magnate.

Caleb tensed up and, softening his voice, said: "Carry on."

"Living with a homeless person is the first stage of your stress test. The second will be to live like one. In fact, you will have fewer resources than any of them. You won't take a credit card, not even food, not even a change of clothes."

"But that's too much, daddy!" Caleb said, trembling. "I'll die!"

"He could indeed die," said Dr. Marco Polo, concerned about Theo Fester's youngest son. "The sentence is very harsh."

"Yes, he could actually die," agreed Invictus, making his statistical calculations.

"You see? My test is too harsh. I won't last a day in that environment. Drug dealers could kill me." And he dramatized: "I'll die of starvation.

And where am I supposed to go to the bathroom…? …On the street? These are unhygienic places; I'll surely get many types of infections," he said desperately, intensifying his hypochondria.

"Yes, there are trillions of bacteria per square meter," affirmed Invictus, and it was unclear whether he was saying that to further terrify the arrogant Caleb or if he just wanted to be helpful.

But Theo Fester did not lighten his test: "You were the son who took the initiative to plan my end. Have you forgotten that? Depending on your behavior, death is actually a possibility."

Dr. Willian knew that in Peterson's stress test, if he failed, which was quite possible, he would at most be emotionally shaken and humiliated. However, if Caleb failed, he would have real chances of being murdered or kidnapped. That's why he also considered the test imposed by Theo Fester unbearable.

"Theo, I'm sorry. I always feared testing my children. When you told me that you would test yours, I felt uneasy."

"And I said they would be able to pass, Willian," affirmed Theo Fester.

"And I replied they wouldn't. And look how things turned out. Now, honestly speaking, Theo, how can Caleb, a son born with a silver spoon, live like a homeless person on the streets of Los Angeles amid drug dealers, gangs, and drug addicts?"

"It's an impossible test to pass, my father," Caleb insisted.

"Maybe it is, if you are as arrogant, radical, and authoritarian as you are with your employees. But your test doesn't stop there; it has a third stage."

"Third stage?!" shouted Caleb.

"Yes! You will not only live like a homeless person but you must help the miserable people you encounter with the utmost kindness, altruism, and solidarity. If you fight with someone or ridicule even one human being, you will be disqualified, disinherited, and you will also go to jail," said his father, deeply hurt.

"An eye for an eye, a tooth for a tooth…! No father in the world has ever done this to his children," commented Caleb, completely distressed and outraged.

"No father in the world has given a second chance to his murderer children. Give up or face this test. The decision is yours," the father retorted.

Dr. Sophia, worried about Theo Fester's children, put her hands on her face. He was right, but it would be a huge risk to put them in front of the predators that were inside themselves. If his children didn't master them, they would be devoured from the inside out.

Brenda began to collapse. The challenge her father was reserving for her could also be terrible. As if he were reading her thoughts, Theo Fester immediately turned his eyes to her.

"Brenda, my dear daughter. I remember when I used to cover my eyes and count to ten and start looking for you. When I found you, I kissed you and felt like the happiest father in the world. Do you remember?" Brenda rescued these real moments, although now they seemed to have occurred centuries ago. With tears, the father declared:

"Today, I search for you with my eyes wide open and cannot find you, my daughter. You got lost amidst expensive parties and social columns. If you had a bit of Kate's heart, your daughter, you would be a different person."

"I am not my daughter" she said, in a harsh voice.

"I don't recognize the woman in front of me. I feel guilty about that. They say I'm one of the greatest entrepreneurs in the world, yet I failed in the most important venture of my life, my family that went bankrupt, fragmented, and self-destructed."

There was a moment of deep silence. Everyone present was moved as the powerful businessman Theo Fester confessed his dramatic vulnerability. He continued: "I try to gather its fragments, not as a remarkable entrepreneur, but as the frailest of apprentices. You, Caleb, wanted me to be one of the top ten richest men in the world. But I tell you, I already am. I always downplayed my wealth. But what you didn't know is that we are really poor."

Theo Fester interrupted himself with another coughing fit and, once he recovered, he continued:

"I taught my children to conquer money but not love." And he quoted the phrase he had taught Kate and Thomas a few days earlier: "Some people lack bread on the table, others lack joy in the soul. Some struggle to survive harshly; others beg for the bread of tranquility and happiness. Who is rich? We are the modern era's beggars, the emotional beggars listed by Forbes…"

Brenda fell into tears again. Moved, she confessed:

"My siblings and I don't love each other, I know. We only came together because we were losing our inheritance."

"Daughter, you have always been more honest than your brothers. I always dreamed that you could take care of the social part of the group. Therefore, your stress test, your challenge for me to look you in the eyes before I die and forgive you, is precisely to fulfill your dream, even if false: taking care of refugees."

Brenda was short of breath.

"You will move to Europe, only with a one-way ticket… and this is the first stage of the test. The second is that you won't have money to return, to eat, sleep, or dress. You will live entirely as a refugee. If you take money with you, or use one of your credit cards or a friend's card, I will know. Thus, you will be excluded from my life and my inheritance. You will be secretly monitored, day and night."

"Monitored? But where are my rights?" She replied desperately, disturbed, and perplexed.

"Of course, you have your rights. You can choose willingly not to take care of the refugees. However, in that case, I will have my rights. Even if I suffer, you will be prosecuted, arrested, and will live in prison. Journalists who mention you every week in the social columns will spread in magazines, newspapers, TV, and social media that you tried to kill your father!"

Brenda began to feel nauseous.

"Do you want to face a women's prison and social judgment? Do you want to have your rights?"

"No, no, no...! I appreciate the opportunity you are giving us. But a month in those places can be an eternity for someone who has only lived in luxury" she said sincerely.

"I know, I know... Maybe, in this small opportunity, you tame the predator within you," said the father, wiping the tears from his face. Then he added: "You will take care of refugees of various nationalities. You will go through the anguish of those who were torn from their homeland, those who lost their home and belongings. You will cry the tears of the elderly, live the despair of children who lost their parents, and parents who lost their children in insane wars..."

Brenda's bulimia flared up. She ate a box of doughnuts that were on the table. This time, she, who had always provoked vomiting away from others' eyes, could not control her anxiety and provoked vomiting in front of her father and brothers.

"What are you looking at? That's right! I've had bulimia for ten years! I eat compulsively and induce vomiting to expel food and my guilt. I tried to hide it from you, from Kate, and from everyone," she confessed, shaken. Everyone was moved.

The woman who appeared most in social columns and TV programs in New York would be tested to the limit.

"And why have you never treated yourself?" the father asked, saddened.

"Shame. Even Princess Diana was ashamed of her bulimia. I will treat the disease now if you give me the opportunity."

"Go treat yourself in the refugee camp. They don't vomit the food they eat because they live in extreme scarcity."

"But, father, think about what you are proposing for Brenda. Imagine the dangers. She could be kidnapped by terrorists," Peterson said, defending his sister for the first time.

"Besides that, Brenda could be raped. And how will she survive? Will she have to prostitute herself? Remember the parable of the prodigal son that mom used to tell us? The father forgave the son," Caleb said, showing a concrete concern for his sister's future for the first time.

Theo Fester once again shed tears when he heard his children's words and fears. They were right; the dangers were enormous. But despite loving them, he did not step back regarding the stress test.

"The parable of the prodigal son is a Christian metaphor. Your mother was a Christian and I am Jewish. I won't give you forgiveness for your fatal mistake without reparations. The choices are yours, and so are the consequences."

After these words, he turned his back and went to his room. But as he walked out, he turned to them and said: "But I'll make your lives a little easier. If you want to give up, call Invictus; if you want psychological guidance, call Dr. Marco Polo. Cancer is bearable; betrayal is not. I hope my resentment doesn't kill me before cancer in the next thirty days."

Caleb looked at his siblings and said in a low voice: "I will die, but I will never call them..." And he didn't finish the sentence, as he was dripping with hatred.

And that's how one of the wealthiest men in the world subjected his children, who lived at the height of social glamor, to go through the greatest human challenges... They had everything to give up or self-destruct; the odds were against them.

CHAPTER 21

Brenda's Madness

Brenda began to pack her things for the most important and risky journey of her life. Kate, her only daughter, had no idea what was going on, but she could see that her mother's expression had completely changed, then she thought it would be better to wait to ask her about it. Brenda hugged her daughter in the living room of their house before taking a taxi and heading to the airport. She had never given her such a long and emotional hug. Touched, tears streamed down Brenda's face, because she wasn't sure if she would survive her stress test. This could be the last time seeing her daughter, perhaps their last embrace and kisses. Kate, at the age of fourteen, was a very smart, talkative, and active girl.

"Are you crying, mom? What's going on? Is Grandpa Theo not well?"

Wiping her eyes, Brenda confessed with a broken heart: "No, honey. Grandpa's health is not good."

The girl became desperate, quickly asking: "What does he have?"

"Grandpa has cancer, my daughter."

Kate burst into tears. Losing her grandfather meant losing her anchor. "No, No, it can't be! It can't be!" She exclaimed. Then, expressing her feelings for him, she added: "I love him so much. He talks a lot to me.

Even if he were the poorest grandfather in the world, I would give everything for him, taking care of him with my own life."

Brenda was devastated. Her daughter loved Theo Fester more than she did. Perhaps Brenda didn't know her father as much as he deserved. Unfortunately, his time was running out and she longed to be at his feet day and night to explore the treasures of this globally admired entrepreneur, but she had an almost impossible mission to accomplish. "I know, your grandpa is amazing!"

"But you always complained about him to me."

"I was wrong, honey."

"Don't let him die, Mom, please don't..." Kate's reactions made Brenda remember what she wished to erase forever: just a little over twenty-four hours ago, she had tried to silence his life. If Kate knew about it, she would never forgive her mother. There would be an uncrossable gap between them. With trembling lips due to overwhelming guilt, Brenda said, "No... I won't... my daughter, I won't..."

But then Kate asked the fatal question: "How long will you be in Europe?"

"Probably a month," she said, afraid of her daughter's reaction.

"A month? Don't you love Grandpa? Who will take care of him? He might die!"

"Honey, I..."

Kate interrupted her quickly and drastically. "I know. You've always been an ungrateful daughter... only loving parties and your millionaire friends. You would call Grandpa only once a month to talk about business."

"Honey, please understand... I'm not going because I want to, I'm going because your own grandpa asked me to."

"What do you mean?!" she asked, disturbed.

With a choked voice, Brenda explained, "Your grandpa asked me to stay a month helping refugees in Europe."

"But you never cared about refugees. You always loved your millionaire friends, athletes, artists, high-class people..."

"I know, I know. Perhaps that's why your grandpa, before leaving this life, wants me to change my path and take care of those in need."

"But do you want to do that?" "Well, I... honestly, I don't know. I... feel that his request, at this moment in his life, is undeniable..." She spoke, again in tears. For the first time, she felt like the most miserable person in the world. Once again, she hugged her daughter. They both cried.

"Sorry, I have to go," she said, distressed. And she advised: "Take care of your grandpa while I'm gone, okay?"

Brenda took a taxi. Thoughtful, she headed to the huge JFK airport. She had a headache, and many doubts with no answers. For the first time, she began to question who she was and what she had become. The great business woman, who, if she had received her father's fortune, would be one of the richest and most powerful women in the world, felt at that moment like one of the most insecure people on earth. Her money, her social status, and her networking were worth nothing, at least not on this risky journey. As soon as she got off at the airport, two individuals were waiting for her, Dr. Marco Polo and Invictus, but she didn't notice them. She carried a huge suitcase and a very expensive Louis Vuitton bag. It would be a bargaining chip in case of extreme need. Invictus touched her from behind and said:

"Ma'am!"

Startled, she turned around.

"Invictus?"

"Yes, I need to check your suitcase and your bag."

"I didn't know I would be investigated before boarding. But, please, feel free to go ahead and look at my things..." she said, trembling.

Invictus, being very clever due to his CIA techniques, not only searched her bag but also the lining and found a hidden credit card.

"It will be confiscated, for now," informed Dr. Marco Polo.

"It's your father's orders."

After that, he bent down and started taking the clothes out of her suitcase. She felt violated.

"You have more than twenty changes of clothes. Choose only one" ordered the powerful Invictus.

"Wait a minute, who are you to give me orders?" Brenda said authoritatively.

"Do you want to quit? There's still time," instigated Dr. Marco Polo.

She took a deep breath. She was devastated. Finally, she chose only one change of clothing. Then, Invictus continued to search her suitcase and found two thousand dollars hidden in a secret compartment. Invictus scolded her.

"Your test is off to a bad start, Brenda. I need to report this to your father," said Dr. Marco Polo.

"Unfortunately, you will fail the test immediately," commented Invictus, inflexible.

Brenda panicked. If arrested, not only would she lose all her material possessions and her social image, but also Kate. She believed that her daughter would never look at her with love again, maybe with pity, if she found out everything that had happened.

"I beg you, don't do this, please! It was a small mistake." Then she started walking away.

As she was walking off, Invictus drew her attention.

"Wait." She froze.

"Why to wait?"

"The purse?"

"But you've already searched it."

"It costs thousands of dollars. You could sell it during this period. Was this also a small slip?" asked Dr. Marco Polo.

She started panicking. Breathing deeply, she commented:

"Yes," she agreed. And humbly said: "You can take it too."

A woman without a purse is like a soldier without a weapon. She opened it, took out her perfume, her lipstick, her hairbrush, and other items, but then she thought: "what's the use…?" Handing them over to the cold Invictus, she left carrying only her cellphone and passport. The cellphone could be used to quit the test at any time. She left completely bothered and insecure, while thinking "Who could endure this test?"

Invictus gave the directions to her destination.

"You will work at Porto di Catania."

"Where is that?" she asked, curious and tense at the same time.

"On the Italian coast, in Sicily. A place that receives thousands of immigrants," affirmed Dr. Marco Polo.

"But what will I do there? How will I help people?"

"Occasionally ferries filled with people sink; there are children dying during the crossing; people suffering from infection, without medical assistance. In short, there are thousands of desperate human beings in need of protection. Be generous and figure it out. There is much to do," commented Dr. Marco Polo.

"Besides, there is human trafficking of immigrants," said Invictus.

Brenda expressed her anguish:

"Human trafficking of immigrants? I've never heard of that. How can I help? You took absolutely everything…!"

"We didn't take your intelligence…" affirmed Dr. Marco Polo.

Brenda turned her back on them and went to check in. On the way, she posted her daily message on Instagram. "Be honest. Honesty is the beauty of the heart!" The woman saturated with falsehood once again wore the skin of a character. Brenda didn't know herself. However, in less than ten minutes, she had 22,205 likes. Many compliments. She rejoiced, but suddenly came to her senses. She felt undressed in front of the airline counter. She stood in the economy class line. She waited a long half hour to be attended. When she was in front of the agent, he saw her distressed.

After receiving her almost empty suitcase, the agent asked, puzzled:

"Where are the other suitcases, miss?"

"I only have this one."

"How come? It's empty, it weighs only four pounds!"

"It's all that I have," she said, filling sad and worried.

"You are the woman I have checked in with the least amount of luggage throughout my whole career," said the agent, confused.

"I know..." Brenda replied.

"Are you feeling okay?"

"A little headache, nausea, but it will pass, I hope."

"Alright. Have a good trip." And as Brenda was leaving, the agent still asked: "Wait, aren't you carrying a handbag?

"It's with a friend..." she said, leaving. She didn't want to answer anything else.

So, she headed to the boarding gate. When they called the first-class passengers, she got up, as she always did, and stood in line. When the agent checked her ticket and passport, he said:

"Your class is economy. You'll have to wait, madam!"

"Ah, that's true! I'm sorry," she said embarrassed.

For the first time in her life, she would travel in economy class.

A friend who attended her extravagant parties and was in the first-class line recognized her.

"Brenda, how are you?"

"Hi, Lucy!" She exclaimed, intimidated.

"Why did you get out of the line? Aren't you boarding?"

Embarrassed, she lied once again. Lying and concealing were part of her existential dictionary.

"I forgot my purse on the seat. I'll board shortly," she said, inhibited.

"Oh, okay! The great Brenda wouldn't travel in economy class, of course!"

The proud Brenda, the expert in expensive fashion and perfumes, caught the hint of prejudice and rebuffed her party friend: "By any chance, aren't the people in economy class human like us?"

"No, it's just... it's stuffy, it smells like sweat..."

Brenda turned her back on her. Minutes later, she boarded. Just as she sat in an aisle seat, another familiar person passed by her. This time, one of the thousands of employees of her companies.

"Mrs. Brenda? Are you here, in economy?"

Startled, she said, once again embarrassed:

"I'm in training."

"Training? What kind of training?" asked the employee.

"Researching the perfume that classes C and B use and how they dress," she said, trying to disguise her shame.

There was an elderly man nibbling on a sandwich he brought from home on the seat next to her. She looked at him somewhat scandalized. Noticing her gaze, he kindly offered her one.

"You want one? I have another one in my bag..."

"No, thank you" she declined the offer without looking at the elder's face.

"You'd better take it because the airplane food couldn't even feed a bird!"

Brenda, the woman who used to spend more than two hundred thousand dollars a month on her extravagant parties, declined a five-dollar sandwich. However, during the journey, she began to think about situations that had never crossed her mind. "Will I go hungry in Italy?"

"How will I get money to eat?" "What will I eat?" "If I have to beg, who would give me money?" "If I identify myself as the daughter of the great Theo Fester, I will be worldwide news, a scandal on social media, I'll lose a million followers in less than a day." Brenda was a slave to her fame.

When the flight attendant brought the snack, she had an instinctive reaction, thinking of saving it for when she disembarked. She took the motion sickness plastic bag and stored part of what she received.

"Smart, huh?" said the elderly man to Brenda. "Why weren't you honest when I offered you the sandwich?"

She looked at him and, feeling the pain of hunger for the first time, as almost a billion human beings feel it, commented:

"I am honest, sir..."

"On second thought, no one is fully honest, girl. We lie or deceive at least five to seven times a day, especially concerning our personal image."

Amazed by the intelligence of the elderly passenger in economy class, a man who seemed so simple, Brenda inquired:

"Who are you?"

"The important thing is who you are."

"Are you a spy for Theo Fester?"

"Spy? Do you believe in conspiracy theories?"

"I'm sorry, my life has turned upside down lately." And she rested her head on the headrest.

For the first time, Brenda began to recognize that she represented a character in society. The world expert in women's fashion wore many masks. She was starting to come into contact with her mental prisons and to discover the emotional vampires that were draining her peace and joy of living. She was a beautiful and unhappy woman.

CHAPTER 22

Peterson's Deviousness

Peterson said goodbye to his son, Thomas. He was an ultra-arrogant man, a lover of social status, a father skilled at pointing out his son's flaws, therefore, capable of fixing machines but not of shaping free and thinking minds. Fortunately, the grandfather, Theo Fester, educated Thomas more than his own father. He stimulated his intellect to be transparent and not to fear life, but to fear not living it intensely and intelligently. A week before his father tried to close his grandfather's eyes, Theo Fester once again urged him to think:

"Thomas, there is no heaven without storms and no success without accidents!"

"Why do you say that, Grandpa?" asked the curious boy.

"Your father and millions of other people prepare their children for applause, but I want you to be prepared to deal with failures, jeers, and humiliations."

"But have you ever failed? Have you been jeered at?"

"Many times! In the business world and in life itself, heaven and hell are very close. At one moment, your sky is full of stars, and in another, it's filled with dark clouds; the exchange rate changes, the interest rate rises, a war breaks out, a natural disaster occurs, a wrong investment, a new technology that outdates yours. If you're not minimally prepared to endure the traps in the business world, it's better to be an employee."

"Wow, Grandpa, I didn't know that!"

"No one is worthy of success if they don't use their failures to nourish it. Sooner or later, we stumble, fall, plunge into the mud of our smallness. Today, I'm an admired entrepreneur, but I've been booed, kicked out, labeled as crazy."

"My father never told me that! But, is it possible for an entrepreneur to avoid nightmares?"

"Some can, but not all of them. If you want to think differently and do differently, prepare yourself to face the criticism of closed minds. They will slander you, spit in your face, call you irresponsible, reckless, an adventurer, claim you will go bankrupt. But once you succeed, they will be the first to applaud you."

Grandfather and grandson talked on the phone almost every day. Theo Fester transferred the wealth of his experiences to him, trying to thaw the coldness coming from Peterson, a banker who was as hard on his son as he was with clients in debt. Departing for an extremely long month to care for cancer patients, with no power, no status, and not a penny in his pocket, he had a different attitude. He approached Thomas and for the first time in a long time, gave him a long and heartfelt hug.

Thomas pulled away from his father, looking into his eyes, and said: "What's going on, Dad?"

The executive who believed he was transparent, but was, in fact, an expert in concealing his feelings from his son, once again used trickery.

"Nothing is happening, son. Everything is fine. I'm just going on an extended trip."

"You always go on extended trips! But why did you hug me this way?"

"In what way, kid? I hugged you as I always do," he replied, altering his voice. "It's just that this time we won't see each other for a month."

"A month?"

"Yes, I'm going to take care of a cancer patients project."

"Cancer patients? Since when do you care for the needy? Is Grandpa going with you?"

"Umm, no."

"It seems his health isn't good. Wouldn't it be better to stay with him?"

"His health is excellent," falsely assured the father.

"Excellent? He often has coughing fits... Are you sure...?!" Thomas asked, suspiciously.

"Of course, do you think I would lie to you?"

"You lie, deceive, and manipulate, sir Peterson," Thomas replied honestly, with some irony, causing his father's authoritarianism to soar.

"Shut your mouth, you rebel! I'll cut your allowance and your credit card!"

"Cut whatever you want! But don't cut grandpa out of your life. Don't walk out on him, please," said Thomas, already shedding tears, leaving the room.

"Do you think I would have the courage to abandon your grandfather? No one takes better care of him than I do!" He affirmed without hesitation, trying to disguise the fact that he had tried to murder him the day before.

Thomas stopped walking, turned to his father, and delivered a blow – he spoke of the terrible news that his cousin had told him not long ago:

"Kate called me less than an hour ago, she was overtaken by anxiety. She told me that grandpa has cancer."

"I was going to tell you..." Peterson tried to fix the unfixable.

But Thomas was inconsolable.

"Father, I'm sorry for you. You don't know that there are cancers in our mind... Lying is one of them."

Peterson was shaken. He was emotionally unresolved but not a psychopath. He didn't know how to deal with guilt and reinvent himself. Seeing his son leave in tears was an unforgettable experience. His relationship with Thomas, which had always been bad, went further down the hill.

Peterson would travel to Houston, where he would be a volunteer at the MD Anderson Cancer Center, a complex with over a million square meters, employing more than twenty-two thousand people. When he arrived at the JFK airport, Invictus and Dr. Marco Polo were waiting for him.

"You again?" asked Peterson, harsh and apprehensive. Like Brenda, he also carried a huge suitcase.

Devoid of generosity but not impolite, Invictus commented:

"I need to check your luggage, please. It's part of the deal. I'll also scan your body."

"Wait a minute. This is an invasion of privacy!" He reacted angrily.

"The decision is yours," commented Dr. Marco Polo, picking up his phone and starting to make a call. Possibly to Theo Fester.

"Wait, wait," said Peterson. He took a deep and anxious breath and gestured for Invictus to open his luggage.

Invictus opened the suitcase and took out expensive suits, ties, and shirts. He threw them on the floor.

"You'll have to take just one change of clothes."

"But it's cold in Houston!"

"And who said you're going to Houston?"

"But the deal was for me to go to the MD Anderson Cancer Center."

"Your father changed his mind. You're going to India," commented Dr. Marco Polo.

"India?"

"Yes, your test will be to work in a country with much greater need than the United States. You're going to the Kashmir region."

Kashmir is a small state with about thirteen million inhabitants. It has been disputed by India and Pakistan since the end of British colonization. The war that started in 1947 led to the division of the region, and much of it is under India's control. An area of conflicts, it is a place where various terrorist attacks occur.

"Kashmir? The conflict region between Pakistan and India?" Questioned Peterson. He knew how to calculate risks. And he added: "There are extremist Muslims there. An American like me won't survive in such a region. I'll surely be killed or kidnapped."

Dr. Marco Polo commented:

"You've already been kidnapped by your fears and your pride."

Peterson started having a panic attack. It seemed like he was going to die with a racing heart, shortness of breath, and intense sweating on his face.

"Do you want to give up?" asked Invictus.

"No, no! It's just that India is a poor country; I'm thinking of how to help it."

"You will help as a human being, just as a person, an eternal learner, nothing more than that," said Dr. Marco Polo.

"I hate you, Marco Polo."

"Hatred is harmful to the host. And the worst is hating yourself."

Then, he signaled to Invictus, who called several luggage carriers and gave them Peterson's brand-named clothes. The carriers were ecstatic with Armani suits and Peterson's other brand-name clothes. While his clothes were being donated, he gritted his teeth in anger, like a dog that doesn't want to let go of the bone. The mega-banker was vain, jealous of his very expensive suits and ties.

After donating Peterson's clothes, Invictus continued his search for valuable items, credit cards, and cash hidden in his suitcase. He found five thousand dollars in fifty one-hundred-dollar bills, very well hidden in the fabric's folds. It was enough money to eat and maybe live without worries. He wouldn't have problems eating, sleeping, moving around, or dressing.

"You guys are dishonest," commented Invictus.

"Don't talk to me like that," said Peterson, shouting and trying to punch him.

Invictus easily avoided the punch and gave a small punch to Peterson's chest, causing him to fall. The executive had bleeding lips. As he struggled to get up, Invictus discovered three credit cards.

Then, he felt his blazer and found another card in the right sleeve. Dr. Marco Polo put an end to Peterson's stress test:

"I'll call your father now. You are disqualified."

"Wait, wait. For God's sake, don't call him." And, crying, he added: "Forgive me, it's just that everything is new to me... I'm desperate! I'm not a psychopath. I'm very afraid and with a tremendous sense of guilt."

Dr. Marco Polo stopped, took a deep breath, and said:

"You are among the mentally incarcerated. Because of your plea, as the leader of the *Prisoners of the Mind* project, I will grant you one last chance."

"Am I part of this project?" Peterson asked, astonished.

Dr. Marco Polo remained silent. Invictus commented:

"You better believe it."

Peterson, in one of the rare insights about himself, began to realize that he had always been a prisoner living in a free democracy. His financial power, social status, awards, interviews for newspapers, and economic magazines concealed an imprisoned mind. While checking in, he was sweating. Like his sister, he realized that the economic class was exhausting, and felt ashamed of being middle class, actually embarrassed to be himself a simple, flawed, and mortal human being. Boarding the plane, he tried to cover his face so that those in first class wouldn't see him, much like people do when they are arrested in front of TV cameras.

His drama had just begun on the long journey to Kashmir. He sat next to an obese man weighing three hundred and ten pounds, whose name was Alfred. His arm occupied part of Peterson's seat. Feeling anxious, he rubbed his hands on his face. He couldn't believe that this was happening to him.

"Am I bothering you?" Alfred asked Peterson, with an angry look.

"No, not at all, sir. These are personal problems."

"Sir, you seem to be having a panic attack..."

Peterson remained silent. He preferred to suffocate his mental demons and swallow his sorrows. Prejudiced, he wouldn't hire obese people to work in his bank. He didn't understand that beauty is in the eye of the beholder.

The obese man continued:

"It's not easy being obese, sir. In addition to carrying the weight of the body, you carry the weight of prejudice."

Peterson looked at the man and said:

"I can imagine."

"And the comfort I have to accommodate my arm in the seat doesn't neutralize the anguish of not being able to share the space properly with you. I'm sorry."

Peterson remembered that a month ago he had called the head of the human resources department and sent out the word: "Thirty percent of Americans are obese. Avoid hiring them as they get sicker than average. Besides, if they don't take good care of their own bodies, they won't take good care of my money."

Peterson was a mentally obese man. Obese with prejudice, vanity, arrogance, pride. He went to his stress test feeling like one of the heaviest human beings he had ever known.

CHAPTER 23

Caleb's Frauds

Caleb, on the other hand, didn't live in New York but in San Francisco, California. His stress test would be in Los Angeles, in his own state. Apparently, an advantage. What a stupid mistake! Since he wasn't married and had no children, he had no one to say goodbye to. Loneliness infected him amid the crowd.

He was an expert at not criticizing himself. He didn't delve into deeper layers of his personality, trying to appease his guilt by telling himself that he hadn't planned the murder of his father; he just wanted to alleviate his suffering. Escaping from himself was a herculean task, but he tried. He never lacked bread on the table but begged for the bread of joy and was so emotionally impoverished that he anchored his motivation to live in the valuation of his startups.

Disguising his feelings, he entered JFK Airport humming the famous song immortalized by Frank Sinatra, praising the global metropolis.

"New York, New York..."

Suddenly, someone touched his arm. It was Invictus, accompanied by Dr. Marco Polo. He jumped back, frightened, indicating that his relaxed state was a farce. His mood went from heaven to hell.

"You are following me here too?!" He shouted, drawing the attention of several people around.

"We're trying to make you rewrite your mistakes and your story!" Said Dr. Marco Polo.

"Rewrite my mistakes? You're kidding. You set a trap for me. You made me stumble. I'm an upright man."

"So why are you afraid of confronting your inner Self? Don't avoid reality. Face your own pride!" Dr. Marco Polo said.

"Pride? You're a cheap manipulator of sick minds."

"I feel sorry for you," said Dr. Marco Polo.

"Don't feel sorry for me. Feel sorry for yourself! I will pass this test and, rest assured, after making my billions, I will use a large part of my fortune to pursue you to the ends of the earth, as well as this fake humanoid. I will hire an army of mercenaries to capture and dismember you."

Dr. Marco Polo commented sarcastically:

"Your aggressiveness blinds you; it leads you to build your own grave."

Caleb was intrigued by these words. Dr. Marco Polo added:

"You have just been filmed by a camera contained in Invictus' eyes. All your words and madness have been recorded again. Therefore, as the leader of the *Prisoners of the Mind* project, I say you are disqualified. You will go to the bars of justice." And he began to make a call, indicating that he would announce the decision to Theo Fester.

Caleb was disturbed and tried to salvage the deal acting like a Hollywood artist.

"You are so naive! I got you good. Be a little more humorous! Do you think I, who loves money, would spend billions of dollars to pursue you? Get real! Don't be foolish."

Dr. Marco Polo knew that Caleb was using a disguise, so he didn't spare him. He was straightforward, dissecting the arrogant mind of this Silicon Valley icon.

"The youngest of the Festers is in a mental asylum, emotionally old."

"Emotionally old? You're kidding. I'm only thirty-two years old."

"Anyone who complains about everything is ten years older than their biological age. Anyone who wants everything fast adds another ten years to their emotion. Anyone with a low frustration threshold doesn't work well with their frustrations; another fifteen years. Anyone with poor social skills who can't pacify their ghosts at least a little, adds another fifteen years. Anyone who doesn't contemplate the beauty or make a spectacle of small things adds another ten years to emotional age. Therefore, you are sixty years added to your thirty-two years of biological age."

"Ninety-two years is the emotional age of this boy! Not even an artificial intelligence machine can handle you like this," Invictus said to Caleb, confirming Dr. Marco Polo's diagnosis.

"It's not possible! Are you bluffing? Where did you get this information?" Caleb asked, perplexed.

"Forget it," said Dr. Marco Polo, not wanting to get into details. "You, like many entrepreneurs, know how to make money, but you don't know how to date life. You don't understand the most basic equation of capitalism: money doesn't bring happiness, but the lack of it almost guarantees unhappiness. You have capital in the bank but you are in debt to the emotion bank."

Caleb held his head with both hands. He had never felt so afraid as in that moment. In a sincere reaction, he said:

"Wait, Dr. Polo, please."

"You don't have another chance" affirmed Invictus. "You humans give too many chances."

But Caleb pleaded, something that wasn't part of the menu of his intellect.

"I humbly request you: if I don't know this equation, disqualifying me now is to take away from me the opportunity to learn it! If you are the thinker my father trusts, the author of a revolutionary project, the *Prisoners of the Mind*, you have to believe at least minimally in the human being. You have to believe in me, at least once."

Dr. Marco Polo took a calm and deep breath and then nodded, showing that he had given in. He looked at Invictus, asking him to hand over the tickets and give him some instructions.

"Brenda went to Italy, and Peterson to India. And here is your ticket to Los Angeles, but I'll have to search and scan you."

"Well, at least I'll stay in my country and in my state, California. Alright. You can search me."

Dr. Marco Polo soon commented:

"This watch cannot go."

He called another baggage carrier and gave him the watch as a gift.

"Wait. It costs fifty thousand dollars; it's exclusive."

"Great. You made this man happy" said Dr. Marco Polo.

The baggage carrier didn't understand a thing. He was so happy that he handled it suspiciously. He couldn't imagine that a watch could cost so much. Dr. Marco Polo observed Caleb's face, and he was intrigued to notice that the calmness of the smartest and most audacious of the Festers returned quickly. Invictus searched through his entire suitcase and handbag. He threw the excess clothes in a trash can. But he found nothing. He scanned his body, patted him down. But again, nothing.

"Satisfied?" asked Caleb, calmly.

"Yes. Apparently," expressed Invictus. It seemed that the watch would be the only life insurance he carried.

As soon as Caleb left, Invictus looked down at his shoes and intervened:

"Wait. Take off your shoes."

Caleb said:

"But this is too much!"

"Take them off," he requested firmly.

He took them off, but after a thorough analysis, Invictus found nothing. Caleb left silently and went to do his check-in. But Invictus, observing his walk, caught up with him and said:

"Give me your shoes again."

He did it. It was then that Invictus took out a pocketknife and cut the sole. There was a space in each sole hiding a thirty-gram gold bar.

"The smartest and most dishonest of the Festers," concluded Invictus.

And he signaled to Dr. Marco Polo to disqualify him.

"Don't take back your word! These gold bars are part of the old Caleb, not the Caleb you gave a chance."

Invictus said:

"Dr. Marco Polo, this farm-raised chicken won't last a day among the drug-dependent and homeless on the streets of Los Angeles. He'll either die or become a drug dealer. It's not worth it."

"All choices involve losses."

In the end, the psychiatrist gave him another chance to try to rewrite his story. He gestured for him to leave... Indeed, Caleb's chances were almost zero, not only to overcome the stressful challenge that lay ahead him but also to survive in a harsh and dangerous environment.

CHAPTER 24

Brenda's Dramatic Stress Test

Brenda disembarked after a layover in Catania, Sicily, arriving at six in the morning. She walked back and forth unsure of what to do or where to start.

Now she was just Brenda, not "Brenda Fester". She had never felt so insecure and frightened. By nine o'clock, she still hadn't found the courage to leave the airport. Hunger began to bother her. The sandwich the elderly man had given her during the flight was her momentary salvation.

Hungry and without money, she salivated while eating. The bulimic, who used to eat compulsively, tried to moderate herself, eating slowly, feeling the taste of the carbohydrates in a way she never had before, beginning to experience the real feelings of a refugee.

At ten in the morning, she dared to leave the airport. She walked aimlessly through the beautiful port city and still didn't know what to do. Without resources, she had to walk on foot, not looking for refugees, initially, but for a place to sleep. Survival was more important than helping the unfortunate. With her broken Italian, she went to a three-star hotel, but it was unaffordable in her current conditions.

Then, lowering her expectations, she went to a run-down pension. The owner also scared her with the price.

"It's thirty euros per day!"

"Thirty euros? That's too expensive!" Said Brenda, who only stayed in five-star hotels with a minimum daily rate of five hundred euros. But times had changed.

The lady still gave her some bad news: "I need an advance payment for fifteen days, four hundred and fifty euros."

"I'm sorry, but I don't have that. I promise that after I find a job, I'll pay you."

"Get out of here," the owner said harshly. "In this land of refugees, everyone comes here with the same story." And she slammed the door in Brenda's face.

Never before had someone slammed the door in her face. The beautiful Brenda used to be treated like a princess everywhere, even by the English court. Used to take two baths a day, she was eager for a shower, but got nothing. In a run-down hotel near the port, a very poor area, Brenda had the courage to tell the elderly lady who owned the hotel that she could work as a chambermaid.

"Please, I need a place to stay, sleep, and take a shower."

"Only with an advance payment for a month," the lady said.

"I could pay for the pension by making the guests' beds and washing breakfast dishes."

The lady looked into her eyes and felt compassion.

"I see desperation in your eyes, my daughter. You seem to have refined manners, but despite wanting to help, I can't. The two chambermaids have been working with me for over twenty years."

"And cleaning the bathrooms?"

"They do everything."

For a woman who lived in a mansion of thirteen thousand square feet with eight suites, not being able to find a tiny room, without a bathroom, without clean clothes, was an invitation to despair.

It was 3 pm and the desperation of finding a place to rest was replaced by the pain of hunger. She had landed over nine hours ago.

She had never thought about having something to eat, only about what to eat; but now, more than ten trillion cells that made up her body were distressed. She saw a restaurant across the street. Several people were eating outside. She tried offering work in exchange for food to the owner.

"Sir, I'm looking for work."

"I don't have a job opening."

She was frustrated, but insisted.

"I'll accept any salary."

"Get out of here, I said I don't have a job opening."

Brenda insisted a little more.

"I can work in exchange for..." But she didn't have time to finish the sentence. She was rejected.

"Get out! Can't you see you're bothering me?"

The daughter of billionaire Theo Fester left humiliated, as if she were the lowest of women. Entering another restaurant a hundred meters from the first, she was anxious, feeling completely unprotected, while looking for the owner, who wasn't there. She encountered a rough manager, around sixty years old.

"Sir, I'm hungry. I don't have a job. Could you get me a job?"

"One more person bothering me. You're the fifth today. Are you a refugee?"

"No, at least I don't think so..."

"But it's still annoying. Get out of here."

Fear and despair began to intoxicate her emotions and thoughts. In her house she had two cooks and, every day, they would throw away half of the food served. The waste was impressive. She dreamed of rummaging through the trash in her mansion and began to realize that her world was unreal and sick. She remembered her last party. There was French champagne, twenty types of appetizers, caviar, salmon, filet mignon, cod loin, puff pastry, and many other dishes. She squandered two hundred thousand dollars... an amount that might be enough to buy the restaurant that had denied her a plate of food.

She went to sleep at a square, with an empty stomach. While trying to lean back on the bench, she saw other homeless people also settling down in the open air. Brenda cried. A lady, who seemed equally helpless, perhaps a refugee, hearing her sobs, approached her.

"Why are you crying, my child?"

She spoke depressed:

"I have many reasons. I hurt the one I loved the most... I threw away everything I had. Today, look at what I am, less than nothing..."

"Haven't you had dinner?"

"I haven't even had lunch."

The compassionate lady gave her a piece of stale bread. Brenda ate it eagerly. It was little, but it was a lot considering it was all she had.

"And you, where are you from?"

"I'm from Ethiopia."

"And where is your family?"

"I lost them at the sea. Italy, Germany, and France refused to take us, and we ended up shipwrecked."

"And what about you?" Brenda asked.

"In the middle of the shipwreck, they saved me. Imagine, me, an old woman, survived. But I wish I had perished also. Sometimes, the pain is so much that it seems like nothing existed, that I have no past... Is my brain playing tricks on me?"

Just as mysteriously as she appeared, the lady left in the darkness of the night. Brenda laid her head on the park bench again. She curled up from the cold. Fortunately, it was summer. She slept out of fatigue, because her mind begged for a break; she was exhausted.

She woke up with sunlight bathing her eyes. She looked for a place to have breakfast, but found nothing. She saw a hibiscus tree; she knew the flowers were edible. She ate them, but they didn't satisfy her. By one in the afternoon, her insides twisted, demanding portions of protein and carbohydrates.

She checked her social network, but she was not in the mood to find out what they were saying about her. She went to another restaurant and repeated the same fate.

"Please, is the owner here?" she asked, tense.

"He doesn't live in the city. I am the manager."

She pleaded again for work in exchange for just one lunch.

"Sir, I'll do anything in exchange for food."

The manager was over fifty years old. He was a fat man, with bushy mustaches, a mind polluted by sexuality, and a sharp tongue to hurt others. He made an indecent proposal:

"Anything?" And he looked Brenda up and down. With a sarcastic laugh, he said: "Let's go to my bed at the back of the restaurant, then I'll give you something to eat."

She looked directly into the eyes of that rude man and responded at the same level.

"This is sexual harassment!"

"No, this is the reality of this port city, miss." And, with more sarcasm, he said something that disturbed Brenda even more: "Many refugees get food for their children this way."

At that exact moment, a woman came out of the back of the restaurant crying, passing by Brenda with a small lunchbox in her hands. Behind her, a short waiter with devious eyes came out, adjusting his pants.

Outraged, Brenda said:

"You're lucky. In other times, I would have bought this restaurant and kicked you out of this pigsty."

"A prostitute exuding luxury?" he said, mocking Brenda.

The other waiters, not caring about the few customers, whistled at her. The powerful daughter of Theo Fester left in tears. Her stress test had barely begun, and she felt defeated, shattered.

It had been almost a day and a half since Brenda had had a decent meal. In her desperation, she started asking for money at a traffic light. However, the words she heard were ones she wished never to hear. Most pretended she didn't exist. Others said:

"Go work, you bum."

And others mocked:

"Get in my car, you prostitute."

Brenda had never given money to beggars who looked good because she believed they were lazy, irresponsible people who made begging a way of life. It had never crossed her mind that some well-dressed people also faced surprising humiliations.

She tried her luck at another restaurant. This time, it was a large establishment with tables both indoors and outdoors. The owner didn't even hear her.

"Get out, get out!"

"But, sir..."

"I said: get out!" he shouted. And yelled: "Don't disturb the customers, or I'll call the police."

There was no need to call; the police arrived and threw her out, warning her: "Next time, you'll be arrested."

She quickly moved away from that place. Her eyes welled up with tears again. She remembered Kate, how many times her daughter waited for her to have lunch and dinner, and she simply didn't show up.

She spoke aloud:

"Oh, Kate! Forgive me, my daughter."

Then, she remembered her grandfather, Josef. She recalled some of the stories he told from the Nazi concentration camps. It seemed surreal to know that he had eaten cockroaches, rats, and spiders to survive. Now, for the first time in her life, she understood how far the desperation of a human being could go.

She remembered her father's words when she was only fifteen years old: "In concentration camps, many Jewish people hid food from each other. Some did dirty work for the Nazis. And do you know why?" "I have no idea," Brenda had answered. "Because the instinct for survival is stronger than solidarity. Only with extreme generosity can one share the little that one has with those who have nothing."

After bringing these images to her mind, she saw a customer from another restaurant leaving the table, leaving some spaghetti on the plate. At that moment, the woman of refined habits was overcome by instincts. She triggered the brain mechanism, opened the hunger window, the anchor settled, and the memory circuit closed. Survival was all that mattered. She sneaked in, grabbed the leftovers with her own hands, and stuffed them into her mouth. Then, she saw another empty table with leftovers from a lasagna on the plate. She did the same thing.

Her bulimia crisis was triggered. Anxiously, she tried to induce vomiting. But suddenly, she came to her senses, withdrew her finger from her throat, composed herself, and regained self-control. She began to question whether bulimia and anorexia existed in the land of scarcity.

While eating compulsively, a young woman of about twenty-five saw her and took a photo. Admiringly, she said:

"It seems like I know this hungry woman."

Of Brenda's eleven million followers, more than five hundred thousand lived in Italy, the majority of whom were young women. And that one seemed to have identified her. However, she couldn't believe that the great Brenda, who reported her luxury parties on social media, who flaunted enviable glamour, and who ran one of the world's largest fashion store chains, was begging for food in front of her. It was just unbelievable!

The photo was posted on the follower's social media. It went viral. Was it Brenda? Theo Fester's powerful daughter went into despair when she learned of the incident, an hour later. There were already thousands of shares. She told herself: they've destroyed my image.

The false image she had constructed of a mature, emotionally stable, and always motivated woman began to crumble. She went to sleep outdoors at a square, feeling the most miserable and unjustly treated woman. In reality, she didn't sleep; her sleep was interrupted by nightmares and night terrors. She woke up startled like sheep going to slaughter.

The next day, she woke up from her light sleep with a little black boy, about four years old, beating her back.

"I'm hungry!"

Brenda shouted in fright. Seeing her shock, he also got scared and ran away. She was also hungry; she hadn't had dinner.

She tried to catch up with him, but he ran too fast. She decided to forget her own woes and went looking for the refugees.

"Where are the refugees?" she asked a man in a suit and tie. She didn't know he was far-right.

"The plagues infesting our nation?"

"Why are they plagues? They are as human as you are!" Brenda retorted, indignantly.

"Humans are us, Italian people, who have lived here for millennia."

"But whose land is it? It's a convention that it belongs to Italy, France, Germany, Brazil, or the United States. Doesn't the planet belong to humanity? Doesn't it belong to all species?"

The man was intrigued by this question.

"Where are you from?" the man asked, aggressively.

"The United States."

"I knew it. You sweep Mexicans from your land and want us to receive Arabs and Africans in Europe." And he turned his back on her.

A hundred yards ahead, Brenda asked again about the refugees. A woman at about fifty years old questioned her:

"And why do you want to know where the refugees are?"

"I came from afar to try to alleviate the pain of some of them."

Generously, the woman pointed to where the boats with refugees were being received. Brenda took another walk and found a middle-aged bald man in front of a shop.

"Please, where can I find the refugees?"

"Are you blind, woman? They are scattered everywhere. Look, they're begging for food, disrupting sidewalk traffic, in the streets, stealing from stores like mine. Years ago, we suffered from the gypsies who came from Romania, now with the Africans."

Nearly a half a mile ahead, Brenda finally found the port of Catania. The wealth of luxury yachts contrasted with the misery of makeshift boats. The concentration of refugees from Syria, Iraq, Ethiopia, Bangladesh, Uganda, and many other places had increased significantly.

"Please, give me some coins" a black woman asked, nursing a child at her breast, with two other small children at her feet.

Brenda was shocked. The older boy was the same one who had woken her up, saying he was hungry.

"What's your name?" she asked the mother.

"Emma."

"And your older son?"

He answered himself:

"Salah."

Then, he pleaded:

"We're hungry…"

"I'm sorry, I don't have any money either."

"But my brother won't stop crying. We're going to die of hunger…"

Brenda was devastated. At four years old, Salah already had the responsibility of supporting his family when he should have been playing and studying. His life was desolate, and she needed to build an oasis for him, at least for one day. She forgot her own misery and began desperately searching for food for Salah and his family.

In desperation, Brenda called her father. The phone rang several times. Theo Fester's eyes filled with tears when he saw his daughter's call. He wanted to answer, but Brenda was trapped in a futile life. She needed to learn life's most important lessons, in an environment where she was just a human being, unprotected, insecure, and frightened. So, she called Dr. Marco Polo, who also did not answer. She called Marc Douglas and was answered, but not by him.

"Invictus, at your service."

"Invictus, I need money. There are children who are starving here!"

"What is hunger?" He responded with a question.

"Don't be insensitive!"

"Insensitive, me? How many times did you remember, at your expensive parties, that there were children starving? Help those in need with the resources you have."

She fell silent. In fact, she had never thought about others' pain in a real, solid, and actual way.

"But I have no resources!"

"No human resources? Don't you know how to sing, dance, do manual labor, plead, cry, or to reinvent yourself?"

"Am I supposed to steal or prostitute myself as well?"

"It seems those are also options."

Brenda hung up the phone and brought her hands to her head, distressed. She asked for food from one person, from another, and yet another. But in that region, people were hardened. They had lost sensitivity. Two hours had gone by, and she had failed. It was so easy to use a credit card, but now she was financially bankrupt. She returned to that family and tried to calm them.

"I still haven't succeeded" she said, completely frustrated.

Salah and his younger brother clung to each of her legs, begging for food. Brenda was desperate. And she cried along with the hungry kids. It was an epic moment in which a billionaire, who had never known the pain of hunger and had never thought that the children of humanity, the kids, suffered so much. She discovered that she was a powerless, and profoundly fragile human being.

She looked up and saw a supermarket, a hundred yards away. She had no doubts. She would steal products to feed those children. She entered and looked for some small, high-energy foods that were easy to hide. She took chocolates and other products and put them under her blouse. While heading to the exit, she was caught by the manager. A man over fifty, slender, with a long beard. She was being filmed.

"You thief!" the manager shouted, grabbing her arm.

"Please, I stole to feed children!" she said, desperate.

"These immigrants drive me crazy. You will feed your children in prison."

"But they are starving," she said, pretending as if the children were her own. She thought that way the manager would have compassion.

"You are going to prison!" insisted the manager.

"I can do anything to make up for my mistake," said Brenda.

Then, the manager looked her up and down and pushed her into his office. And there, Brenda was raped. It was horrible. Theo Fester's daughter didn't resist much, as it was the only way to provide food for those children. She cried as that man violently invaded her intimacy. Many immigrant mothers were raped by monsters who claimed to be human.

She left the supermarket, staggering, all battered and shedding tears. She reached the kids and handed over the food. They were overjoyed. The mother asked:

"Why are you crying? You succeeded."

"The price was too high."

"I know, my daughter, I've already paid that price five times."

Brenda kissed Salah and his brother, and she left. It was another extremely difficult day. She slept that night outdoors again, among various refugees begging in Sicily. It was a horrible and unsafe environment. She thought several times about giving up, but the pain of others fueled her courage. She called Kate almost every day. There wasn't a time when she didn't get emotional.

"Where are you, Mom?"

"I can only tell you that I'm helping the poor."

"Come back home, please! I miss you!"

"I miss you even more, my daughter. But I'm on a mission, meeting incredible people, trying to be a spark of hope for those who suffer."

"But aren't you risking your life?"

"I am..." And her voice choked. "But in my parties, I also took risks."

"What risks?" Kate asked, curious.

"They are different risks."

"Come back, Mom."

"I think about coming back every day. But please, give me strength to continue."

Kate, in sobs, said:

"Then keep going, mom. Give your best."

Brenda tried. She went out to sea several times to rescue refugees, fed malnourished children, and took care of the elderly. She was beaten once and sexually abused twice. She cleaned bathrooms to survive, went without dinner ten times and without lunch nine times. Despite losing weight yet she didn't have a bulimic crisis. Every day brought dramatic experiences. The woman who launched globally desired perfumes encountered the foul odor of the streets and of prejudice. In those eternal thirty days of stress, Brenda discovered an unimaginable world.

CHAPTER 25

Peterson's Powerful Stress Test

Peterson had a connection flight in the capital of India, New Delhi, to reach the main city of Kashmir, Srinagar. Kashmir, with its mountainous terrain, is the northernmost state of India. A nation with almost 1.4 billion inhabitants, which is becoming the most populous in the world. It was more than fourteen hours of flight, a long and tiring journey.

The financial sector executive was completely lost upon arriving in Srinagar. More afraid than hungry, he left the airport. The human mind is so powerfully creative that, when it has no enemies, it creates them. Prejudiced, Peterson looked around to see if there was any radical Islamic about to detonate a bomb, explode their body, or kidnap him.

The beautiful region, in constant conflict with Pakistan, was a socially tense environment; however, theoretically, it would be the ideal place for Peterson to exhibit noble behavior, capable of redeeming himself from past mistakes before his father. But Theo Fester was far away, perhaps in New York or San Francisco, and certainly not watching him. He didn't see anyone suspicious filming or photographing him during the flight. He thought about some tricks he could use to turn his thirty days in the desert into a mild oasis. While walking down a quiet street, he received a message from a boy, written in English, Spanish, and French, the three languages he mastered.

"Run, American."

He read it in terror and began to focus on various angles to determine if the message was generic or addressed to him, Peterson Fester. Suddenly, he was approached by two men asking for his wallet. He thought they were undercover soldiers. He handed over his documents.

"Where's the money?" the tallest one asked.

"I don't have any, gentlemen" he said, trembling.

"How does a foreigner come here without money?" One of them questioned loudly.

"Are you perhaps a drug dealer?" the other asked.

"Under no circumstances," said Peterson.

They stole his cellphone and pushed him. The banker fell to the ground and scraped his right hand, which had a small cut. He went to look for a hospital that cared for cancer patients. He didn't find a specialized institution, only a general hospital. Clever, he tried to secure a privileged place in the facility, maybe as manager or counselor. He sought out the director of the place and showed his fake credentials.

"My name is Peterson." But he didn't mention his last name. "I have worked as a manager for large hospitals in the United States. I would like to contribute to your noble institution for a period of two months."

The director pondered.

"It is interesting to receive a visit from a hospital management expert in this remote mountainous region. What brought you here?"

"Philanthropy. I have affinities with Buddhism; I appreciate contemplation and meditation."

"Do you meditate every day?" Asked the doctor and manager.

"Whenever my schedule allows it," the executive affirmed.

"But is it you who makes your schedule, or is your schedule making your routine?" The doctor questioned.

"What? I didn't understand!" Said Peterson.

"I see that you are not a meditation expert. Are you really a hospital manager? Where have you worked?"

Every time Peterson was criticized, it triggered the cerebral switch, it opened a killer window, the anchor closed the memory circuit, and he externalized his allodoxaphobia, the irrational fear of dealing with other people's opinions.

"Who are you to doubt me? Do you know who you're talking to?" He threatened the man in a harsh voice, as if he were still a financial executive. And he thought that if such insolence had come from one of his subordinates, they would be out of a job. But he came to his senses. He was in Kashmir, without status, without money, without power.

"Calm down, sir. I just asked," said the director, startled by his reaction.

Peterson began to stutter.

"S-s-sorry. It's just that I hate it when someone doubts... my... integrity."

"A person who claims to love contemplation shouldn't be offended by a little disagreement. You should react with gentleness," commented the director.

Peterson tried to explain: "I'm fatigued from the long journey. I can assist you in managing the hospital during this period if I have a good bed and reasonable food."

The administrator looked him in the eyes, nodded, and invited him into his office. Peterson was pleased. He thought he had taken the bait. He would work comfortably. Kashmir would not be a desert.

After looking at some papers and checking computer reports, he gave Peterson an opportunity.

"I have a job opening for a chambermaid or a cleaner of rooms and the surgical hall."

"Are you kidding me?" said, loudly again, Theo Fester's eldest son.

"It seems that the one playing with life is you," expressed the indignant director.

"Do you happen to know me?" Questioned the powerful Peterson.

"Perhaps you are a king who cannot do humble work?" The director asked in sequence.

Peterson turned his back on him. He left outraged. As he crossed the hallway, he saw a familiar picture. He couldn't believe it. It was of his father. And underneath it was written: "A man who loves Kashmir."

He returned to the administrator and asked, impressed:

"Why is there an old photo of Theo Fester in the corridor?"

"Because he donated a significant amount of money for the construction of this institution. A great man, one of the best I have ever known. Do you happen to know him?"

"No, I mean, I've heard of him," said Peterson, surprised. He had never imagined that his father was a philanthropist.

Peterson looked for another health institution. He had been in the region for eight hours and had not eaten anything. Hunger knocked at his door. But he didn't have the courage to ask to work in a restaurant as Brenda did. He passed by a grocery store that sold food and fruits displayed on the sidewalk. He couldn't resist. He stole an apple. But he was seen by someone across the street.

"Thief!"

It was a commotion. Peterson didn't know what to say. He had no money to repair the damage. The only thing left for him was to run. The banker who chased after his debtors, executing mortgages, expropriating properties, was now in debt. He had never run so much and in such a humiliating way. He threw the fruit on the ground to see if it would end the relentless pursuit. But the more he ran, the more the human horde behind him grew. He was afraid of being lynched. Desperate, he entered a Buddhist temple, merging with the monks and repeating a mantra with them.

The banker didn't meditate at all because every two seconds he looked sideways to see if his pursuers had entered the temple. But they respected the environment. After the false meditation, he walked fearfully to the temple exit. An elderly monk, observing his anxiety, invited him to visit the monastery.

Willingly, Peterson accepted. During the journey, he was perplexed because it was not a classic meditation monastery; it was a place where patients with chronic wounds, some cancerous, others infectious, were taken care of.

Peterson felt nauseous seeing some of the open wounds and smelling the stench that came from some of the patients. He wanted to quickly dispense with the horrifying tour, but the monk prevented him:

"Calm down, son. Sooner or later, it will be us lying in a bed like this."

Stunned, the man who managed almost a thousand bank branches and over thirty thousand employees had never imagined that one day he would be a wretch depending on others. He acted as if he were eternal.

"The situation of these patients is painful," commented Peterson, almost voiceless.

He entered another room. There were two patients. One unconscious and the other groaning in pain.

"Oh, I can't take it anymore! Let me die, monk!" Said the desperate patient.

He had skin cancer. The entire front part of his right leg was taken over by cancer. There was a large bandage to prevent contamination. And dressing him was a torment because it hurt the nerve endings, causing great pain.

"Patience, my friend. Patience," said the monk.

"Amputate my leg, please," begged the agonizing man.

"No, we will continue using the bandages."

"But the nurses here are rude. The pain is unbearable," he said, groaning again.

"But I brought someone who knows how to bandage wounds like no other."

"Who?" Peterson asked, looking around.

The monk put his hands on the executive's shoulders and said:

"You!" And looking at the patient, he affirmed: "This man will bandage you perfectly."

"Me? How can you say..." he said harshly, not completing the sentence. And then, not to torment the dying man even more, he spoke to the monk in a reconciling tone: "I have never put bandages on a wound. You are mistaken."

The monk stopped, took a breath, and looked deep in to Peterson's eyes:

"If you were so skillful in escaping a lynching and so creative in pretending to meditate for half an hour, you will certainly have the skill and creativity to apply the best possible bandage on this suffering man."

It was then that the ultra, proud, and relentless Peterson took a deep breath. He remembered his stress test. It was his opportunity to start his dramatic philanthropic saga. As if he were about to go to his own funeral, Theo Fester's son took the materials the monk gave him and began to do what would have been impossible just a week ago.

He tried to cover his nose with his left hand to avoid the horrible smell of the decaying skin. But it was impossible to dress the wound with only one hand. The man screamed in pain.

"Oh, I'd rather die!"

Peterson was sweating, panting, and had palpitations, as if he were facing a predator. However, the predator was his own prejudice against a dying person. As he removed the bandages and the man's skin came off in his hands, the executive began to feel nauseous. Hearing the man groan, he had an authoritarian crisis.

"Shut up!" said the banker, impatient. And then, he tried to calm down: "I'll do my best."

"I can't take it anymore!" said the man, crying.

While applying antiseptics and ointments to the patient's skin, the man's pain was so intense that he sat on the bed and vomited on Peterson's face. The powerful banker, who only had intimate relationships with celebrities and political hotshots, was washed by the vomit of that poor man, entirely infected, devoid of any social status. Peterson wanted to die. He let out an aggressive and desperate scream.

"I can't take this! I can't! My father is a torturer! I've had enough!"

He wanted to run away. But where would he go to? The only option would be a prison in New York. And for a moment, he thought that imprisonment would be less unbearable. And it was only the first day of his stress test.

After screaming like a predator, he stood up, covered in vomit, and tried to justify his reaction to the gentle monk.

"This guy infected me with his bacteria."

"But the bacteria of your mind are more infectious than biological bacteria," replied the monk.

"What does this monk mean with such words?" He thought. He said goodbye without finishing the bandaging, leaving the place with indignation.

The son of Theo Fester had suffocated his humanity. He had failed to build bridges even with his son Thomas. He had not transferred the capital of his experiences, only money. On Thomas's last birthday, when Peterson gave him ten thousand dollars as a gift, the boy, with teary eyes, said:

"I don't want your money, dad. I want you... Don't you understand?"

However, Peterson was a money-making machine and did not understand. He no longer knew what it was like to be a simple human being. As he withdrew, the man whose bandaging Peterson did halfway, spoke gently to him:

"I'm sorry, sir, for vomiting on you. If I were healthy, I would give you a bath to relieve you..."

Peterson didn't say anything comforting; he felt completely uncomfortable because that was the only outfit he had. He would have to sleep in it and wake up in it. While walking through the monastery, he found a poorly maintained bathroom, smelling bad, without shampoo, with only a piece of soap. For the first time in his life, he washed his own shirt. He also washed his head, face, and chest. But the smell of vomit was stuck in his nostrils. Shortly after finishing washing, he met the monk again.

"I understand you," said the monk.

"Is there any room outside this wing where I could stay?" The banker asked.

The monk replied:

"I'm sorry. Every day, many people ask us for lodging. But, for outsiders, we only give the privilege of caring for the wounded for one day; then they have to leave."

"Could you at least give me a piece of bread?"

"From here, no one takes anything; one can only give. Unfortunately, that's the rule."

Peterson turned his back. Yet the monk, seeing his misery, said:

"Wait. Go back to the room of the man you tried to do the bandaging. Take the piece of bread from the man next to him."

"But when he wakes up, he'll be hungry..."

"He won't wake up anymore," the monk stated categorically.

Peterson was stunned. He hesitated, but then, crushed by hunger, gave in. He walked to the room, entered silently, and, in an instinctive reaction, took the small piece of bread and left, swallowing the bite. He was beginning to discover the prisons hidden in the basements of his mind. He shed a few tears as he left the monastery and chewed on that stale and hard bread. He slept outdoors that day.

In the following days, Peterson continued his journey, not aware that it was a search of himself. A difficult task for someone who didn't know how to penetrate the basements of his own mind and identify the vampires that were draining him. Every day brought a new experience. A week later, being clever, he managed to work in an underground house that lent money at high interest rates. During this time, he also took care of children and adults with cancer. He had more contact with his madness than in decades of his life.

CHAPTER 26

Caleb's Unimaginable Stress Test

Caleb disembarked at the huge Los Angeles airport, feeling uneasy. However, since he lived in San Francisco, it seemed like home, after all, they were cities in the same state. Besides, he had a beautiful apartment in the city. Being a master of disguise, he just needed to employ some strategies to sleep comfortably. As soon as he left the airport, he looked left and right and didn't see anyone suspicious watching him. Despite not being a man of many friends, he had many sycophants and admirers in Los Angeles. All it took was a blink, and they would come to his aid. He was so at ease that he said to himself...:

"I conned the fools! Los Angeles is the entertainment capital. It will be a delightful month!" ...Opening his arms as if he was embracing the city.

Suddenly, a man who had just crossed his path looked at him and said: "The problem with smart people is thinking that everyone else is a fool."

Caleb was intrigued. He wondered if his words were a warning from someone who was watching him or if he spoke it randomly. He preferred to believe in the latter option. It didn't take long for the young billionaire to be recognized. A young woman called him from behind.

"Sir Caleb? Sir Caleb? I'm an economic journalist from Bloomberg."

"Yes" he answered curtly.

"How is your father?"

"Why don't you ask about me first?" He questioned the journalist.

"Oh, I'm sorry. How are you, sir?" The reporter asked, embarrassed.

"I'm very well," Caleb asserted, always bordering reality.

"And what about your father?"

"He's also great," he reported, without expressing that Theo Fester had terminal cancer.

"I admire him a lot."

Caleb stopped, thought, and replied: "Theo Fester is an interesting man."

"Not just interesting, he is exceptional!"

"I'm exceptional, my dear. I'm a much-improved version of him," he said sarcastically.

Whenever he spoke, Caleb had the gift of causing discomfort in others. The journalist noticed his arrogance.

"A brilliant father helps his children shine…" she innocently asserted. But she received a fitting response.

"Wrong again. I have my own shine."

"But didn't he contribute to your upbringing?" the journalist asked, indignant.

"As an entrepreneur, a bit, but I'm self-made. A large part of what I am, I achieved myself."

"You talk as if you were a god."

"A god? Yes… perhaps a god of the Silicon Valley."

It was seemingly impossible to corner the executive, quick-witted and proud. There was no dialogue with him, only a monologue. When the journalist turned her back, he said:

"Wait. Journalists should know that the press must be free but also intelligent. Next time, ask more interesting questions."

She left fuming with anger. She had heard that Caleb Fester was a difficult person, but not unmanageable. Minutes later, Caleb was recognized by a group of three business student girls. They shouted the famous entrepreneur's name as if they were cheer leaders.

"Caleb! Caleb!"

His ego swelled:

"Here I am, my fans."

"Can we take some selfies with you," they requested, euphoric.

"Of course," he said, beginning his stress test on a high note.

"Could we intern at your office in San Francisco after we graduate?" The beautiful brunette ventured.

He impolitely approached their ears and said:

"I'm very selective with my interns! But surely, you've already passed the test."

They said their goodbyes.

Caleb became excited: "I am the best!"

At that exact moment, someone touched his shoulder from behind.

"You're the best at what? Being a killer, a thief, a scoundrel, an egomaniac? Come on, speak!"

Caleb was startled. He took a step back. It was a homeless man, wearing a black and torn up blazer, with long shaggy hair and a poorly kept beard.

"Get out!" Caleb said to the intruder.

But the homeless man retorted: "Get out of where? Out of your life, this city, the planet?"

"Who are you?"

"I am like the shadow that appears with the light and disappears with the night" the ragged man expressed poetically.

"What do you mean? Where did you get that from?"

"Don't you know poetry?" The homeless man inquired.

"But a, a..." Before Caleb could complete the sentence, questioning the culture of the ragged man, the homeless man qualified himself.

"A homeless man, a beggar... can't know poetry! I don't study poetry; I make poetry. Nice to meet you, I am Vince Williamz," and he extended his hand to Caleb.

"Nice to meet you too. I am Caleb Fester." And he extended his hand, but the prison of his hypochondria spoke louder, withdrawing it immediately. He didn't want to greet someone who didn't take a bath and probably didn't even wash his hands. It was an invitation to contamination.

"What made you pull back...? My viruses or your prejudice?"

"No, nothing..."

"Besides being fragile, you're a liar," the homeless man observed, walking away.

In the next moment, Caleb thought, "Where am I going to?" He had no money for a taxi. Suddenly, he saw a young woman selling bouquets of roses. He went up to her and asked:

"How much is it?"

"Five dollars."

"I'll pay ten." The young woman was overjoyed. She couldn't believe the kindness of the stranger. But Caleb had another deceitful reaction: "I forgot my wallet at the car and need to go there to get the money Can I take the bouquet now?"

She was so ecstatic with the sale that she agreed:

"Of course. I'll wait for you." Caleb took the bouquet and left while the young woman was distracted with another customer. Twenty meters ahead, he found a very well-dressed lady. He seduced her with his false words, one of his specialties.

"Time hasn't passed for you. Red roses for an incredible woman."

The lady was flattered. She then asked:

"How much is it?"

"Only fifty dollars."

"But it's too expensive!" The lady complained.

"Doesn't a queen deserve a fifty-dollar bouquet from Dubai?"

"Do they grow roses in Dubai?" She asked, curious.

"Only the special ones," the charmer spoke in French. And then, he repeated the same phrase in English.

As he spoke another language and was well-dressed, she believed him. Excited, she opened her wallet and paid what he asked. Caleb left without going back to pay the young florist. However, a hundred meters ahead, she found him:

"Hey, what about my ten dollars?"

"I was looking for you and couldn't find you." And he gave her the fifty-dollar bill.

"You lied to me. I saw you selling my bouquet for fifty dollars. How did you do that?"

"Girl, I am one of the greatest entrepreneurs in the world. I would get rich anywhere and under any circumstances."

"But your price was unfair."

"It depends. How much are you worth?"

"I'm priceless!"

"First, sell yourself, then your product. Enchant your customer, and the clay you possess will be worth as much as gold."

The young woman listened to Caleb's lesson. She started selling herself, doubling her price. Indeed, she had never earned so much money in her life. After this incident, Theo Fester's youngest son forgot about his stress test, took a taxi with the money he had left, and went to the Dolby Theatre, the venue for the Hollywood Academy Awards ceremony. As an investor in film and series production companies, he had attended previous Oscar parties.

The entrepreneur was a paradox. He claimed to be a vegetarian, disliking animal cruelty, but he didn't mind hurting and eliminating people along the way. He didn't kill them physically, but destroyed their dreams, relationships, and energy. He used to take care of his diet, but was an irresponsible emotional consumer, suffering in anticipation, needing to be the center of attention, and not caring about his mental prisons.

After admiring the immense Dolby Theatre once again, he felt the most unforgettable of stress stimuli in his gut: hunger. He had paid the florist and spent thirty dollars on the taxi, reached into his pocket, and saw that he only had ten dollars left. It wasn't even enough for a glass of one of his favorite wines. He tried to find a restaurant selling light food near the famous theater. Embarrassed, he asked about the self-service price. He didn't have enough money. The waiter said ironically:

"Ten dollars? Is that all you have? There's nothing at our restaurant for that measly amount, my boy."

If that waiter was his employee, Caleb would have banished him. He left humiliated. After walking about a hundred yards from the Dolby Theatre, he saw several tents piled up in front of an old AT&T building. It was curious; it had never crossed his mind that there were homeless people near the Oscar party. He approached a man around fifty but who looked eighty, named Darren Johnson. The hardships of the streets, eating poorly, not sleeping well, and the lack of medical assistance punished the man's body. The life of the homeless in the United States was harsh.

"By any chance, are you extras in a movie scene?" Caleb asked naively, believing that the tents were part of a film production, even though there were no cameras around.

"Yes, I'm a part of it," Darren Johnson said without hesitation.

"Which movie is being produced?"

"The one about my life."

"Are you an actor?" The son of the magnate asked excitedly.

"Young man, are you an alien or plain stupid? Didn't you know that the movie capital is also one of the capitals of homelessness?"

"What do you mean?" Caleb asked innocently.

"We have fifty-eight thousand homeless people here. And what's worse, three out of every four of these people live on the streets, without a shelter to sleep."

"Fifty-eight thousand homeless? Wait, sir, you must be talking about São Paulo, or Buenos Aires, Ankara, Johannesburg... but not Los Angeles!"

"These ignorant Americans disgust me," Darren Johnson expressed to Caleb.

"But why do you accept this shameful condition? Why don't you look for a job? Why don't you fight?"

"Who are you to ask us these ignorant questions?" The homeless man questioned.

"Well... I'm an entrepreneur from the Silicon Valley," he said, surprisingly shy.

Darren looked into his eyes and said:

"Do you think we are in this dump because we want to? How many failed attempts do you think we've made before ending up on the streets? We are the sewage of society. No one believes in us, no one gives us opportunities," Darren said with tears in his eyes.

Caleb was impressed. He was starting to get to know a very different world from the beautiful offices of the Silicon Valley.

"But did living on the streets become a way of life for the conformists? Innovate! Reinvent yourselves!" He said arrogantly once again.

Caleb, like many of his peers, lived in a bubble in the Silicon Valley. It wasn't the real, concrete, raw, and suffering world of millions of human beings in his nation. If he had no idea that in the richest country in the world, the United States, there was a large caste of impoverished people, imagine his ignorance about what was happening in the rest of the planet. He never knew that there were more than three billion human beings living in extreme poverty, with less than two dollars per day, and about one billion and one hundred million people living with only one dollar per day. It wasn't even possible to minimally nourish the ten trillion cells in the human being's body. Caleb also wasn't aware that numerous children went to bed hungry and crying.

Dr. Marco Polo, on the other hand, had insomnia and cried because he was fully aware of the hunger and misery afflicting the human species. Once, the psychiatry thinker left international leaders perplexed with his dramatic comment:

"Anyone who can't put themselves in the place of others and feel their pain is not worthy of being a social leader or even be called a human. One of the ideas of the *Prisoners of the Mind* project is to solve the prison of hunger that plagues humanity once and for all." But the prime ministers and businessmen looked at each other, astonished and one of them countered:

"This is a utopia! Hunger has always been a part of our species; it has never been eradicated."

Dr. Marco Polo knew that, and being a student of human history, he proposed a solution:

"All world exports and imports should pay 0.25 percent in tax, generating billions of dollars in revenue, which would be part of a fund to eliminate world hunger, administered by the UN. In four years, the hunger of all peoples would be sustainably eradicated. Such a low tax rate wouldn't harm any nation and would solve this global problem once and for all, because the issue isn't the lack of food, but its distribution. Hunger in humanity would be a problem to be solved by the UN, no longer by governments, as some leaders use it for electoral purposes. Immigration involves other factors, such as violence, deprivation of freedom, lack of opportunities, but hunger is the main one. Once the hunger variable is resolved, the flow of illegal immigrants living in inhumane conditions in the richest nations can be significantly reduced. The surplus from this fund could be used to develop social, agricultural, and educational projects in the poorest nations."

Many leaders applauded Dr. Marco Polo with enthusiasm, but they took no action. They were unworthy of the power they possessed. They were short-sighted, slow, and not very intelligent in solving the afflictions of humanity.

Caleb dramatically rejected learning about the *Prisoners of the Mind* project. For him, being rich was about filling his pockets, and for Dr. Marco Polo, being rich and emotionally healthy was about giving the best of himself to make others happy.

Mary, a middle-aged homeless woman who had overheard Caleb's arrogant words to Darren Johnson from a distance, came up behind him and gave him a strong slap on the head, saying: "Get out of here, you daddy's little boy!

The famous Silicon Valley star fell to the ground, almost unconscious. A ringing sound echoed in his ears. Theo Fester's youngest son was beaten by a homeless woman. Furious, he got up and went after the assailant. He pushed Mary, who fell to the ground. In the meantime, four homeless people came out to defend her. In addition to hitting Caleb, they held him so that Mary could slap him in the face again. His father had never laid a finger on him, but that day, Caleb received the first beating of his life. Darren Johnson shouted for the attackers to stop. Caleb was injured, with a bleeding upper lip and bruises all over his body.

In addition to being beaten, his assailants took the ten dollars he had and gave it to another homeless person begging on the streets. Darren dragged him into his tent. Caleb groaned in pain. He couldn't speak. He slept for five hours. He woke up with his whole-body aching. A woman was placing wet cloth on his wounds, trying to alleviate his pain. When he looked at her, Caleb was shocked. It was Mary, the same woman who had slapped him. She was a friend of Darren. Seeing Caleb's surprise, she said:

"Relax, I'm not mad anymore!"

"I've never been beaten by anyone. Especially not by a woman…"

"But you deserved it," she said. "Next time, be less arrogant, and I'll be gentler."

Inside the small tent, there was also another homeless friend of Darren's, Bill Rollin. He was a former Silicon Valley entrepreneur who had lost his image, his money, and his children. He struck up a conversation with Caleb:

"I heard you say you were a Silicon Valley entrepreneur. Did you lose everything like me?"

"I lost a lot" Caleb affirmed.

"The gods of the Silicon Valley owe humanity a debt."

"Why are you saying that?" Caleb asked, still sore but curious.

"They have made more money in two decades than successful men in two millennia. But they didn't minimize the pain of discrimination, social exclusion, depression, self-abandonment, hunger. It's no wonder the suicide rate in the Silicon Valley is so high. I lost both my children at once…" And, with tears, he left without the need of giving further explanations; his face revealed a shocking suffering.

Darren Johnson looked at the injured and hungry young man and offered him the only thing he had, a cold hot dog.

"Sausage? I hate it. I'm a vegetarian."

"But you haven't eaten in a long time."

At that moment, overcome by the instinct of hunger, he swallowed his pride and ate the hot dog. Never had a hot dog, costing less than three dollars, been so delicious. He remembered his father, who loved this cheap type of snack. He remembered two of his father's sayings: "You eat your past" and "The best food is the one you eat with pleasure." Caleb wanted to deny his father, hide from everything he represented, but it was impossible. The brain's biographer, the AMR phenomenon, recorded Theo Fester in countless ways in the depths of his unconscious mind.

In that stress test, Caleb faced daily surprises that were never programmed by his intellect. It was an eternal thirty days in which he roamed between emotional heaven and hell. The virus of pride and the neurotic need to be the center of social attention insisted on infecting his mind. The mental prisons of hypochondriasis, impulsiveness, and the need to cheat others often suffocated him. He was supported, cared for, and taught by people he never thought could offer any kind of teaching or help. However, Theo Fester's youngest son was a resistant mind, little open to learning or thinking about other possibilities.

He was beaten several times, humiliated many times. At times, he hated his father for the test he had imposed on him; at other times, he admired him deeply. He wanted to give up in certain situations. But he withdrew at the thought that he would face global rejection for planning the murder of his own father and that he would be locked up in a prison.

Emotional time was different from physical time for Caleb Fester. The day didn't seem to have only twenty-four hours but an infinite number of them. He tried to cheer himself up by betting on the possibility of becoming a billionaire. But his father was more present than he imagined, observing with eagle eyes the steps of his beloved son. In many moments, instead of applauding him, Theo Fester cried upon learning about his behaviors. Passing the stress test was an almost impossible task for the young man who thought of himself as a god and now discovered that he was a mere mortal, fragile, arrogant, depressed, and embraced by countless insanities.

CHAPTER 27

Incredible Dialogues Between an Entrepreneur, A Psychiatrist, and Artificial Intelligence

The stress test for Theo Fester's children was coming to an end. Days before the final analysis, the magnate was walking through the vast gardens of Forest Castle. Dr. Marco Polo was on his right side, and Invictus on his left. Solemn moments of silence permeated their minds. Even Invictus, the *Robot sapiens*, dared not express opinions. He read on his creator's face that silence was better than the thundering of words.

Peterson, Brenda, and Caleb were being observed by disguised cameramen who filmed their reactions, edited them, and broadcasted them to their father. Although Theo Fester saw them separately, he preferred to see the whole picture to make the most impartial judgment possible of his own children. Dr. Marco Polo was concerned about the results. He ventured to say to the magnate:

"Mr. Fester, as a Jewish person, you know that according to the Torah, the exodus of the people of Israel from Egypt, wandering through the desert with nothing in their hands, was a dramatic stress test."

Theo Fester replied:

"I know, I know. But the Jewish people failed that test. They created conflicts, complained, rebelled, and wanted to go back to the *comforts* of Egypt in every possible way."

Dr. Marco Polo took a few more steps and added:

"Perhaps you don't know, but there is a psychiatric analysis of the sacred texts of Christianity that also reveals a spectacular stress test."

"Oh, really? What is it?"

"It reports that a carpenter from Nazareth rejected the honor of being the Son of God. And this man, who carved wood, dreamed of carving human minds and used all means to train and test his students, who only gave him headaches. He trained them not to discriminate against prostitutes or people with leprosy. He taught them to empty their egos, to be empathetic, to think before reacting, to manage anxiety, to judge less, and to embrace more."

"Interesting stress test," said the billionaire. "I never thought about that."

"At the peak of his fame, when entering Jerusalem, his followers expected him to use a royal carriage, but he entered the city on the back of a small and clumsy animal. Another dramatic test."

"And what about the result? Did they pass the test?" Theo wanted to know.

"They failed tragically…! Peter, the strongest, denied him. The most educated, from the political party of the Zealots, called Judas Iscariot, betrayed him. And the others abandoned him when he needed them most."

Theo Fester took a deep breath. He paused strategically to think.

"Will my children fail the test?" He rhetorically asked himself.

Invictus decided to make a comment.

"Sorry for interfering. Except for the stress test in the Torah and the one in the sacred book of the Christians, I have no memory of a father in any culture who has tested his children as intensely as you, my creator."

Theo Fester observed some tulips in front of him, approached them, smelled the fragrance, and commented:

"Human life should be an eternal spring, but winters are inevitable. I didn't think about the Torah or the book of the Christians when I subjected my children to the stress test. I thought about my role as an educator, leader, and entrepreneur."

"Are you sure you want to make this judgment? Your attitude may have no historical precedent in humanity. Your children won't be adapted if you take everything from them. Rich people think about dying when they go bankrupt, celebrities lose their reason to live when they fall into anonymity, athletes become depressed when their performance levels decrease," Dr. Marco Polo pondered, trying to soften the billionaire's judgment.

The mega-entrepreneur looked into Dr. Marco Polo's eyes and commented:

"Genetic ties define whether a human being will be their father's heir. It's not by merit, gratitude, affection, generosity, and certainly not by respect for their parents, but rather by passing down genes. I've always treated people based on meritocracy throughout my life."

"But your children are not your employees," Dr. Marco Polo asserted.

"Of course not! But if parents evaluated whether their children truly deserved their inheritance, which was earned with sweat and tears, sleepless nights, and crises... would they pass the test?"

"Many would not pass," Dr. Marco Polo affirmed.

"Approximately ninety percent of them would not pass," said Invictus, always more logical. "According to the statistics I have, most siblings quarrel after their parent's death, becoming bitter enemies in the battle for the money they didn't earn. Given their brief existence, why are humans so complicated?"

"Emotion either turns them into monsters or into generous human beings," said Theo Fester. "If, in evaluating my children's behavior, I was to disapprove of them, do you think there would still be a solution for them, Dr. Marco Polo?"

"As a psychiatrist and a thinker in psychology, I believe that 'behind someone who hurts, there is a wounded person'. I have even come to believe that psychopaths and sociopaths are not hopeless, at least for those who want to overcome their mental ghosts."

"Even a psychopath? Wouldn't that be psychiatric romanticism?"

"It's not possible to be a humanist without doses of romanticism. However, the few psychopaths who recover have risks of committing suicide."

"Suicide? Why?" Questioned the billionaire.

"Because they have acquired an awareness of the pain they inflicted on their victims. As psychopaths, they are not adapted to the feeling of guilt, and when they experience it, they dramatically collapse, excessively punishing themselves. Therefore, they run the risk of attempting to end their lives. So, it is vital to lead them to transform tears into growth, not self-punishment."

Theo Fester pondered on that information. Undoubtedly, it would be easier to just give his inheritance to his children, like any father would do. However, he couldn't. As one of the world's greatest entrepreneurs, he always thought outside the box.

Invictus, reading Theo Fester's expression, said:

"I would like to feel some of your frustration with your children, but I can't."

"Artificial intelligence has significant limitations," stated the investor.

"I can't feel guilt, but I am to blame for the state you're in."

"Why do you say that, Invictus?"

"Remember? I suggested that you test your children to check if they truly loved you for who you are, not for what you have. It was my suggestion to solve this emotional equation, something I don't understand."

"I remember well. I had just received the cancer diagnosis and didn't want my children to know about my fate at that moment."

"I can say 'I'm sorry' a thousand times, but I can't feel the meaning of that expression" commented Invictus.

"Invictus, it wasn't you. For years, I've known that my children were unworthy of the power and inheritance they would come to have. It wasn't even the attempted murder they carried out. That was just the straw that broke the camel's back of my unfathomable disappointment."

Theo Fester also mentioned that his past made him care more about the return of his children than most of other parents: "To this day, sometimes I wake up in the middle of the night recollecting my father's nightmares about the sufferings he went through in the concentration camps, caused by hunger, beatings by the Nazis, and imminent death. Without a mother, at the age of five, I should have been playing, but I had to comfort him because of his nightmares. I became a shy, terrified child, with ragged clothes, and ridiculed. I was not loved by anyone... only by my father. And today, my own children don't love me."

"You became one of the richest men today, but also one of the neediest men in the world... That's not necessarily bad. It makes you human" concluded Dr. Marco Polo.

"I wanted to feel needy, to become more human," confessed Invictus.

"Nietzsche expressed that fragility makes us excessively human," commented Theo Fester. "I am not as powerful as many believe. In fact,

I am a needy man. The wealthy are sterile, yet the needy are creators, hungry and thirsty to venture, to be recognized, admired, and loved."

"Am I the result of your neediness, sir?" Asked Invictus.

"Yes. I seek in you what I do not have from my children. But this search will not succeed."

"But I can blindly obey you."

"It's not enough."

"But I can serve you like a slave."'

"Not enough either!"

"But I can applaud and praise you like few others."

"Still not enough."

"But what would be enough?"

"Only love would be enough."

"Wait. If no child would serve a father as I would, then you humans seek something rarer than gold."

Dr. Marco Polo smiled and responded before Theo Fester could:

"Perhaps. Perhaps."

The Silicon Valley magnate was amazed, so ecstatic about the opportunity to have such an intelligent dialogue with a psychiatrist and with Invictus, a rapid and insightful *Robot sapiens*. Revealing his great intellectuality, he was enlightened to conclude something he had never thought of before. He commented:

"Evaluating our dialogue, I understood something staggering: the God in whom the Jewish people believe, which is the same as the one Christians and Muslims believe in, is also a needy God, in the good sense of the word…"

"How come?" Dr. Marco Polo asked curiously.

"When it says in its first commandment 'Love God above all things', it is revealing His vital need to be loved. Doesn't this reflect His tremendous emotional need?"

"You're right" said the psychiatrist, thoughtful. "I'm not religious, but I can notice that unlike all kings and powerful figures, He didn't demand obedience, servitude, or flattery, but pleaded to be loved."

"What? The Creator of creators is a needy being too?" Invictus asked. "My super memory is malfunctioning right now! You drive me crazy!"

"My mind is also malfunctioning," Theo Fester affirmed. Dr. Marco Polo concluded:

"Maybe that's why there are millions of emotionally ill and mentally imprisoned religious individuals. They exalt the power of their God, not love; they exalt His justice, not tolerance and patience," analyzed the psychiatrist.

Theo Fester was shaken by this analysis.

"Do you think I am mentally imprisoned, Dr. Marco Polo?"

Dr. Marco Polo did not soften his tone.

"Do you feel like a prisoner?"

Theo Fester had another coughing fit.

"I suffer for the future and dwell on my past! I demand too much from others. My brain is constantly exhausted; I wake up exhausted! Without a doubt, I am a prisoner in my mind. And you, illustrious psychiatrist, do you have your mental prisons, or a free mind?"

Dr. Marco Polo smiled and honestly pointed out:

"I demand too much of myself. I give myself to others but I forget to love my own health. I confess, I neglect my own needs, putting myself in a place unworthy of my own agenda. I need to cherish my life more. These are some of my mental prisons, Mr. Fester. And I hope that among yours is not the difficulty of forgiving," said the psychiatrist, reminding the magnate that he would soon judge his children.

Invictus began to hit his own head several times, looking as if it were trying to self-destruct.

"What's happening, Invictus?" Theo Fester asked, extremely concerned.

"My programs are disoriented once again. I can't reason. I can't understand the language and the elements you are using. What are mental prisons? What is forgiveness?"

"Forgiveness is giving a new chance to someone who has failed," Dr. Marco Polo stated.

Invictus raged. He raised his voice:

"But it's mathematically impossible. There are no algorithms to produce forgiveness. There will never be." And turning to his creator, he concluded: "You deceived me, Theo Fester! I am not made in your image and likeness!"

"Calm down, Invictus. Forgiving is not my specialty, but I wish it were."

Peterson in Kashmir, Brenda in Sicily, and Caleb on the streets of Los Angeles lived through innumerous emotional crises, social conflicts, and existential experiences that are impossible to describe in their entirety. Some of these experiences were worthy of the most notable applause; others, of tears; and yet others to be forgotten forever. If they were told in words, they would turn into many books. The verdict of a father does not change the destiny of his children, but this time it would change forever...

CHAPTER 28

Peterson's Trial

Peterson, Brenda, and Caleb finally entered the immense hall of the Forest Castle where Theo Fester was. Caleb was using crutches, all wounded. He had difficulty walking; his right eye was bruised; and there was a deep cut on his forehead. Brenda had a bruise on the right side of her face. Peterson had no apparent injuries.

The magnate was sitting on a simple chair, not on a judge's armchair or a throne as a king would. It was the sentence from a wounded, frustrated, disappointed father, but still, someone who loved them. Peterson, Brenda, and Caleb approached step by step and kissed him. Then, they sat in front of him.

Apparently, they were not the same people who had arrived at that palace over a month ago, proud, haughty, arrogant, assuming they were above the mere mortals. There was no one else to be seen in the immense hall. Dr. Marco Polo, Marc Douglas, Invictus, and Dr. Willian were watching the trial from another room.

Theo Fester took his notes, furrowed his brow, and looked firmly at his eldest son. However, before opening his mouth, he took a remote control and started broadcasting Peterson's first behaviors in the distant regions of Kashmir. Peterson was astonished, unaware that he was being filmed, he started having an anxiety attack. He thought his father had paid someone to spy on him from a distance, but the possibility of detailed video records of his behavior hadn't crossed his mind. He and his siblings had only been filmed in the Forest Castle because it was a controlled environment.

"You didn't say we would be filmed," Peterson anticipated, with his voice trembling. And he began to feel a tightness in his chest as if a heart attack was happening.

"Yes. We weren't informed that we would be filmed," said Caleb, also indignant; it seemed like he was anticipating his own defeat.

"But how could I judge you fairly if my evidence were based on assumptions?" The father commented without mincing words, pausing the images. Having said that, he continued to broadcast them.

The radical and ruthless banker began to crack his fingers. His heart was racing like a wild horse resisting the reins. His father commented:

"Look, Peterson, my dear eldest son, you lied that you were a hospital manager, lost your patience with Mr. Igor, the director. Moments later, you stole an apple and fled from your pursuers. Then you started well. You were bandaging a poor man's wound, while bathed in vomit. Screaming, you interrupted your ritual of solidarity and, on top of that, called me a torturer."

"But..." Peterson tried to interrupt.

"Calm down. Despite everything, for someone not used to giving, you did reasonably well on your first day of the stress test."

Peterson opened a smile. He couldn't contain his happiness. Euphoric, he said:

"Kashmir taught me to be a better human being. Unforgettable lessons."

Theo continued to broadcast the images and judge them... Suddenly, instead of transmitting images from Kashmir, he showed images from the deck of the yacht where Peterson held his frequent parties with politicians and businessmen. In this image, Theo's eldest son, drunk, humiliated an employee who was sweeping the floor.

"Look, Peterson, how you offended this simple employee who was cleaning the yacht by calling him 'Dumb! Stupid! Blind, can't you see that you left those paper napkins on the deck?'".

Irritated, Peterson said:

"I didn't know you would use old images to evaluate me!"

"And who said I wouldn't use them? They are comparisons, you before and after."

The banker quieted down. His father continued:

"Those napkins had been deliberately thrown by one of your guests to see how you, who are completely impatient, would react. And the politicians who were with you enjoyed seeing the waiter being humiliated. That waiter and millions of other taxpayers are the ones who pay those politicians' salary, but it seems that they don't know they are employed by the people. They are unworthy of the power they have. Just like you, unworthy of the power I gave you."

"But that waiter was a terrible employee; he had already left other trash behind. He couldn't see the obvious."

"I investigated his story. He couldn't see because he had a severe case of myopia that was never treated."

"But I didn't know that."

"Horses, because they wear blinders, they never know what's happening next to them. Humans, when they refuse to see, do worse."

When Theo Fester made this accusation, Peterson had a coughing fit, just like his father. The fear of criticism was taken to new heights. He wanted to lash out at him but held himself back with great difficulty. And his father continued:

"For years, I've been investigating your behavior, Peterson." At this moment, Brenda and Caleb shivered.

"I know," said Peterson.

"You know?"

"You have been a judge much more than a father to me," he accused.

"A judge? A son who doesn't listen to his father's advice might need a judge. How many times have I told you that no human being deserves to be treated with stupidity? ...Not even our enemies."

When his father made this comment, the atmosphere became tense. The children began to believe that no one would pass their rigorous trial. Peterson collapsed. Desperately, he tried to undermine his father's analysis.

"This episode was before the fascinating lessons I had in Kashmir. It was there that I brilliantly experienced my stress test. It was there that I humanized myself. It's not fair to judge me based on my past."

His father frowned and showed Peterson in Kashmir, cleaning the floor to earn a few coins for a meal. He was sweating and wiping his forehead, audibly saying, "I can't believe I'm doing this pig's work. Me, the owner of banks and yachts! I hate you, old man!"

Peterson did not know where to hide his face. Worried, he said, "I was just blowing off some steam. It wasn't how I really felt."

His father pointed out: "The great banker was cleaning the floor to get dinner because he hadn't gotten money for lunch... the same job as the yacht cleaner you humiliated and earning less than him. I wonder if the children of today's millionaires would survive if they weren't to inherit their parents' wealth. Some wouldn't even be able to do manual labor."

"But you wouldn't survive without your money," Peterson said.

"You're wrong, my son. I was an office boy, I cleaned restaurants, washed bathrooms for two years, I was a cook... before becoming an entrepreneur. Before becoming a billionaire, I learned the lessons of being poor. I went bankrupt five times and reinvented myself with each bankruptcy."

Peterson broke into a cold sweat. He was wondering whether he should stay or run away. But his father began to praise him and show some clips.

"You took care of ten injured people, assisted women with breast cancer undergoing chemotherapy, walked through highs and lows, sometimes surprisingly. But you still complained a lot. From the audio recordings I have, you said 'I can't take it anymore' thirty-two times and 'I hate this!' twenty times. You lacked solemn doses of love."

"But who could endure that?" Peterson asked.

"*That* was **people** who were suffering!"

"But you don't seem to be someone who cares for those who are suffering."

"Didn't you see my photo in that hospital…? Do you think I just sent money? I was there! I helped people, not as Theo Fester, but as a human being. I personally took care of my father until he died of cancer when I was twenty. I helped children in orphanages. Did you know that I cleaned bathrooms even after becoming a billionaire?"

The children doubted. But Theo showed shocking scenes. He already had gray hair, and he was cleaning bathrooms.

"I did it in secret to never forget that I am a simple, fallible, imperfect mortal."

"But you never told us anything about it," observed Peterson.

"I didn't talk about what I did, but I tried to guide you many times – *You will go to the loneliness of the grave like any mortal. Be careful! Poor money management impoverishes as much as its absence!*"

The children remembered those words. Then, Theo showed a film in which he helped feed the children in orphanages. Thomas, Peterson's son, was with him sometimes, and other times Kate, Brenda's daughter.

"I tried to save your children, Thomas and Kate. I wanted to teach them what I wasn't able to teach you."

Peterson, Brenda, and Caleb were surprised. The daughter said: "I only knew you on the outside. Now I can see who you really are!"

In the many occasions that Theo Fester talked about giving, his children figured he wanted to soften the guilt of being a billionaire.

"You wanted to know about numbers; no longer listening to the language of feelings. But this is my fault too. When you were children, I worked a lot. I failed; I recognize that."

And Theo Fester turned to Peterson to give his verdict.

"Do you remember, on your fifteenth day in Kashmir, that three-year-old girl you picked up? She sneezed on your face. You dropped her immediately, and she fell. Fortunately, it was on the bed. But she could have fallen on the floor." And he showed the clip – It was shocking.

"I was afraid she might infect me," Peterson replied, trying to justify his actions.

"But she was the one with low immunity. Actually, she could have been infected by you."

Then his father showed him working in an underground company that lent money.

"When you started working in that financial agency, you went back to being a banker. You began lending money. If working for an underground company wasn't bad enough, you lent at an interest rate of ten percent per month...!? In Muhammad Yunus's homeland... the banker to the poor, who's biggest concern is boosting small entrepreneurs with low-interest rates? You committed financial rape!"

"But that was the market rule" Peterson defended himself again, while his lips were trembling.

"The rule of the underground market. Why didn't you break the rules to favor those in need?" His father asked. And after a pause, he continued:

"But what shook me the most, my son, was harassing the nurse at that poor clinic. But wait, let's go to another episode on the yacht."

Peterson turned red, breathless, with palpitations. In the footage, he was with some politicians and four models, two blondes and two brunettes, and there he was, trying to grab one of the girls by force. And since she did not give in, he assaulted her: "Don't be a hypocrite; you like powerful men."

"You invited me for a ride, not to compromise myself. You're drunk" she said, trying to break free.

"I am Peterson Fester; I am one of the richest men in the world. Any woman would love to be at my feet."

After showing this scene, his father only commented:

"And the politicians, businessmen, and two actors who were with you still had the courage to applaud you. They applauded a sexual predator!"

"Once again, going back to the past..." Peterson said, standing up, knowing he was about to fail his stress test.

Next, his father showed him harassing a poor Indian nurse. She and Peterson were on a deserted street. The video showed him promising the world to her...

"I am a very rich man. I will get you out of this hell."

"But how? You don't look rich at all!"

"I am here undercover. Look at who I really am." And he showed her images from his yacht parties, mingling with socially important people. He tried to seduce her with his power, as he had always done with so many other women.

"Wow! I had no idea," said the humble nurse, surprised.

At that moment, Peterson thought she had fallen into his trap. He took her in his arms and tried to kiss her. But she refused.

"I am engaged. I am getting married."

"Forget your poor fiancé! With me, you will have a future!"

And he tried to grab her again. But she avoided him. Peterson got enraged and slapped her.

"Then die in this miserable place, taking care of your patients."

And he turned his back on her. As he walked away, she said:

"I prefer to take care of these poor patients than live with a mentally ill person!"

When his father played this video, Peterson lost his voice. Theo Fester said calmly:

"Sit down. I won't give you my verdict now. I will analyze your brothers' behavior and then inform my decision to the three of you."

Peterson sat down cowered. He couldn't argue. Tormented, he looked at his two siblings, and suddenly a statement crossed his mind: "The success of others causes me envy, but the misery of others consoles me." He believed that his siblings would also fail. Caleb, especially... undoubtedly. At least, he wouldn't be the only one going to jail and live in misery. "But who knows, maybe my father will give me a consolation prize for facing Kashmir?" He thought for a moment.

CHAPTER 29

Brenda's Trial

Theo Fester deeply breathed in and out three times. He was shaken by the analysis he had made of his eldest son's behavior; he needed a moment to meditate and relax. Then he began to analyze his only daughter's behavior. He locked eyes with her and replayed her extravagant parties: Brenda would dance, drink uncontrollably, and, at times, use drugs. She loved status, but on social media, she posted messages like: *Humility is the garment of wisdom.*

"Brenda, you play a character on social media and another at the lavish parties."

Brenda tensed up. She was a woman who lived on the surface, not exploring deeper topics, not even with her daughter, Kate.

"Mom, let's go to the movies?" Kate would ask.

"I don't have time, my daughter; I am hosting a party."

On another occasion, Kate said:

"Mom, can we go to the zoo?"

"I hate animals. I prefer to be with humans."

"But I am human, and you don't like being with me," the girl said intelligently.

"Kate, stop complaining for no reason. I am always with you."

"Always on the phone, not with me."

"But I'm working!"

"Your followers are more important than I am."

"Stop being foolish. Why do you say that?"

"At least you send messages to them and answer their questions."

And Kate would leave crying. After showing these videos, Theo Fester asked:

"What do you think of this? Are you going to say, as Peterson did, that the past doesn't matter, what actually matters are the thirty days in Sicily?"

Brenda cried. It took her a while to respond.

"This is not part of my stress test, I know, but nothing justifies my behavior. I was an irresponsible mother. I confess, I lived a character. I was an expert at deceiving myself. I mistreated those I loved the most."

Theo Fester was surprised that she did not try to explain herself, for admitting her madness.

"The worst prisoners are those who believe they are free minds because they live in free societies. I congratulate you for admitting your madness."

Peterson was uncomfortable with his sister's praise. Then, Theo Fester played the first days of Brenda's test. He showed the scenes where she was raped to get food at the supermarket. At that moment, Theo himself couldn't hold back and cried. Brenda also broke down. Caleb was stunned. Peterson, horrified, accused his father:

"How can a father subject his daughter to such a situation?!"

Brenda continued crying. Theo Fester couldn't utter a word. In tears, she defended him: "No, Peterson. It wasn't our father who... led me to the rape. But the human beings who, trapped in their mental prisons, become predators to one another. I... spent sleepless nights hating my rapist, that monster... I washed my intimate parts several times. But the worst nights were when I was disgusted with myself..."

Caleb took Brenda's hands and, for the first time in adulthood, comforted his sister. Then, he asked:

"Why were you disgusted with yourself, sister? You're not to blame."

"I was disgusted with the superficial and arrogant life I led. I lived in a gilded cage, alienated from the pains of such fascinating people, admirable children... Children drowning... Do you remember the Syrian boy who drowned on the beaches of Turkey and became a symbol of disregard for refugees? The world was moved, so was I, but in my comfortable mansion. However, unfortunately, several other boys have died. Some in my hands, but the press doesn't report that... Oh, my Goodness! I was so blind!"

Theo Fester looked at his daughter with admiration. She was right. Her life was a mud bath sprinkled with expensive perfumes and crowned with diamonds.

"But you fought for the helpless. You demanded that rescuers went to the boats to rescue Africans with their children to give them a place in the sun in Europe, fleeing unscrupulous dictators or ruthless hunger."

And so, Theo Fester played a video in which she herself dived into the sea and rescued a drowning child.

"You put your life at risk to save the most fragile..., something you had never done before. You shared your bread, even though being tortured by hunger, with the kids and their mother."

Brenda said:

"I need to go back. The misery of those people is unbearable. Many children are developing the 'resignation syndrome'."

"I don't know this syndrome," Caleb said.

"Dr. Marco Polo taught me about it."

"You talked to this..." Peterson was about to insult Dr. Marco Polo, but Brenda cut him off.

"Scoundrel, Peterson? Opportunist? Deceiver of fragile minds? Do you think our father, with the resumé he has, could be deceived by someone? Do you think with such clarity and culture, greater than the three of us combined, he could be fooled by a psychiatrist? If he wanted to, he would outsmart any mental health professional. Dr. Marco Polo won him over with his intelligence...Yes, I talked to him almost every day!"

Peterson swallowed his words.

"What is the 'resignation syndrome'?" Her younger brother asked again.

"It was diagnosed in many children in Sweden. Children and teenagers who have become emotionally disintegrated. They stopped eating, speaking, walking, living. Some go into a coma."

"How awful!" Caleb expressed. "But why?"

"According to Dr. Marco Polo, the brains of these boys and girls go into a dramatic and unbearable state of exhaustion when they become aware that they and their parents will be deported to their countries of origin, to war zones, to hunger and misery."

"My Gosh! What are we doing to the children of humanity?!" Theo Fester exclaimed. The man who did not use to cry became much more sensitive in recent months, like never before in his story.

Brenda, sympathetic to everything she had seen, showed the photo of the boy who clung to her legs, Salah, who had motivated her to steal food in the supermarket.

"This syndrome occurs in several countries, but it is not properly diagnosed. After I brought food for Salah and his family, this lovely boy became my friend. See..." And she showed a video in which she chased

Salah, who hid behind the lampposts and trees in the squares for Brenda to look for him.

"I love you, Brenda" Salah said in the video she recorded on her phone.

And Brenda revealed the worst:

"But when Italy decided to deport his mother with his two brothers to Ethiopia, to the chaos of hunger and scarcity, Salah stopped sleeping, he would wake up in panic in the early hours. I had to console him. He was only five years old, but he worried about his mother and brothers. I fought for them at the immigration center. I shouted, made a scene, but it was no use. The government insisted…"

Brenda started crying again.

"And what happened?" Peterson asked anxiously, remembering his son Thomas.

She showed the video.

"In one week, Salah went through a stressful emotional burden that would take an adult decades to experience. He exhausted his brain. He gave up on living. He became some kind of zombie. He wouldn't get out of bed anymore, quit talking, and didn't want to eat. He gave up on everything and everyone. Days later, he disappeared…"

Her father and her brothers were silent for a few seconds. Then, Theo Fester ventured to comment:

"Are we rich? Or are we miserable living in palaces? Soon, we will go to the solitude of a grave. Will we go with dignity…? …With a clear conscience that we helped soothe, at least a little, the pains of humanity? How many *Salahs* could be rescued if we were less egocentric?"

"You're right, Dad. I've thought about it day and night," Brenda agreed.

Despite being impacted by his daughter's actions, Theo Fester continued to unlock her mental prisons. He did not soften his judgment. He was more penetrating in her insanities.

"You began to have this awareness of the brain exhaustion that the system ruthlessly causes in children. But you also exhausted the brains of countless children and teenagers. You put them in a concentration camp."

Brenda was speechless. Then, disturbed, she asked:

"How did I do that, Dad?"

The father saved the revelation for later. He only concluded his reasoning.

"For years, your grotesque actions embarrassed the Festers. They embarrassed the past of your grandfather, who was a victim of the concentration camps, and humiliated me, your own father."

"It's not possible! This is a very serious accusation! I don't recall committing such an atrocity," she said, anguished, thinking that her father was exaggerating.

Theo Fester was incisive.

"Adolf Hitler considered Jewish people, Slavs, Romani people, and homosexuals as sub-races, especially Jewish people, which were considered subhuman, disposable objects. Himmler, the executioner of the political police, the SS, was a bumpkin in his youth, uncultured, and an obsessive animal breeder. He made genetic improvements. He was responsible for the extermination camps, ethnic cleansing. What do you think of that?"

"Horrible! Horrible!"

"But what do you think of the concentration camp created by the fashion world?"

"What do you mean?" She said, with trembling lips.

"You, as the owner of one of the largest global women's fashion chains, imposed an atrocious beauty dictatorship that entered the collective unconscious mind of millions of women. You and your team of stylists selected bodies as Adolf Hitler selected Aryans."

"But, but... Have we been so cruel to women?"

"I have no doubts. Once, you rejected a model who was ready to walk the runway because she had gained only six pounds."

"My Goodness...! Who?"

"Julia, a sixteen-year-old Italian teenager. You said, 'You are disqualified.' And sentenced, 'You are fat. Look at your belly!' The girl panicked. Disturbed, she said, 'But... I only gained six pounds. Please.' 'No. You will scare away customers from my collection.' And the girl said: 'This is cruelty!' Then you answered: 'It doesn't matter. Models have to be hangers. It's not their bodies that should stand out, but the clothes.'" The father showed the video and said aloud:

"Do you know what happened to her?"

"I have no idea. I never heard about her again."

"Of course, you discarded people like objects. She had a monstrous mental prison that generated intense depressive crises. She ate compulsively and gained one hundred and ten pounds in less than a year. She is morbidly obese. Five seconds can change a story for better or for worse, my daughter."

"My Goodness, what I have done!? I need to find her, apologize, help with her treatment."

"I've been doing that. She became a second daughter to me. She is in treatment." Then, the father concluded: "You were cruel to the models, cruel in selecting women within the tyrannical beauty standard to work for you, and cruel to your daughter, Kate. You scold her every day, saying that she should eat less!"

Brenda once again did not try to defend herself.

"You're right. I was really cruel. In Sicily, I saw so much misery that seeing a chubby girl made me happy; it was a sign of good health. I was relentless with my daughter. But I understood, in my conversations with Dr. Marco Polo, that raising my voice, criticizing, and repeating the same things activated the brain's biographer to register killer windows, finally promoting what I detested the most." After this moment, brutally opening her mental wounds, she confessed:

"I enforced the dictatorship of beauty. I am also its victim which is why I suffer from bulimia. Normal women, who are chubby, and lack the idealized curves, nose, breasts or lips are indeed excluded, rejected just like illegal immigrants or refugees. They are treated as sub-human, scum, or social waste, while hundreds of millions of women are massacred by the tyranny of beauty."

And, in a unique and emotional moment, she dared to sentence:

"Honestly, my father. I deserve to be held accountable, not only for attempting to murder you but for trying to kill the self-esteem of millions of women, as well as adolescent girls and boys."

Peterson, desperate to hear his sister condemning herself, put his hands on his head.

"Brenda, are you sick? Don't be so cruel to yourself!" Her older brother desperately shouted.

But she did not listen to him. She was disappointed with herself and ashamed of how generous life had been to her and how she behaved like an executioner of innocent people, teenagers in the fashion world, and employees. She did not feel sick; she was just a human being fully aware of her madness.

CHAPTER 30

Caleb's Trial

Caleb was as shocked as his older brother, if not more so. He rubbed his hands on his head and checked his pulse, fearing he might be having a stroke. His hypochondriasis crisis had reached its peak. It was time for his trial.

He struggled to condemn his father. He believed a father shouldn't judge his children, but embrace them. However, it was surprising how Theo Fester conducted a fair judgment. Caleb began to admire his father like never before. He realized that, as his father exposed the wounds of his children's personalities, he was thrusting a knife into his own soul.

Caleb hoped his father would take a brief pause, as he did with Brenda, before starting to dissect his stupidity, insanity, and arrogance without anesthesia. But Theo Fester didn't need a strategic pause to initiate "Caleb's case". He thought: "I'm lost, I'm going to be crucified."

"As for you, Caleb," Theo spoke with a determined voice: "Your ego soars to the clouds and breaks down into a storm over the heads of those who oppose you. It's surprising how you never tire of repeating that you were awarded as the greatest entrepreneur of your generation. It's surprising how you promote yourself!"

Caleb rubbed his hands together several times. What would come next? However, he still tried to soften the situation: "I didn't do anything with ill intentions. No one gives what he doesn't have."

"You're right. We only give what we have." At that moment, Theo Fester showed a shocking video. Caleb was at a party in the Silicon Valley. Several successful startup leaders were present, celebrating their stock market success and the billions they earned. But there was a twenty-five-year-old man called Peter, whose startup hadn't taken off. Caleb looked at him and, in front of his victorious friends, asked: "What is this loser doing at this party?" People publicly mocked him.

"I was invited," the young man replied, embarrassed.

"But there are only winners here. Leaders of successful startups."

Bewildered, the young man tried to explain: "I'm not a failure. I'm reviewing algorithms, strategies, and processes. Our company will still take off."

"But don't count on my investments anymore. You're out!"

"Don't walk out now, Caleb, please!" Then the arrogant Caleb commented, "I'll only invest more if you drink all the champagne in this glass." And he spat into the glass. There was a macabre chorus: "Drink! Drink!" In disbelief, desperate, with no resources and fearing bankruptcy, the young man closed his eyes and drank it in front of everyone. Many felt nauseous at his gesture. Then, Caleb mocked him and went back his own word. "I'll invest a thousand dollars."

"A thousand dollars? We agreed on a million dollars."

"Weak! I wouldn't invest in someone without a backbone, without self-esteem. A thousand dollars and nothing more."

Caleb, watching that scene from the past, was so stunned that he said: "This happened a year ago. Considering the richness of details in the footage, you had been planning to test us for a long time. It wasn't just because of the disappointment we caused you in this Forest Castle about a month ago."

"Yes, several years ago. You're clever, my son. But I'd prefer you to be less intelligent and more generous."

"But you're also a bulldozer. You run over people."

"Yes, I confess. This is one of my many mental prisons: I detest people who are slow, I have an aversion to those who don't dare, and even more to those who live with the conformist syndrome of *I was born this way, I'll die this way*. But publicly humiliating people is not listed in my mental prisons. I would have praised the failure of young Peter."

"But he was a real failure."

"Yet he ventured in uncharted territories. He dared... Do you know what happened to this young man you humiliated and made drink your spit?"

"No." He shook his head, trembling. "Am I his guardian by any chance?"

"He tried to commit suicide three times. The third time, he jumped off a five-story building..." Theo Fester fell silent.

"Oh no! What have I done to Peter?"

Theo paused, emotional, and continued:

"But he didn't die. He had a traumatic brain injury. He fell into a coma. I visited him ten times in the hospital. The eleventh time, he came out of the coma. And do you know what were the first words he said? 'Give me another chance, Caleb.'"

"I've been a despicable person."

"He became a paraplegic."

"Oh no!" Caleb shouted, feeling completely saddened, looking at his crutches, fully aware of how horrible it is to be unable to move.

"But fortunately, he has no cognitive sequelae."

"That's good!" he said, somewhat relieved.

"But his father couldn't handle it. He had a fatal heart attack."

"My God, I've been so cruel... I need to help him, to confess my terrible mistakes, and try to be his friend!"

His father was pleased to hear this and said:

"I already did that for you. I became his second father and his best friend."

"You? How? You seemed so unsociable!"

Theo Fester did not say anything. He called Peter and put the phone on speaker. Peter, upon seeing the magnate's number, commented excitedly and loudly:

"My master...! I'm so glad you called!"

"How is your treatment?"

"Unfortunately, I'll never walk again. However, I learned from you that I may not have legs, but I can fly." And he paused, struck by emotion. Then he continued: "Thank you, Mr. Fester, for believing in me!"

"I'm not Mr. Fester; I'm your second father, my son. Thank you very much for existing. You make me very proud."

Peter paused again. Then, joyfully commented:

"The company is doing well. Are we going public next year?"

"Yes, but without me."

"Why?"

"My health..." The magnate said, shaken.

"Aren't your children taking care of you?"

"Sometimes."

"And what about Caleb?"

"I'll talk about him later. He roots for you," he said, looking at Caleb, who nodded in agreement.

"But don't forget that the only company that can't go bankrupt is your mind."

"I know, I know..."

"See you soon."

"Wait, don't hang up," Caleb unexpectedly intervened. "Peter, it's me, Caleb."

"Caleb?"

"I'm proud of you. Forgive me, man... I was stupid, arrogant, inhuman. I always knew you'd become better than me... I was consumed by jealousy."

"I understand."

The moment was intensely emotional, and words could not express the depth of their feelings. Peter and Caleb couldn't say anything else. Peterson, feeling extremely jealous of Peter, spoke up: "You never treated me like you did to this Peter guy."

The father was impressed with this observation.

"No? Look at your phone records. I called you fifty-nine times just this year. But a mere mortal never manages to speak with a person who considers himself a god. You answered my call four times, but you were always busy. I called Brenda seventy-two times; she answered nine. I called my youngest son eighty-two times and I only managed to speak to him twice, and we live in the same city. And still, he only talked about numbers, results..."

Brenda commented, disappointed: "For a long time, we pretended to be a family."

"I didn't; you did," the father asserted. And, after a pause for reflection, Theo Fester commented: "Caleb, you caused fifteen disturbances, got hit ten times, and received five beatings. What do you think of that? You broke the world record. The last beating resulted in these crutches," he affirmed.

"I confess, I have no self-control; I'm a sick man."

"Indeed, you've always been uncontrollable," Peterson pointed out, secretly delighted by his brother's misfortune. At least, he wouldn't be alone.

"Are you a masochist, Caleb? Do you like to mutilate yourself?"

"No!"

"Look at the first disturbance. Despite being unaware of the predicament of the homeless, you've already prescribed the solution. It's too much arrogance for a fallible boy under forty!"

Caleb lowered his head. He fell silent, submitting to his father's judgment.

"Aren't you going to try to defend yourself?" The father asked, raising his voice.

"Are there justifications for clearly stupid actions?"

"Indeed, clearly stupid, unjustifiable," the father affirmed. Then, he began to play videos of the first hours of Caleb as soon as he landed in Los Angeles.

"Invictus was with you, following in your footsteps."

"How is that possible?" he asked in amazement.

"He was in the shoes of that man who crossed your path and warned you when you said, *I'm the best*. Invictus was also the homeless man who welcomed you," Theo Fester said, indicating that he was the first to receive him in his tent.

"Mr. Darren Johnson? He was a *Robot sapiens*? No way!"

"Why?"

Caleb took a deep breath and replied:

"Because I saw him cry. We cried together."

"You also cried? The most insensitive of my sons also cries? You are bluffing."

"No. Not this time!"

"But I don't have that recording."

"It was in the dark of night, on the fifth day of the test. Darren Johnson told the saddest chapter of his story, the reasons why he became a man wandering the streets." And Caleb recounted this chapter:

"Darren loved his wife, but she had been diagnosed with breast cancer. Due to financial difficulties, it took a while before she sought help. The cancer spread throughout her body. A year later, she died. A month before the cancer diagnosis, the couple, despite being poor, decided to share what little they had with a pre-adolescent girl. They adopted Elisa, a ten-year-old girl. Those were extremely happy days. Before dying, his wife asked him to take care of Elisa with the utmost love and attention. But exactly a year after his wife's death, a drug-impaired driver tragically ran over the girl who was Darren's joy. Mr. Darren said: *I couldn't bear it, Caleb, I couldn't bear it. I failed as a father. I cried day and night because of little Elisa's death. I would give my eyes for her to see, my lungs for her to breathe, my heart for her to come back to life.*"

Theo Fester's eyes started tearing up. And his youngest son continued:

"I hugged Mr. Darren. I never imagined that a father could love his child so much. As I hugged him, his tears flowed down his face and wet my only shirt, which I had been wearing for over ten days."

Theo Fester, touched by the story, said:

"I failed as a father too. I stopped dreaming so that my children could dream, but I didn't tell that to you. I lost many nights of sleep so that my children could sleep well, but I kept silent about my insomnia. Like many parents, I was a small hero, but I was terrible at personal marketing. Like many of them, I'm treated as a villain by my children, who only know how to observe my flaws."

The children fell silent in the face of their father's profound reasoning and the intense love he had for them. They discovered late that he loved them much more than his money and work. Revealing his own insanities,

Caleb confessed: "More than my siblings, I am an expert at pointing out your flaws. I think I'm fit to deal with machines, but not with human beings."

Upon hearing these words, Theo Fester had a heart palpitation and shortness of breath. It seemed like his life was fading away like the flames of a candle. It was too late to redeem his children. At this moment, instead of easing the scalpel, he cut into the flesh of his egocentric son even deeper: "Anyone who is not transparent has an unpayable debt with themselves. Your record of dishonesty is astonishing, Caleb."

"What are you talking about?" Caleb wanted to know.

"Nine months ago, you promised the employees of one of the startups where you were the majority investor that if it valued over a billion dollars in a year, you would distribute ten percent of the profits to all employees. They were ecstatic. They gave their all to achieve the results."

Caleb was stupefied.

"I'm your son. How can you accuse me like this?"

"A son who shames my story. I saw the report; you manipulated the numbers just to avoid keeping your word!" the father said, exasperated.

Caleb fell silent again. The father made a deeper cut with the scalpel: "You are unworthy of the money you have. You were a scoundrel. Your god is money, it has always been." And, after a brief pause, he continued, "But don't worry; once again, I cleaned up your mess. Once again, my children acted as predators, and I took the fragile prey from their jaws."

All three were stunned by the metaphor their father used. As for Caleb's betrayal, his father told him, "You promised ten percent and didn't deliver, but I gave twenty percent to the entire team."

"Twenty percent? That's too much!"

"Now I'll give fifty percent." And Theo Fester added, "And, to my disappointment, even on the streets of Los Angeles, you were dishonest."

Caleb broke down.

"It seems I can never get it right!" He shouted. "When was I dishonest? When?"

"When you stole what little they had from those who had almost nothing. How could you, Caleb Fester?" Accused the father.

"Where? How? Show me the evidence," challenged his son.

"Watch this clip, boy. You stole ten dollars from a man older than me, over eighty years old!"

"But…"

"There are no *buts*."

It was then that his son explained:

"You are mistaken; Mathew is sixty-seven years old, but due to hunger, contempt, and ghosts from his past, he looks like he's ninety. Yes, I confess, I took twenty dollars from his wallet."

And without saying anything else, Caleb made a call. He put the call on speaker mode, just as his father did with Peter. Someone answered on the other end.

"Hello?"

"Teacher," said Caleb, respectfully.

The proud Caleb had never related to middle-class people, let alone a ragged person.

"Caleb, my dear student!"

"I want to apologize a thousand times."

"Why?"

"Ten days ago, I took twenty dollars from your wallet."

"Why are you apologizing? The money was yours. Every time you earned something, you shared it with me. On that day, you put forty dollars in my wallet. Later, seeing a hungry child, you took ten dollars. Then you took another ten dollars to buy a bouquet of flowers to put on little Elisa's grave together with Darren Johnson. With the twenty dollars, I ate for four days, my son…" Mathew generously commented.

"Have you been studying Sartre?" Caleb asked.

"Yes, humans are condemned to be free! A child tries to escape from its mother's arms in search of freedom, a teenager risks new friendships to venture out, a prisoner dreams day and night of escaping from prison, a subjugated people sooner or later rebels against their tyrants."

"Sometimes, I think Sartre was delirious. It seems like I'm not condemned to be free but to be incarcerated," said Caleb.

"Wrong. Even a suicidal person doesn't want to end life but to escape pain. No one gets rid of the thirst for freedom."

Theo Fester was amazed by the dialogue his son was having with a homeless person.

"And Nietzsche, have you been studying him?" Caleb asked again.

"These days, I read that Nietzsche spoke about the ideal man, incorruptible, autonomous, a superman, in short. But the Superman only exists in DC Comics. There are no perfect actors in the theater of humanity. We are all flawed, foolish, stupid, arrogant, such false humble beings that we take pride in our humility," said Mathew. "And what about you... have you been drinking from your arrogance?"

"I'm addicted, just like an alcoholic."

And then, the two-bid farewell with tenderness and hung up. After that, Caleb commented that some people do not have a bed to sleep in, others sleep on soft mattresses but do not rest. Some do not have homes to live in; others live in beautiful houses or apartments but live like emotional beggars with no protection.

CHAPTER 31

The Verdict

Theo Fester, one of the greatest entrepreneurs in history, was appalled by the dossier that he compiled over the past years, regarding his children's behavior. They were infected with neurotic needs for power, to being the center of social attention, to control others, and to always be right – four powerful and destructive neuroses. Theo constantly asked himself, in the silence of his mind: "Have I raised monsters or human beings?" The modern family had become a group of strangers, but the magnate's family had gone further, it had become a dangerous sham. Now he would deliver his verdict. His children would either go to prison or to freedom, to the valleys of social shame or to glory, to financial misery or to the possession of a fortune that few heirs had ever owned. There was too much at stake. Peterson, Brenda, and Caleb were feverish and breathless.

After analyzing various clips that they had played of the past and reflecting deeply on their behaviors over the last thirty days, the Silicon Valley magnate would finally give his verdict. With less than two months to live, Theo Fester wanted to rest with a clear conscience in his grave. He began his verdict with Brenda, fixing his eyes on his daughter's pupils and said:

"Brenda, my beloved daughter, I would like to come up with words of praise for you, but you have left a trail of unprecedented pain in the story of countless people. For years, you were a promoter of the dictatorship of beauty in the most sordid sense. You excluded people based on aesthetics, belittled women because of their appearance. Moreover, you used your social status like a heroin user who injects drugs into their veins. And what you did to your lovely daughter was no less serious. You spent only five minutes a week, on average, in Kate's presence. I reiterate: five minutes a week, but you spent more than five hours a day on your social networks, living an unreal, artificial, fictitious character, deluding millions of followers with your body cult, utopian happiness, and false optimism. You hid bulimia when you could have helped thousands of women by being true, speaking of your mental struggles."

Brenda collapsed upon hearing her father's words.

"And worse still, the meager five minutes per week you spent with your daughter without using digital devices were not to rescue her, to dig into deeper layers of her story, to ask about her joys, dreams, nightmares, or the ghosts that haunted her. Instead, it was to scold her, criticize her, and point out her weight issues when, in reality, she was only slightly overweight. You were a cruel mother and a cruel businesswoman."

Brenda put her hands on her head upon hearing her father's conclusions. Then, he continued:

"Finally, for the love of money, you tried to silence my existence, the existence of the one who generated you, caressed you, took care of you, taught you how to speak, and acquainted you with the nuances of life. And to alleviate your guilt, you elevated your hypocrisy to the heavens, praying at the exact moment your brothers supposedly tried to suffocate me. Nevertheless, I want you to know that I already felt suffocated by your behavior and that of your brothers in these past years. However, in recent days, you tried to reinvent yourself. Now, as I analyze your reactions to the stress test, my verdict is..."

Brenda began to sweat. She believed herself unworthy of her freedom. But she hoped for a spark of compassion from her father. She was certain that she would go to prison and lose her entire inheritance.

"... favorable to you, my daughter. You passed your stress test with flying colors, Brenda!"

Brenda burst into tears. Her brothers stood up and applauded. Her father, already in tears, continued:

"You have my forgiveness! I won't press charges for attempted murder. I will praise you wherever I go, for the little time I have left. And your inheritance will be restored. Moreover, the chain of six hundred and fifty stores you manage will be yours, entirely yours."

Brenda continued to cry. She couldn't contain her joy. She hugged her father. She kissed him several times and said with a choked voice:

"I couldn't be happier. Overnight, I went from prison to walking freely, from poverty to becoming a billionaire. But I am much happier for your forgiveness...! I know, Dad, that you are not perfect, that you have your flaws, but I discovered that you are the best father in the world, at least for me. You had so many sleepless nights so that I could sleep. A thousand apologies... A thousand apologies... for everything I did to you, for the many people I hurt professionally, for hurting my daughter Kate..."

Suddenly, the door of the large room of the Forest Castle opened. They heard the footsteps of a person. To their surprise, it was Kate, his daughter. Brenda, fascinated, ran to hug her as she had never done since she grew up. She showered her with kisses. Kate stepped back a little from Brenda, opened a smile, and said:

"Mom, congratulations, congratulations, you passed grandpa's stress test."

"Kate, you knew about it?" she asked in amazement.

"Yes, I knew."

"Did you know about my biggest mistake?" she asked, embarrassed.

"Which one?"

"I know there are many... The one I wished your grandfather wouldn't live..."

She couldn't bring herself to say that, along with her brothers, she planned to murder her own father.

"I know everything. Grandpa is my great friend. He didn't hide anything from me." Then, she looked at him. He smiled slightly at his granddaughter. And Kate added: "Don't punish yourself, Mom. Start your story anew..."

Kate began to cry upon seeing her transformed mother.

"...Mom, I want... to get to know this wonderful person you're becoming... and that grandpa discovered."

"I still have serious flaws. I was a fan of celebrities, but I promise you that, from now on, I'll be your biggest fan. I'll tell you stories, even if I'm not very good at it; I'll sing for you, even if I'm off-key, just like I did for the refugee girls in Europe. Thank you so much for existing."

After saying these profound words to Kate, Brenda made another pause, looked her father in the eyes, and to everyone's amazement, she added:

"You just gave me six hundred and fifty stores spread around the world. I know it's one of the largest international chains of women's fashion. But I'll keep only ten percent of the shares."

"What do you mean, my daughter?!" her father asked.

"I'll use half of the other ninety percent to create a fund to repair the damage caused by the dictatorship of beauty that I and other institutions have inflicted on the collective unconscious mind of people, especially women, children, and teenagers. I want to hire psychologists, psychiatrists, and social workers to treat eating socioemotional disorders, such as bulimia and anorexia. I'll invest in socio-emotional projects so that humanity knows that beauty cannot be sold, compared, or bought; that beauty is a unique heritage of each human being. I'll hire models outside the tyrannical standards of beauty."

"I'll help you, Mom" said Kate, overjoyed.

"Very nice, my daughter, I'll die in peace with you."

"And the other half? What will you do with that?" Theo Fester asked.

Brenda paused, took a long deep breath, and said:

"I want to donate it to the refugee cause! To the NGOs that support it. The pain of mothers and children treated as social scum in engraved my mind."

"What's scum, Mom?"

"Garbage, my daughter."

"I'll help you with this project too," said Kate.

Peterson and Caleb widened their eyes. It was unbelievable that their sister would give up a large part of her fortune. They were astonished.

Brenda confessed:

"I have lost nights of sleep thinking about what happened to an incredible boy named Salah."

Kate's eyes teared up, and she said:

"I know, Mom, I know… You were raped… while trying to get food for him… Finally, when he found out that his mother would be deported, he gave up on living…"

"I have nightmares seeing him lying on a bed: I try to wake him up to life, but I feel completely powerless…" Brenda confided.

Suddenly, the main door of the room opened once again. Everyone turned to it because the creaking was very loud. In the dim light, it was possible to see someone walking slowly towards them, but no one could see his face. Suddenly, the silhouette of a small black boy appeared, and he shouted:

"Brenda! Brenda!"

Brenda felt like she was entering a movie, a surreal scene. It was that familiar voice. She opened and closed her eyes a few times to check if she wasn't dreaming.

"Salah? Is that you?"

She and the boy ran to each other's arms.

Her father opened a broad smile.

The magnate had rescued him.

"I am arranging the documentation for him and his family to stay legally in the United States."

After these emotional moments, Kate led the boy out of the Forest Castle room to explore the gardens.

Brenda stayed to find out what her brothers' verdict would be. She hoped they would meet the same fate as she did.

Then, Theo Fester took a sip of water. Caleb and Peterson were moved but quite apprehensive because they did not know what awaited them. They did not know if the world under their feet would crumble or stand firm. The billionaire looked down and observed his notes.

Finally, he looked up and said:

"Caleb, I'll start with you."

Peterson was intrigued by this change in order. Perhaps because he would be better evaluated, he thought. Caleb tensed up. He took a long and deep breath. Never had such quick moments defined the course of a long story. His father was poetically sharp.

"Caleb, your arrogance is as deep as the oceans, your egocentrism is as abundant as oxygen, and your unhealthy need to hurt others is as penetrating as the sharpest blades. In recent years, your behavior has caused irreversible consequences, not only in spectacular young people like Peter but in many others that I investigated, who were unlucky enough to cross your path. Michael, your former manager, suffered from depression. Helena, your new business manager, had panic attacks. Gutenberg, your financial manager, has developed social phobia. Robert, one of your minority partners, promised to kill you when you publicly humiliated him, saying he was 'an idiot, a shitty investor,' at a meeting of entrepreneurs in the Silicon Valley. How many more have you suffocated? You are a mental prisoner promoting other mental prisoners."

Caleb put his hands on his head. He knew he would be condemned. He would either receive his father's forgiveness and inherit ten billion dollars, or he would end up in misery and physical imprisonment. There was a lot at stake. Overwhelmed by guilt, he spoke without arrogance but with genuine concern:

"Are you ashamed of me?"

"I have more reason to be ashamed than to be proud," his father replied.

"Am I redeemable? Do you think I'm a psychopath?" Caleb asked, trembling.

"I refuse to give you a diagnosis; I'm not a psychiatrist. All I know is that, with your past record, humanity has worsened. You were financially efficient and emotionally inefficient. With you, the human species became more predatory and less altruistic, more ferocious and less viable, even though you raised fifteen billion dollars for my group in the last three years."

Never had a father spoken such words to a son. They were extremely heavy, cutting through the mind like a scalpel, splitting intellect from emotion, separating the monster and the human, as if it was a double-edged blade. Caleb began to stutter, and his father sensed the desperation. Theo Fester took another sip of cold water and concluded:

"However, despite suffocating many people, you brought air and life to this young man among the homeless." Theo showed the video where Caleb helped a teenager who was having a cardiac arrest due to cocaine abuse. Caleb was seen performing chest compressions and mouth-to-mouth resuscitation on the young man, this time, without worrying about germs, bacteria, viruses... just wanting to save him. The young man had a positive reaction to the resuscitation and managed to recover. "Caleb, even with all your aversion to disease, you had the courage to perform chest compressions and mouth-to-mouth resuscitation on this young man and saved his life."

"No, Dad, he saved my life. After witnessing that scene, I completely eliminated cocaine from my story. I decided never to let myself be dominated by drugs again."

"Very well, my son. Analyzing the grotesque and monstrous actions in your past and comparing them with your behavior in your stress test, trying to minimize the immense wounds you caused, it is not hard to deliver my verdict. Do you think it's possible to hide your madness, including coming up with the plan of killing your own father?"

"No. I know I can't" he said, shedding tears.

"Very well. That's why my verdict is..."

Caleb stood up in an anxiety crisis, knowing for sure he would go to prison.

"... in your favor, Caleb. You passed the test, my son!"

"What? Are you playing with my feelings?" Caleb asked, not believing what he had just heard.

"No. You really passed the test!"

Caleb put his hands on his face, in tears. And his father added:

"I forgive you. I won't carry to my deathbed the plans you made for my murder. I refuse to dwell on the grievances you imprinted on me in the theater of my mind. My meals will be peaceful, and my nights will be pacified. I won't see you as my enemy or my executioner, but as a beloved son, who was lost, but now I've found."

Caleb ran into his father's arms and gave him several kisses. His father looked into his eyes and warned:

"You've learned many lessons. You surprised me with your humility and generosity. At times, I thought you were a hopeless case. However, you're still in the early stages of rewriting your story. Many monsters still inhabit your mind. You'll need years of training."

It did not matter if he didn't pass his stress test with flying colors like Brenda. What mattered was that Caleb had a new opportunity. At that moment, the youngest and most arrogant son of Theo Fester took the floor and left his father and siblings shocked.

"Will I be a billionaire?" he asked his father, who did not like the question.

"Yes."

"How much will my inheritance be, Theo Fester?" He asked again, leaving his father anxious, having second thoughts on whether or not he should have passed the stress test.

"Ten billion dollars" he replied, embarrassed.

Caleb glanced furtively at his father's eyes and said:

"Well then. I renounce my inheritance."

"What are you saying?" The magnate asked, perplexed.

"That's what you just heard, Dad..." And with a choked voice, slowly, mixed with warm tears, he added: "I've discovered that your forgiveness is my greatest reward, and your love is my greatest inheritance. I just want an allowance to survive."

Peterson entered a state of panic; he did not understand his younger brother's reaction. His father, also perplexed, asked:

"But what will you do with your fortune?"

Caleb smiled and commented:

"Half of my fortune goes to the homeless in this country. And the other half, I want to use it to launch Dr. Marco Polo's megaproject: *Prisoners of the Mind!*"

"But how? You seemed to hate him."

"Well, from now on, I will work with him. This project will be my life's mission too."

"I don't understand" said Theo Fester, in a state of euphoria. "You thought he was a manipulator of fragile minds."

"Much more. I thought he was a scoundrel, a seducer of terminal patients, a usurper of inheritance; but today, I believe that every father should somehow test their children before making them heirs. In these infernal thirty days of stress, I, who am not prone to crying, cried like a child, went crazy like a psychotic person, felt fragmented like a depressed person. And finally, I swallowed my pride and reconsidered my story."

Caleb wiped his eyes with his hands. One of the brightest entrepreneurs in the world, under forty years old, discovered that he had never been a god, but a fragile mortal being. He discovered what many powerful people never did. Caleb added:

"After swallowing my pride, I talked several times in the last ten days with Dr. Marco Polo. I am a vegetarian, I didn't like to see animals bleed, but I didn't care about bleeding your happiness, my father, and the happiness of my siblings, and of the people who worked for me."

"Surprising. But how did you talk to Dr. Marco Polo so many times if I don't have those reports?"

"I knew my phone was tapped. I used my teacher Mathew's phone and begged desperately for Dr. Marco Polo to be a homeless person like me. In response to my request, in the last few days, he also slept in Mathew's tent. By the way, we didn't sleep; we spent the nights talking. He explained to me how the mind works. And I really understood that there are more mental prisons in my brain than in the world's most violent cities. And if we don't transition from the Information Age to the Era of the Self as the manager of the human mind, humanity will be unviable, always producing monsters like me, efficient, rich, powerful, but predators."

Theo Fester couldn't contain his joy; however, he warned his son:

"Are you sure you won't regret donating all your fortune? Life is tough, my son."

"I'm not strong or a hero. But I'm sure I am taking an important and conscious step. Look, I've been a slave to cocaine, I'm impulsive and hypochondriacal; Brenda has bulimia, arachnophobia, and digital dependency; Peterson, allodoxaphobia, tropophobia, and a sick need for power. We are all prisoners in our minds, my father. But I have a requirement for donating everything I have and working on this project."

"And what is it?" his father asked, curious.

"Invictus must be part of the project."

The father stopped, smiled, and remembered that he had said the same thing to Dr. Marco Polo at the UN headquarters.

"Accepted. Invictus technology will be part of the *Prisoners of the Mind* project!"

It was a solemn, unique, spectacular moment. If he only had these two children, Theo Fester could close his eyes to life in peace, but he still needed to judge the oldest one, Peterson. He stopped and quickly read his notes. The initial comments were complimentary, different from what happened with the other two heirs:

"You, Peterson, are my oldest and most dedicated son. You have always been with me in the most difficult moments of my life. You were disciplined and fought for our business group as few sons would have done."

Peterson nodded in thanks. He was euphoric. And his father continued: "However, you loved money more than life, you left the dearest people at the bottom of your story, like your son, Thomas. You treated your wife with inhuman indifference. You stepped on anyone who opposed you. Your pleasure was to gather with people who only fueled your ego, who flattered you day and night. However, in the stress test, you tried to turn things around, attempted to write your noblest chapters on your saddest days. Therefore, comparing your past mistakes with your behavior in Kashmir, my verdict is…"

Peterson interrupted him. By the initial praise and quick criticism, he believed his father's favor was won. He stood up with a slight smile on his face, as he believed he would leave that trial as a billionaire, with incalculable wealth, immeasurable power. His spirits were so high that he preempted:

"I trust in your immense compassion, my father, and I praise your justice!"

These words silenced Theo Fester. Yet Peterson insisted: "I am proud to be your son."

His father made another moment of silence. Suddenly, he let out a tear. Peterson realized something was wrong and began to feel anxious.

"Come on, Dad. Say that I passed, please."

Theo Fester raised his eyes and said:

"You failed."

Peterson froze. His mind went blank. So did his brothers'. Suddenly, his body started to tremble, and he screamed as if being devoured by a predator.

"No-o-o-o-o! It can't be! I hate you… you old man!"

"With great regret, this old man failed you."

That's when Peterson began to assault him with words like he had never done before.

"You're hateful! A lunatic! A cheapskate! An ungrateful! You always sabotaged me! Me, the son who was your slave! The idiot who was always at your feet, who gave his life to the group, excluded from your inheritance!"

Caleb intervened:

"Peterson, shut up!"

"Shut up yourself, you murderer. You are one of the reasons for putting me in this situation! You are just as crazy as this old man. That's why everyone hates you."

"Calm down, Peterson" Brenda requested.

"Calm down? You got a chain of stores and want me to calm down after he took all my fortune, turned me into a beggar, and, on top of that, is throwing me into a stinking prison?"

His father had tears running down his face. He wanted to say something to him...

"Son..."

But Peterson cut him off:

"Don't call me son!"

Peterson quickly took something from his blazer. It was a weapon, a Glock G28 pistol, powerful and super-compact. Desperate, he pointed the gun at his father and then at his siblings. Caleb and Brenda went into shock and stepped back, but the father was not intimidated. He stood up from his chair and took two steps toward Peterson.

"I'm going to kill you, old man, and then I'm going to kill these two children of yours. I'll take everything! Everything!" He shouted, completely out of control.

His father took a few more steps. And suddenly, Peterson said something surprising.

"And you want to know a big secret before you die, Theo Fester?"

"Go ahead" said his father, trying to calm him down. He knew that all of this could end in a terrible tragedy.

"You don't have cancer!"

His father stopped, frowned, and, confused, asked him:

"What are you saying?"

"I forged the diagnosis."

"You're bluffing. All the tests show that I have tumors spread throughout my lungs" the father asserted.

Peterson laughed.

"It's not possible!" Brenda said, indignant.

"Are you upset, Brenda? You just became incredibly rich," Peterson said.

"Why did you do this?" Caleb asked in shock.

"To satisfy your ambition, you little brat, as well as mine and Brenda's. I already knew that this man had been investigating us for years. I knew he was preparing a dossier on our behaviors."

His father remained silent, in disbelief.

"And how did you forge the diagnosis?" Caleb wanted to know.

"Old tricks that you always used. Fake images. Nothing a million dollars can't buy."

"And my coughing fits?" Theo Fester asked.

"Manipulated medicine, you naive one. Ah... Didn't Invictus find that out?"

"But I had chemotherapy and radiotherapy. I suffered a lot in the last month."

"You suffered unnecessarily. But you won't suffer anymore; this is your end."

And he aimed the gun.

Theo Fester was impressed by Peterson's psychopathy. His son was sicker and more aggressive than he could have imagined. At that moment, Theo Fester tested Dr. Marco Polo's theory. He remembered how he shifted the anchor of memory from the boundaries of killer windows to the light windows of the man who was about to commit a massacre in the

UN room. If intimidated by his son, he would be prey; if he attacked him, he would be a predator. In both situations, Peterson would shoot. He needed to surprise him:

"You can kill me, but you won't kill my ideas." These words shook Peterson. And his father took a few more steps.

"Stop!" he shouted, trembling with his father's audacity.

But Theo Fester continued to approach:

"Behind that gun is a human being that I abandoned. I confess! A son who went through pains I never discovered and crises I never investigated. I failed you."

Peterson was perplexed. Theo Fester wanted to make him think.

"You, the Silicon Valley magnate, one of the most powerful men in the world, admitting your insanities? Admitting that you were stupid? That's what fear does to a man's brain, huh?" He mocked.

"You are strong, Peterson, not because you carry a weapon, but because, despite all your mistakes, you have enormous potential to reinvent yourself."

"Shut up! Shut up!" He shouted, trying not to look at him.

"Look me in the eyes. And shoot," said Theo Fester.

Peterson trembled. His father was two steps away from him.

"Shoot. Come on. I'm not afraid of dying; I'm afraid of losing you." And tears streamed down his face.

Peterson couldn't do it. He broke down in tears. Then his father hugged him.

Caleb picked up the gun. Peterson sat on the floor, collapsed like a desperate and helpless child. Then, Theo Fester said:

"I will withdraw your entire inheritance, Peterson."

Peterson, with his head down, said:

"I know. And you'll press charges, arrest me... What else?"

"I'm not going to press charges."

He looked up and asked, perplexed:

"What?"

"I forgive you!" said the father, sobbing.

"I won't go to prison?"

"No. But your mistakes were many. And there is one condition," said Theo Fester.

"What?"

"You will live for a year in one of the most dangerous slums in Rio de Janeiro!"

"A slum in Brazil?! I'll be killed...?"

Theo, raising his voice, reproached his son's prejudice, saying:

"In the slums of Rio de Janeiro, over ninety percent of the people are more ethical, peaceful, and heroic than in many places courted by the world, including New York, where you live, and the Silicon Valley, where your brother lives. You will learn, my son, to be worthy of those people who are deserving, although they live in an unworthy social environment. You preside over banks; go learn with them how to preside over your mind."

"But what will I do without money?"

"The same as billions of people do. Fight to survive, having dreams and discipline to grow."

Brenda stood up and said:

"Dad, I want to give Peterson part of my shares."

However, her father forbade her.

"No..."

Suddenly, again, the main door of the immense hall of the Castle of the Forest opened. The creaking diverted their attention. Only Peterson continued looking at the floor. A boy entered very slowly, approached Peterson, and gently called him:

"Dad..."

"Thomas? My son. What are you doing here?" He said, getting up.

In tears, the son said:

"I'm here because, despite everything, you are one of the most important things in my life."

The father's crying intensified.

"It's not possible! You know that..." Peterson began to speak but did not have the courage to list his mistakes.

"I know everything that happened in the Castle of the Forest."

"You also know that I failed in Kashmir?"

"Yes."

"You know that your grandfather disinherited me?"

"Yes."

"You know that I pointed a gun at your grandfather?"

"Yes. I watched everything from another room..." he said, wiping his face with his hands. He was a boy in distress.

"Are you afraid of me?" the father asked, anguished.

"No, I have compassion for you" Thomas replied, moved.

"Do you know that I'm going to Brazil to live in a slum in Rio de Janeiro? Do you know the dangers I'll face there?"

"I know that your aggressiveness might be as intense as that of violent traffickers. They traffic drugs; you trafficked hatred and arrogance," replied the son, intelligently and honestly. "Yet I know that there are incredible human beings there, better than us."

"Where did you get these ideas?"

"I wasn't just around my grandfather; I was raised by him."

"Your mother is going to file for a divorce."

"I know... She also suffered too much. She never wanted a rich man; she wanted a good man."

Peterson could barely speak.

"Your father will be a slum dweller. Will you keep your distance from me? Will you turn your back on me?"

"Yes, I will turn my back..." Thomas affirmed.

"I figured you would...," said the father, lowering his head.

"I will turn my back on all I have here..."

"What do you mean?"

"I will go with you," his son declared.

"My grandson, don't go" advised the grandfather.

"Your grandfather is right; you don't deserve to face the hardships that I will certainly encounter," said Peterson.

"I will go because I love you... And I have always dreamed of going to Brazil."

"You would do that for me? Even knowing that we might go hungry?"

"Even so! I will show you how much the love of a son is worth, the love that you couldn't show as my father..."

Peterson paused and, almost voiceless, said:

"Thank you very much for not giving up on me, Thomas. I am ill. But I want to get to know you... And even get to know the tears that I caused you to shed... which you had never had the courage to tell me about."

After that, Peterson fell to his knees, and his son did too. At that moment, they hugged each other for a long time. Theo Fester also burst into tears, and Brenda and Caleb couldn't contain their tears either.

Dr. Marco Polo watched everything on video, from another room. He was also very moved. Invictus, in an unprecedented move, picked up a tear from the psychiatrist with one of its fingers and placed it on its right eye, letting it run down its face. It wanted to feel what was impossible for androids and robots. The Fester family was a sham, a family of gods who fought each other, but after running ultimate risks of self-destruction, they finally became human again. And so, the *Prisoners of the Mind* project began. Humanity would never be the same...

Acknowledgment

I express my gratitude to all the patients I have attended in over twenty thousand psychotherapy sessions and psychiatric consultations. I considered them not as patients but as a world to be discovered. As a researcher of the thought-building process and the Self as the manager of the human mind, I became an explorer searching for a hidden treasure within its ruins. And I have always found it! In this journey, I discovered that we are all prisoners in our minds, seeking freedom.

Rousseau claimed that humans are born good, and society corrupts them... In reality, humans are born in construction. The worst prisoners are those who believe they are self-sufficient.

Augusto Cury.

Review Request

Before you go, can I ask you for a quick favor?

Would you please leave this book an honest review on Amazon?

Your review won't take long, but it can help this book reach more readers like you.

Thank you for reading, and thank you so much for being part of the journey.

-Augusto

www.ingramcontent.com/pod-product-compliance
Lightning Source LLC
Chambersburg PA
CBHW022059090426
42743CB00008B/650